"In my culinary heart, there is a little bit of the Chesapeake Bay, which looms large whenever I see John Shields has written a new cookbook. He brings back those recipes I associate with the region, writing about them so refreshingly they are new again. I feel so happy to have this book to read and cook from, and so will you."

—Nathalie Dupree, coauthor of *Mastering the Art of Southern Cooking*

"John Shields has done an amazing job showing us how to preserve the traditions of the region while also respecting the environment around us—he understands how important it is to maintain our local food economies so that future generations can also know the beauty and the bounty of the Chesapeake Bay."

—José Andrés, Chef/Owner, ThinkFoodGroup & minibar by José Andrés

"John Shields's recipes, from the classic to the contemporary, continue to sizzle. *The New Chesapeake Kitchen* includes lots of yummy treats for perennials and millennials."

—Barbara Mikulski, former US Senator

"The Chesapeake Bay is huge, but John Shields brings it right to your tongue! His recipes are distinctive and delicious, and remind us how our food choices relate to the environment. Think globally, eat locally and sustainably! Doing right by the Bay has never tasted better."

—Will Baker, President, Chesapeake Bay Foundation

"To eat a John Shields meal is to truly taste the Chesapeake. He understands how the food we grow here shapes us, from the verdant fields around the Baltimore suburbs to the soft-crab delicacies and flaky rockfish caught on the Eastern Shore. His words are beautiful and heartfelt; his food even more so."

—Rona Kobell, Chesapeake Bay writer

"John Shields is the greatest chef of the Chesapeake, and he's also the wisest—demonstrating that you don't have to be a killjoy to be an environmentalist. This gorgeously illustrated book mixes Bay-friendly culinary advice—such as the endorsement of farmed oysters and smaller portions of meat—with local recipes so rich with flavor they feel decadent. You can save the Bay without losing your taste."

—Tom Pelton, author of *The Chesapeake in Focus: Transforming the Natural World*

THE
NEW
CHESAPEAKE
KITCHEN

JOHN SHIELDS

PHOTOGRAPHS BY **DAVID W. HARP**

JOHNS HOPKINS UNIVERSITY PRESS
BALTIMORE

Johns Hopkins University Press
2715 North Charles Street
Baltimore, Maryland 21218-4363
www.press.jhu.edu

Library of Congress Cataloging-in-Publication Data

Names: Shields, John (John Edward)
Title: The new Chesapeake kitchen / John Shields ; photographs by David W. Harp.
Description: Baltimore : Johns Hopkins University Press, 2018. | Includes
    bibliographical references and index.
Identifiers: LCCN 2018000280 | ISBN 9781421426501 (hardcover : alk. paper) |
    ISBN 9781421426518 (electronic) | ISBN 1421426501 (hardcover : alk. paper) |
    ISBN 142142651X (electronic)
Subjects: LCSH: Cooking—Chesapeake Bay Region (Md. and Va.) | LCGFT:
    Cookbooks.
Classification: LCC TX714 .S5345 2018 | DDC 641.59755/18¯dc23
LC record available at https://lccn.loc.gov/2018000280

A catalog record for this book is available from the British Library.

Special discounts are available for bulk purchases of this book. For more information,
please contact Special Sales at 410-516-6936 or specialsales@press.jhu.edu.

Johns Hopkins University Press uses environmentally friendly book materials, including recycled
text paper that is composed of at least 30 percent post-consumer waste, whenever possible.

Book design by Kimberly Glyder

TO OUR AMAZING CHESAPEAKE FARMERS, WATERMEN, AND CULINARY ARTISANS, PAST, PRESENT AND FUTURE. YOU ARE OUR HOPE.

AND, AS ALWAYS, TO THE ONE WHO KEEPS ME ON AN EVEN KEEL IN THE WATERS OF LIFE, JOHN FRANCIS.

CONTENTS

Acknowledgments....................................IX

Introduction 3

1 STARTING THE DAY....................................13

2 APPETIZING BITES 35

3 SOUPS AND ONE-POTS............................ 57

4 OVEN FIRED 93

5 PASTA AND FLATBREAD............................ 115

6 BEANS AND GRAINS 131

7 SALAD BOWL....................................153

8 VEGGIES GALORE....................................173

9 BREAD BASKET....................................197

10 DESSERTS AND SWEET TREATS................213

11 PUTTIN' IT UP....................................233

12 CHEERS!.................................... 253

Key Local Resources....................................261

Suggested Reading 263

Index 265

ACKNOWLEDGMENTS

IT NEVER CEASES TO AMAZE ME how many people it takes to bring a book to life. This has been one long session in the delivery room, so there are many thanks in order.

First and foremost I must thank my longtime friend, co-conspirator in crime, confidant, and collaborator, Bonnie North. She traveled with me throughout the Chesapeake as we visited and interviewed many of the folks featured in the book. Bonnie kept the project moving and organized—well, at least as organized as it is possible to keep me. Bonnie's research and vast knowledge of our local food communities were instrumental. Many of the sidebars in the book were the vision and product of Bonnie's efforts. What can I say, Bons? Couldn't have done it without you.

The idea of a new Chesapeake kitchen was incubated with assistance from the talented individuals at Johns Hopkins University Press. Kathy Alexander kept at me for many years about writing this book and publishing with the JHU Press. When it seemed we had lost our way my niece's cousin, Sara Cleary, who happened to be working at the Press, contacted me out of the blue and got our project back on track. My dear, sweet editor Catherine Goldstead and I had numerous lunch meetings discussing the book—and sampling desserts. Managing editor Julie McCarthy plotted out our course of production with great skill and precision. Having worked with Deborah Bors on the 25th anniversary edition of *Chesapeake Bay Cooking with John Shields*, I kept my fingers crossed, hoping that we would get a chance to work together again. I got my wish. Debby is amazing. Her dedication to this project and attention to detail is brilliant.

Everyone loves a beautiful book, and for this I am indebted to book designer extraordinaire, Kimberly Glyder. And photographs are essential. For this we enlisted the help of one of the Chesapeake's finest photojournalists, David Harp. Dave is a good friend and has been involved with every aspect of this work from beginning concept to finish. He's a true artist and a true lover of the Chesapeake Bay. Barbara Harp, Dave's wife, worked side by side with us putting together the gorgeous photos in the book.

Mike and Sarah Baugh are the hosts with the most. They opened their home and its beautiful waterfront location in Cambridge, Maryland, for us to shoot the cover photo for the book. They are an amazing couple who raise their own animals, tend magazine-worthy kitchen gardens, and keep longstanding homesteading traditions alive.

We did quite a bit of food photography for this book, as one might imagine. We enlisted the ever-energetic, wildly enthusiastic, talented food artist-stylist-chef Rita Calvert. We have worked on many projects together and Rita is a pro. I always feel totally confident with Rita at the helm.

So Rita makes things look pretty, but somebody has to cook all those dishes. A big shout-out to Gertrude's Executive Chef Doug Wetzel for overseeing the shoots, and a double shout-out to Sous Chef Steve Balcer for expertly cooking every dish and arranging all the food shots.

Once a book is written, the next challenge is letting people know it exists. And for this we have a marvelous team. Jack Holmes of JHU Press connects us to the world of publishing and beyond. And my longtime buddy, Washington, DC, publicist Bunny Polmer, knows how to make a match. She keeps me moving with tons of interviews and appearances, and helps me schlepping demo ingredients. Love those 5am television spots, Bunny!

A belated thanks to my longtime agent, Angela Miller, for putting together the book deal with JHU Press, a match made in heaven. Another well-deserved thanks to my dear, dear buddy, chef–food journalist–tv host and all-round fabulous fellow Patrick Evans Hylton, for connecting me with some of the coolest food people to be found down in the Hampton Roads, Virginia, area.

Just as I was nearing completion of the writing process, I got stuck. Like really stuck. But I was re-motivated by an inspirational pep talk/kick in butt from my cardiologist, Dr. Sonia Baker. Thank you, Dr. Baker, you rock.

And back to the big, amazing thanks. My Gertrude's family. Running a restaurant and writing a book do not always go together. So many times management struggled, and there are only so many hours in a day. But my friends and crew at Gertrude's were there 100 percent and gave me the space, the time, and the continuous support to help bring this book to fruition.

Lastly, but really first, is thanks to my life and business partner, John Gilligan, for being by my side and keeping me grounded. It's easy to veer off course and I am eternally grateful to have such a loving spouse keeping me pointed in the right direction.

THE
NEW
CHESAPEAKE
KITCHEN

INTRODUCTION

SO WHY A *NEW* CHESAPEAKE KITCHEN? At this point in the twenty-first century, I believe it is a perfect time to reevaluate just where we are in relationship with the Bay and its environs. Things have changed greatly since I published my earlier cookbooks. Most of the recipes that constituted those works were derived from eighteenth-, nineteenth-, and twentieth-century dishes and styles of cooking. The Bay we know today is much changed from the Chesapeake that existed then. There are many seafood varieties that, once plentiful, are now either completely gone or in danger of collapse. We now have species of fish never before seen in the Bay that have established themselves as "invasives," meaning they have no predators and threaten to disrupt the entire eco-diversity balance of the Bay.

The human population of the Chesapeake watershed has soared and put stress on the Bay and its surrounding environment. Concentrated animal feeding operations (CAFOs), a form of factory animal production, have increased the number of animals processed for food consumption to all-time highs. The ensuing "waste" from these facilities puts enormous stress on our creeks, streams, waterways, and groundwater and severely diminishes the water quality of the Chesapeake.

Much of our agricultural land (we were once akin to California's productive Central Valley) has been relegated to mono-cropping, mostly soy beans and corn, which are too often genetically modified (GM) strains. A large percentage of our soil has been ravaged and stripped of all vitality and nutrients. It is now saturated with synthetic fertilizers and chemicals, which further degrade the soil and the water quality of the Bay.

That's a lot of bad news in three paragraphs, but that is *not* the focus of this book. It is simply the plain fact about where we are living in the Chesapeake region in the twenty-first century. And we cannot address problems until they are acknowledged as such. A wise, spiritual visionary, Richard Rohr, said that we must name the darkness, because if we do not, we run the risk of calling darkness the light.

This book is about hope. It is about the future of the Bay. It tells the tales of the heroes, the dreamers, and the visionaries who live and love the Bay. It tells stories of young, innovative oyster farmers who are revitalizing an industry while helping to restore the Bay's water quality. And about small, nonprofit groups that devise systems to utilize invasive species, while feeding the least among us. It is the story of multigenerational watermen who have transitioned into oyster farming while developing school curricula for children living in small coastal communities. It is about the love and care that our new generation of farmers has for their animals, tending them with great compassion in harmony with the environment, while creating some of the finest cheeses and food products in the world. It is about the soil and the farmers, biologists, and environmentalists who are rebuilding the Bay and the soil. They are responsibly planting heritage grains and heirloom vegetables and in so doing are rebuilding the soil and their communities, both urban and rural.

In these early decades of the twenty-first century, although we may feel overwhelmed by the problems that surround us, we can see these rays of light shining in cities, towns, and villages around this vast Chesapeake watershed. They give us hope and are leading the way to a new era for the Chesapeake. Through their efforts, and all of ours, we can rebuild our local food economy. Through a new Chesapeake kitchen, we can then cook our way to health.

WELCOME TO A NEW CHESAPEAKE KITCHEN

Okay, let's now step into my new Chesapeake kitchen. We need to keep one foot in the past to see our way to the future. Legend has it that Captain John Smith, upon entering the Chesapeake, wrote in his diaries that the fish were so plentiful that "we attempted to catch them with a frying pan." That sums up Chesapeake cooking—fresh and simple. Taking the best of what we have growing (or swimming or grazing) in the Bay's watershed and treating it simply, letting all the flavors and nutrients shine through all on their own, is the best approach.

As a longtime author specializing in Chesapeake Bay "cuisine" (I was actually once reprimanded while interviewing a waterman's wife. She said, "We don't have a 'cuisine,' it's just the way we cook"), I have three Chesapeake cookbooks under my belt. When researching and writing the third, *Chesapeake Bay Cooking with John Shields*, which was a companion book to a public television series, I wrote (and still stand by) the following:

> A new vision for the Chesapeake kitchen becomes necessary as we enter the twenty-first century. Here on the shores of the Chesapeake and its far-reaching tributaries, it seems appropriate to sit back and reflect on what happened during the past century in our communities, families, and homes. Where are we now in our relationship with the Chesapeake, and how can we modify our lifestyles to make changes that will improve the quality of our lives and the surrounding environment? It is apparent that some of these changes are crucial for the Chesapeake Bay and mankind's survival. When we begin to think about the many issues involved in the sustainability of mankind on this planet, it can become overwhelming. But as we have seen in recent times, sometimes the most effective change is a small action, on the grassroots level. And it often happens right in our homes.
>
> A new eating "trend" (the locavore) that has become popular is really the oldest method for recipe planning: using seasonal foods. Simply put, it means using fresh foods grown in your region during the season in which they are grown. If there is too much of one crop being harvested, you preserve the surplus, and by doing so, you supplement your recipes during the winter months. Studies have found that using seasonal foods in your diet helps your body obtain maximum nutritional benefits. And purchasing seasonal

foods is not only good for you, it is good for the local economy and local communities. Small farmers begin to thrive. A climate is created for people who want to continue or return to farming, and for those who want to begin, thus reducing the acres available for urban sprawl. And by shopping locally we begin to reconnect with others in our communities and thus the daily task of purchasing food becomes more social and enjoyable.

How does this kind of thinking and behavior affect our environment? When we take time to prepare our meals with care and understand how our food nurtures us, we cannot help but develop a heightened awareness of our natural environment. It's all connected. Let's look at the spectacular Chesapeake Bay. For us locals, it is our lifeline—we are blessed with a region rich in seafood, game, waterfowl, and an exceptional array of produce. Just by using these wonderful, local, seasonal treasures, we become constantly aware of the Chesapeake and our common link to it.

I regard the Chesapeake Bay as our communal soup pot. When creating a delicious meal for loved ones, what kind of cook would pour dirty motor oil into the soup pot? Would you throw in a cup and a half of battery acid, or a touch of oven cleaner? I hope not, but when we put blinders on and believe our day-to-day actions are not the same as mixing these types of toxins into our soup pots, we are sadly mistaken. Again, this awareness is paramount, and we can begin right in our own kitchens, stores, local farmers' markets, or right in our own backyard vegetable gardens.

All around the Chesapeake Bay and the United States, communities and organizations are forming as people come together, join hands, hearts and minds, and say, "No more. We will not allow monetary interests to destroy our precious national treasures, and ultimately the fabric of our lives."

HOW IT WORKS

REBUILDING OUR LOCAL FOOD ECONOMY, ONE TOMATO AT A TIME

1. Try to Buy as Much of Our Food as We Can as Locally as Possible

Farmers' Markets. The easiest way to do this is at a farmers' market. Fortunately, there are farmers' markets galore these days. They can be found throughout our region in places like schools, fairgrounds, church properties, vacant lots, and even parking lots. Some are quite formal and more established, while others are just in place for all or part of the growing season.

Why are farmers' markets so helpful? Aren't they just a trend? For one thing, it's great to be able to have a genuine relationship with the people who grow your food. Since I've made the acquaintance of my friend David Hochheimer, who owns Black Rock Orchard in northeastern Carroll County, I appreciate a whole lot more all that it took to grow and bring to market that apple that I eat every day on my way into work.

The food offered at your local farmers' market is grown by small family farmers who are personally, philosophically, and financially invested in their lands, which in turn means they really practice responsible farming. Due to the increase in the popularity of farmers' markets, older farmers are better able to hold onto their land while mentoring a whole new younger generation that is eager to farm. When we do our shopping at farmers' markets, it makes it possible for these hard-working neighbors to make a good living and support their families.

And the best news is that the money generated stays within the community. It's not sent thousands of miles away. It is the economic engine that makes it possible to rebuild our local food economy (an economy that was dismantled by an industrialized food system that only came into major play during the last century). And, farmers' markets help us to eat fresh food seasonally, which is really good for our bodies.

The Dupont Circle farmers market is the jewel in the crown for the Potomac/DC area and has helped put the local food movement on the map. Because it draws huge crowds each week, farmers must apply years in advance just to get a spot. Over the years, it has given many farmers and artisanal food makers a fantastic showcase for their products. In so doing, it's made it economically feasible for these folks to expand their operations and continue in the business of farming. Dupont Circle Market is operated by FreshFarm Markets, a nonprofit organization that now runs a dozen local farmers' markets throughout Maryland, Virginia, and Washington, DC.

In the Baltimore area, the Waverly/32nd Street Farmers Market is the granddaddy of them all. It is the only year-round farmers' market in the Baltimore metro area and draws hundreds of neighborhood shoppers each Saturday, with more than fifty local vendors bringing their wares each week. There is also the lively Baltimore Farmers' Market, which operates under the Jones Falls Expressway downtown. It's a virtual festival of food happening every Sunday during the growing season.

Virginia Beach, the largest city in the state of Virginia, is home to two large farmers' markets. The Virginia Beach Farmers Market operates year-round and offers local produce, meat, and seafood seasonally. The newer Old Beach Farmers Market is nestled in the heart of the resort area and features a great selection of produce, cheese, seafood, meats, and prepared creations from local chefs.

Of course, the markets listed above are only the tip of the iceberg. If you visit Department of Agriculture websites from the states within the Chesapeake Bay watershed, you will find an ever-growing list of local, seasonal farmers' markets, usually quite near your own home. So, at least during the growing season, there is never a shortage of places to find local products and have an opportunity to deal directly with the folks who grow, raise, and harvest your food.

Small Independent Food Markets and Grocery Stores. In the olden days, most shops and grocery stores were based in neighborhoods and were, by nature, independent. Globalization and super-sizing of companies has changed all that, and most of the small local groceries have been gobbled up or put out of business by large chains. But not all the independent groceries have succumbed. There are still quite a number of local food businesses all around the region, and they are the next best choice in shopping after the farmers' markets. Money spent in these stores stays in the local community and helps keep people employed. The small independents are normally extremely involved with the community and in supporting community endeavors. Sometimes the small grocery is a bit more expensive than well-known chain store alternatives. That's because they cannot buy in the same huge quantities as the large chains. But most of the independents I've shopped at have been more committed to buying local products and local produce than many of the large chains. It's a little extra money well spent.

Larger Regional Markets. In many areas around the Chesapeake region there are only large, chain grocery stores. There is nothing wrong with these stores at all, and they employ many in the community. For those of us who are committed to a local food economy, I find the best strategy is to develop a relationship with the store management. Let them know what you like to buy and the plus sides of buying local. Help them make contact with local farmers and the producers of local goods.

It could be they had just never thought about buying locally. And should they start bringing in local products, make sure to support them and send other customers their way. This is how change happens—through face-to-face relationships.

2. Make Most of Our Dishes Plant Centered—Bay- and Body-Friendly Food

If we look at past civilizations from around the world, almost all diets were primarily plant based. Stews and other dishes that were mostly vegetable/grain based were augmented with seafood, meat, game, poultry, and the like, and have been the staple of the human diet all over the globe. Animal protein was scarce and mostly reserved for the rich. With the advent of industrialized food production and the ample availability of cheap animal products, most of us have become able to eat like the rich. But with this new access to food came new illness and new health issues. The land and water that have always nurtured us got "sick," too.

So, what does that mean? You shouldn't eat meat, poultry, fish, fowl, or crab? Of course not! But let's think about the ubiquitous Chesapeake crab cake. It is said that God created the crab cake on the seventh day for those too lazy to pick crab. The first thing we locals normally think of when considering a crab recipe to prepare are crab cakes. They are quintessential Chesapeake cuisine, but there are some problematic elements here in our twenty-first-century kitchen. In recent decades, the amount of crab harvested from the Bay has decreased drastically. And locally harvested crabmeat does contain a fair amount of mercury and PCBs (polychlorinated biphenyls), so we need to be mindful of how much of it we eat. Still, crab cakes are an iconic regional dish and we all love them. And in imagining our new Chesapeake kitchen, I am not suggesting giving up crab cakes! What I am suggesting is a general turn toward stretching the protein in everyday meals. I'm talking about looking to the past to see our way to the future.

Keeping the preceding thoughts in mind, here's an example of the approach I'm proposing, something I like to call Bay- and body-friendly food. Normally, one pound of crabmeat can make enough crab cakes to feed three to four people. But instead, let's look at Maryland crab soup. I'm not talking about cream of crab, but rather the traditional vegetable crab soup. The bulk of the soup is made from fresh vegetable ingredients—tomatoes, potatoes, green beans, onions, corn, lima beans, and cabbage—that, when in season, can be found at your farmers' market, at local groceries, through community-supported agriculture (CSA), or perhaps even in one's own backyard. Some folks add a little grain, such as barley, to the pot to thicken the soup a bit. The last ingredient added—and in the smallest quantity—is the crabmeat. That one pound of crabmeat, which would have fed three to four people as a crab cake entree, will now feed eight to ten as a hearty crab soup. Another plus in choosing a dish like a vegetable crab soup is the amount of fresh vegetables that one consumes just by eating a large bowl. And by preparing more crab dishes with this in mind, we naturally take away some of the stress on the crab population and on our bodies. It's a win-win. It's both Bay and body friendly!

Likewise, let's consider chicken. Factory-farmed chicken is perhaps a too-abundant protein source that now contributes to a variety of major environmental problems in our region. All that cheap fast-food fried chicken and those chicken nuggets aren't doing such great stuff for our health,

Community-Supported Agriculture

On our local farms, all may seem quiet and at rest in winter, but inside those farmhouses, folks are busy planning for the next season. You see, farming is a business like any other—and it's a risky business. Many farmers assume massive debts. A local farmer once confided in me that his farm goes into hock to the tune of almost $200,000 each spring! You have to really love what you're doing to put everything you have on the line just to stay in the business of farming one more year.

A CSA is a community of individuals who pledge to support a farm operation by purchasing "shares" or "subscriptions" to the coming year's harvest. Members help the farmer pay the up-front costs of seeds, equipment, and labor, and in return, the farm provides a healthy supply of seasonal fresh produce throughout the growing season.

The community-supported agriculture concept has been gaining momentum since its introduction to the United States in the mid-1980s. It originated back in the 1960s in Japan, where women interested in safe food for their families and farmers seeking stable markets for their crops joined together in economic partnerships. This arrangement, called "Teikei" in Japanese, translates to "putting the farmers' face on food." CSA agreements are fluid and take many forms, but all have at their center a shared commitment to building a more secure, local, and equitable agricultural system. The CSA arrangement is an important tool in the effort to prevent our smaller farms from being lost to suburban sprawl or swallowed up by large transnational corporations that have little interest in our local economy or ecology. You're assured the highest quality produce, often at below-retail prices. In return, farmers and growers are guaranteed a reliable market for a diverse selection of crops. Sounds like a win-win deal, doesn't it? It is.

Now, this doesn't totally eliminate the risks involved, but it helps to spread the risk around a bit. It also gives us a sense of greater rootedness in our own growing region, its weather, and its seasons. Perhaps most important, it fosters in all of us a greater sense of personal responsibility for the health of our soils and of our waters.

Every farm pick-up or drop-off day brings an exciting new challenge: Here are your latest ingredients. Now, what are you going to create with them? The inevitable bumper crop of the season (all those zucchinis!) presents the opportunity to brush up on those forgotten skills, such as canning, pickling, fermenting, and freezing—time-tested ways of preserving nature's seasonal bounties for later consumption. What could be more satisfying in bleak February than to crack open the jar of tomatoes that you yourself "put up" last August and smell the luscious aroma of last summer's harvest? That's the way it was always done!

either. But let's take a glimpse into the past and a look in my Grandma Gertie's kitchen. My grand-mother lived right in Baltimore City, and two doors down the block was Mr. Krumholtz's neighbor-hood store, complete with a barnyard outside. Gertie would get an obviously local, freshly killed, free-range chicken (which was not cheap), and from it she would create a Sunday dinner for eight to ten people. The dinner was also chock full of whatever vegetables were in season or that had been "put up"—potatoes, corn, green beans, kale, spinach, lima beans—and served with stuffing, sauer-kraut, biscuits, gravy, and so on. The next day the picked-over bird (yes, there was chicken left over) was often turned into chicken salad. And then the carcass and leftover meat became chicken soup with homemade noodles. This is the old Chesapeake kitchen mentality that is sorely needed in the new Chesapeake kitchen and that is part and parcel of celebrating Bay- and body-friendly food.

3. Figure Out What You Like to Eat and Then Plan Your Menus

There was a lot to think about in these first two sections describing how the new Chesapeake kitchen works, but this section is the key to success. How many times have we tried to change our way of eating—fad diets, starvation diets, gluten-free diets, all protein/no protein diets—and failed? The most important thing to consider when pondering your very own new Chesapeake kitchen is: What do you like to eat?

Maybe you're a meat-and-potatoes kind of guy or gal. That's still quite possible with our Bay-and-body food mantra, only now you may be a potatoes-and-meat person, for example. We've just reversed the emphasis on the meat and upped the portion of potatoes (and other veggies of course) in our quest for a more sensible way of eating.

To get the Bay- and body-friendly seal of approval, a dish must nourish us and nourish the Ches-apeake, by sticking to these simple parameters:

- Uses as many primarily local ingredients as possible that are in season
- Contains sensible amounts of seafood, meats, and poultry
- Contains ingredients and products produced in ways that are not harmful to our land, our water, and ultimately our communities and future generations

4. Just Grow

We've talked a lot about farmers, watermen, and the environment in pondering how to rebuild our local food economy, but I believe the most important step we can take is to grow something ourselves. To grow an herb, a plant, or a small fruit tree does not require an enormous amount of space or land.

I've helped lead a gardening series for a number of years, and I always reiterate to the partici-pants, "Just grow," even if it's only some flat-leafed parsley this year. I find the act, the miracle of growing—seeing something spring forth from a seed and make its way into a full-fledged item of food—always amazes me. Always!

By growing, we reconnect with life. We slow down, and the process makes us realize just how precious food is and all the effort and care required to grow it. Food is not a mere commodity. It is life. So, in envisioning a Chesapeake kitchen for the twenty-first century, I think even simple growing, by each of us, is essential. Some sort of window sill, balcony, or driveway container garden will help physically and psychologically reconnect us to the land, the soil, and to our very own local food economy.

May all be fed. May all be healed.
—John Robbins, *The Food Revolution: How Your Diet Can Help Save Your Life and Our World*

Let's cook!

1

STARTING THE DAY

Breaking the fast, which refers to the first meal after not eating during the night, is a tradition in cultures all around the globe. And the Chesapeake, rich with a melting pot of ethnicities, has quite the selection of styles and tastes to fit most mornings. Whether you're rushing out of the house with a fresh smoothie in tow or lingering with the Sunday paper over a plate of hotcakes and eggs, the recipes collected here provide a great basis to begin the day.

Asparagus and Broom's Bloom Cheddar Frittata

A frittata is a beautiful thing. It is unbelievably versatile. Springtime in the Chesapeake means freshly picked asparagus. When the season is on you'll find it everywhere, and a frittata is the perfect vehicle for this wondrous seasonal veggie. Look for a sharp cheese that will brighten the flavor of the tender asparagus. Here, I have paired the asparagus with one of my favorite cheeses, a cave-aged cheddar from Broom's Bloom Dairy, located in Harford County, Maryland. A lovely goat cheese or your favorite combination of Parmesan-style cheeses will work as well. Let your imagination run wild.

The frittata need not be served hot, as it works well at room temperature. With a lightly dressed salad it would make a perfect luncheon or early supper.

Serves 6

- 1 pound medium asparagus, trimmed
- 10 large eggs
- 3 tablespoons milk or nonfat yogurt
- 1 teaspoon salt
- ⅛ teaspoon freshly ground black pepper
- 2 tablespoons minced chives
- 2 teaspoons finely chopped fresh thyme
- ½ cup grated sharp cheddar cheese
- 2 tablespoons melted butter, or extra-virgin olive oil

Preheat the broiler.

In a steamer pot, or in a pan with boiling water, steam or blanch the asparagus for about 5 minutes or until just tender. With a slotted utensil, place the asparagus in a cold water bath to cool quickly. When cool, drain and pat dry, cutting the spears into ½-inch slices. Set aside.

Beat the eggs in a large bowl. Add the milk or yogurt, salt, pepper, chives, and thyme. Whisk together well. Stir in the asparagus pieces and the cheddar.

Heat the butter or olive oil in a 9-inch ovenproof skillet over medium heat. Add the asparagus and sauté until coated, about 2 minutes.

Raise the heat to medium-high and add the egg mixture. Cook for several minutes until the eggs start to set.

Reduce the heat to medium-low and cook until the frittata is almost set but the top is still runny, about 2 minutes. Place the skillet under the broiler. Broil until the top is set and golden brown, about 5 minutes.

Let the frittata rest for several minutes. Using a rubber spatula, loosen the frittata from the skillet and slide onto a serving plate. Cut into wedges and serve.

Huevos and No-Huevos Rancheros

Over the past two hundred–plus years, the Chesapeake region has been home to an amazing tapestry of peoples from around the world. The seventeenth, eighteenth, nineteenth, and early twentieth centuries saw a steady influx of new arrivals from Europe, Africa, Asia, and the Caribbean. Later, from the twentieth century into the twenty-first, a new wave of migration appeared from Mexico and Central America. Latino communities can now be found all around the Chesapeake region, and just as with the ethnicities that preceded, the recipes and cooking techniques of these folk are being absorbed into the fabric of Chesapeake cooking. And they are good examples to follow. Most Latin American cuisine is primarily plant based, with beans, rice, and corn acting as the foundation of the plate, and meat, fish, and cheeses added in smaller amounts.

I lived in California for nearly twenty years, and Huevos Rancheros was found on any self-respecting Latin restaurant's menu. I fell in love at first bite. Lots of options here. You could substitute canned refried beans for the black beans, should you be so inclined. Eggs any-which-way are fine—poached, fried, or scrambled—or, as you can see here, scrambled tofu can even be used in place of eggs. We have two companies in the greater Chesapeake region crafting organic tofu of the highest quality. Whether it's tofu or eggs you choose, this hearty breakfast dish can't be beat for starting the day.

Serves 6

1   (15-ounce) can whole tomatoes, with juice
¼   cup diced onion
1½   teaspoons minced garlic, divided
1½   teaspoons ground cumin, divided
¼   teaspoon cayenne pepper
1   teaspoon salt
3   cups cooked black beans, divided
Salt and freshly ground pepper, to taste
Hot sauce, as needed
Juice of 1 lime
6   large eggs, or 1 recipe Fu-Scramble (*recipe follows*)
6   corn tortillas

Condiments for serving:
Shredded queso fresco, Monterey jack, or white cheddar
Salsa Fresca (*recipe follows*)
Sour cream
Tabasco, or your favorite hot sauce
Slices of avocado
Coarsely chopped cilantro

Into a food processor, place the whole tomatoes with juice, onion, 1 teaspoon garlic, 1 teaspoon cumin, cayenne, and salt. Pulse until a fairly smooth consistency is reached. Transfer the mixture into a saucepan and heat gently.

Place the black beans into a second saucepan and lightly mash. Season with salt and pepper to taste, ½ teaspoon cumin, ½ teaspoon minced garlic, 4 dashes (or so) of hot sauce, and the lime juice. Slowly heat the mixture, taking care not to scorch the beans.

Prepare the eggs (or Fu-Scramble) either sunny-side-up or scrambled. While preparing the eggs, heat a heavy (preferably cast iron) skillet and coat with vegetable oil. Heat the tortillas briefly for about 1 minute per side and transfer to a plate. Cover with a towel to keep warm.

To serve, spread each tortilla with some of the black bean mixture, top with an egg (or scrambled Fu), and lightly sauce with the tomato mixture. Garnish as you'd like with grated cheese, salsa, a dollop of sour cream, hot sauce, avocado, and a sprinkling of cilantro.

FU-SCRAMBLE

1-pound package of extra-firm (or firm) tofu, drained and patted dry

1 teaspoon garlic powder

½ teaspoon turmeric

Salt and freshly ground pepper, to taste

½ red onion, finely diced

½ cup finely diced green bell pepper

½ cup finely diced red bell pepper

2 scallions, finely chopped

Olive or vegetable oil for sautéing

Thoroughly dry the tofu with paper towels and then crumble it into a mixing bowl. Add the garlic powder and turmeric, mixing together with the tines of a fork. Season the tofu with salt and pepper to taste. Set aside.

Coat the bottom of a skillet or sauté pan with sufficient olive oil to sauté the vegetables. Cook over medium heat and add the onion, sautéing for several minutes. Add the bell peppers and scallions and continue to sauté for about 5 minutes, or until the vegetables just begin to soften a bit. Season the vegetables with salt and pepper as needed. Add the crumbled tofu and cook for about 5 minutes longer, or until the tofu is heated through. Serve immediately.

SALSA FRESCA

3 large ripe tomatoes, cored, seeded, and diced

½ red onion, finely diced

1 small serrano chili pepper, seeded and minced

1 small jalapeño chili, seeded and minced

Juice of 1 lime, or more, to taste

1 tablespoon extra-virgin olive oil

1 teaspoon salt

¼ cup finely chopped cilantro

Mix all ingredients together in a bowl. Cover and refrigerate until ready to use.

Blue Cat Seafood Hash

As you may have already heard (*see page 78*), the invasive blue catfish has been taking over most of the rivers and tributaries of the lower Chesapeake. Not a good thing for the Bay, but on the breakfast menu, the blue catfish is the perfect vehicle for a fantastic seafood hash. I like to add a smidgen of smoked fish to the hash mixture, giving a whole other dimension of flavor, with just a hint of smokiness.

Serves 4 or 5

3 cups diced cooked potatoes

2 cups flaked cooked blue catfish fillet

½ pound smoked salmon or other type of smoked fish

8 ounces (1 stick) butter or 6 tablespoons olive oil

1 small yellow onion, diced

3 green onions, minced

2 teaspoons chopped garlic

1 teaspoon Tabasco sauce

1 tablespoon Worcestershire sauce

2 tablespoons fresh lemon juice

3 tablespoons chopped flat-leaf (Italian) parsley

1 tablespoon chopped dill

1 tablespoon chopped chives

Salt and freshly ground black pepper, to taste

Old Bay seasoning, to taste

3 tablespoons or so of vegetable oil, for frying

8–10 freshly poached eggs

Combine the potatoes, cooked catfish, and smoked fish in a mixing bowl and mix well. Melt the butter in a large skillet and sauté the yellow and green onions and garlic until soft. Add the Tabasco sauce, Worcestershire sauce, and lemon juice. Then pour into the bowl containing the potato-fish mixture. Stir in the parsley, dill, and chives, mixing well, but take care to not mash the potatoes. Season the hash with salt, freshly ground pepper, and Old Bay to taste.

Heat the vegetable oil in a skillet and fry the fish hash mixture until browned on the underside. Flip and brown the second side. Divide the hash onto serving plates and serve immediately, topped with poached eggs. For a fancier brunch, you can top the eggs with a Hollandaise sauce and a sprinkling of Old Bay seasoning.

Hominy and Gravy with Turkey Sausage Patties

My number-one culinary hero is my grandmother, Gertie Cleary, who raised me as well as my mother. I spent my early years right by her side in the kitchen of her Baltimore duplex. If I was lucky, she would let me lick the leftover batter from the mixing bowl of a cake she had just prepared, or she would fashion extra bits of pie dough into sweet little nuggets dusted in cinnamon or sugar. One of my favorite memories is waking up and smelling the aroma of her sausage patties and pan gravy cooking on the stove. Gertie believed in the miracle of hominy and would serve it as a side both at breakfast and dinner. It was a great way to make sure all of our family had full bellies, without breaking the bank on too much meat.

More and more farmers at the markets are selling freshly ground meats—beef, pork, lamb, and turkey. Sausage making is really easy to do—you just season the ground meat. I add a little oil to these patties, as ground turkey is quite lean. Of course, if you are not in the mood to make sausage, there are many varieties to be found in local groceries and at the farmers' market—so no worries.

Serves 4

16 Turkey Breakfast Sausage Patties (*recipe follows*)

6 tablespoons flour

2½ cups whole or 2% dairy milk

Salt and freshly ground black pepper, as needed

1 (20-ounce) can hominy, broken apart with a fork (or freshly cooked hominy; *see note*)

1 teaspoon sugar

4 tablespoons butter

Cook the sausage patties in a skillet until well browned but not overcooked. Turkey sausages need to be cooked only until there is no more pink in the center. Remove the patties and keep warm, reserving 6 tablespoons of fat in the skillet. Since turkey is lean, add vegetable oil if necessary.

For the pan gravy, heat the pan with the reserved fat already in it, and stir in the flour. Cook, stirring constantly, for about 3 minutes. Remove from the heat and gradually whisk in 2 cups of the milk. Return to the heat and bring to a boil, stirring constantly. Reduce the heat and simmer for 5 minutes, stirring often. Season well with salt and pepper.

Combine the hominy, the remaining ½ cup of milk, sugar, 1 teaspoon salt, ½ teaspoon black pepper, and butter in a saucepan. Heat to serving temperature. Arrange the sausage patties and hominy on individual plates. Spoon the gravy over the top and serve at once.

HOMEMADE TURKEY BREAKFAST SAUSAGE PATTIES

Makes 16 small patties

1   pound ground turkey

½   small onion, grated

2   teaspoons salt

1½ teaspoons rubbed sage

1   teaspoon crushed fennel seed,
    or ½ teaspoon ground fennel seed

1   teaspoon dried thyme

1   teaspoon black pepper

2   tablespoons olive oil

2   tablespoons apple cider

Pinch of cinnamon

Pinch of allspice

Place all the ingredients into a mixing bowl and combine thoroughly. Place the bowl in the refrigerator for about 1 hour before forming the sausage into patties.

To prepare, take 1 cup dried hominy and rinse it well with cold water. Place the hominy in a heavy-bottomed pot and cover with cold water, about 3 inches above the top of the hominy. Soak overnight. When ready to prepare, pour into a colander to discard the soaking water, and then return the hominy to the pot, adding fresh water. Bring to a boil, reduce the heat, and simmer for anywhere between 1 and 2 hours. Check for tenderness. Just before the hominy is done, stir in 1 teaspoon of salt and continue cooking until the hominy is tender. The hominy is then ready to use in any dish of your choosing.

Note on cooking dried hominy: I really enjoy fresh-cooked dried hominy. It takes a little more time, but I feel it's well worth the effort. Dried hominy can be found in most grocery stores in the Mid-Atlantic, and in other places it can be found in the international section of grocery stores, with the Latin/Hispanic foods.

Apple and Raisin Cornmeal Mush

Polenta is a fancy name for old-fashioned corn-meal grits. With more and more farmers around the Chesapeake growing heritage strains of organic corn, a belly-warming bowl of lightly sweetened grits is a healthy way to start the day. Creative cook that you are, I know you can imagine a zillion different variations for this recipe. So go ahead and make your signature "mush" by adding different kinds of dried fruit, another type of "milk," and whatever fresh fruit fits the season or your fancy.

Serves 4

3 cups soy, almond, or dairy milk

1 cup freshly squeezed orange juice

½ teaspoon salt

1 cup coarsely ground cornmeal (grits)

3 tablespoons maple syrup or honey

1 large, tart apple, peeled, cored, and diced

¼ cup raisins

Chopped toasted almonds, walnuts, or YVOK Granola (*recipe follows*)

In a heavy-bottomed saucepan, bring the milk, orange juice, and salt to a boil. Slowly stir in the grits. When the mixture starts to boil again, add the maple syrup, apple pieces, and raisins.

Reduce the heat to low and partially cover the pan. Simmer the mixture for about 25 minutes, stirring every 5 to 10 minutes to prevent scorching.

Ladle the porridge into bowls and serve the nuts or granola on the side as a topping. A pitcher with milk to add is a nice touch.

YVOK (YOUR VERY OWN KITCHEN) GRANOLA

If you look closely, you'll find that most granolas consist primarily of oats. Yeah, they have some nuts and a tad of oil and sugar, but basically you have a cup of oats. And what could be a better way to start the day? Oats are good for the body and satisfy the early-morning hunger cravings. The thing is—granola really is mostly oats. And oats are not expensive. Making a nice batch of granola is not rocket science, nor does it need to cost an arm and a leg. Experiment with what you like to add to the granola, and eventually you will have your very own signature recipe.

Makes about 4 cups

3 cups thick-cut rolled oats
3 tablespoons brown sugar
1 teaspoon cinnamon
¼ teaspoon salt
⅓ cup honey
¼ cup vegetable oil
1 teaspoon vanilla
½ cup sun-dried fruit of choice (raisins, currants, cherries, apricots, or the like)
½ cup toasted, chopped nuts of choice (almonds, walnuts, pecans, etc.)

Preheat oven to 300°F.

Combine the oats, sugar, cinnamon, salt, honey, vegetable oil, and vanilla in a bowl. Mix well with a spoon or spatula. Spread over a well-oiled baking sheet. Bake the mixture for 15 minutes, then stir once again for even browning. Bake 10 minutes more and remove from oven. Stir again and allow to cool to room temperature before adding fruits and nuts of your choice.

Mr. Al's Old-Timey Chessie Porridge

Al Saunders is legendary in the Baltimore music world and has been delighting listeners for over five decades. But beyond the clarinet and sax, this man can cook. In fact, Al is my personal healthy chef and keeps me stocked up with invigorating soups, stews, and smoothie concoctions to keep me going. One of my favorites is Al's porridge. It's a fantastic, nutty combination of grains that can be enjoyed for days on end, if you whip up a double batch.

There are various types of barley on the market, with pearl and hulled being the most prevalent. The hulled is the way to go, as it is minimally processed and is an actual whole grain. It's the grain in this trio of barley, oats, and rice that gives the porridge its characteristic chewiness. It takes a bit longer to cook than the other grains, which is why Al starts with it beforehand.

Another tip from Al is to substitute half coconut water for the regular tap water. And he likes to sprinkle a little unsweetened shredded coconut and cinnamon on top of his bowl of grains. Me, I'm happy with whatever fruit is in season to top mine off.

Makes 3 to 4 servings

5   cups water, or more as needed
1   teaspoon salt
⅓   cup whole (hulled) barley, well rinsed and soaked for 30 minutes
⅓   cup steel-cut oats
⅓   cup long-grain brown rice
Agave nectar or maple syrup

In a heavy-bottomed pot, bring the water and salt to a full boil. Add the drained barley and bring back to a full boil. Keep an eye on the pot so the mixture doesn't overflow when it boils. Reduce the heat to low and cover the pot. Cook for 20 minutes. Then add the oats and brown rice. Stir well and re-cover the pot. Continue cooking for about 25 minutes, stirring from time to time to prevent burning. If you feel the mixture is getting too thick, add a touch of water. Turn off the heat and allow the porridge to sit, covered, for at least 15 minutes. Flavor the porridge with agave or maple syrup to taste.

Optional add-ons:

Raisins, currants, or other dried fruit
Banana, peeled and cut into pieces or rounds
Toasted nuts, such as walnuts, almonds, pistachios, etc.
Flax seeds

Grit Cakes with a Peachy Compote

The Chickahominys are one of the original tribes that made the Chesapeake region their home. The word *hominy*, in their native language, means "corn." They are the "people of the coarse ground corn," one of the major staples from our region sustaining the populations for countless generations.

Hominy, cornmeal, grits, polenta? It all gets so confusing. Actually, kernels of corn are dried and ground into various types of meal, or cornmeal. "Hominy" is the kernels of corn that are cleaned by a reverse osmosis process, which sounds pretty scary but is just a natural whitening process. So, all from a simple ear of corn we get white cornmeal, yellow cornmeal, a coarser grind producing grits, and its European cousin, polenta. The whole-kernel hominy is known in the Southwest and Mexico as posole.

This is a fun breakfast recipe—a little unusual, but quite delicious. If you are in a hurry, the "quick cook" grits found in the grocery store will work just fine. But you'll need to follow the package instructions for making the grits, as they require less liquid than the stone-ground type.

Serves 2 to 3

2½ cups water

1 cup dairy milk or plant milk

2 tablespoons butter, oil, or vegan butter

1 teaspoon salt

½ teaspoon cinnamon

1¼ cups stone-ground grits

½ cup raisins (optional)

2–4 tablespoons local maple syrup or honey

Vegetable oil, for cooking

Cornmeal for dusting

Peach Compote (*recipe follows*)

Place the water, milk, butter/oil, salt, and cinnamon into a heavy-bottomed pot and bring to a boil. Slowly stir in the grits (and raisins, if using). Reduce the heat to medium and cook for 10 minutes, stirring constantly. Then reduce the heat to low, and continue cooking for about 30 minutes longer, stirring frequently. You do not want the grits to scorch. Lightly sweeten the grits with the maple syrup or honey to taste.

Lightly oil an 8 x 8 inch pan. (If using a different pan, the idea is to have the rounds be about 1¼-inch thick.) Pour in the cooked grits and allow to cool completely. Cut out rounds of grits using a 3-inch biscuit cutter. Coat the bottom of a skillet with a little vegetable oil and bring to a medium heat. Dust the rounds of grits lightly in cornmeal and cook until golden brown, about 2 to 3 minutes on each side.

Place the rounds on a plate and serve immediately with warm peach compote.

PEACH COMPOTE

⅓ cup water

Juice of ½ lemon

4–6 tablespoons brown sugar (depending
on the sweetness of the peaches)

Pinch of cinnamon or cardamon

4 cups fresh peaches (peeled and pitted),
sliced or cut into pieces (about 6 peaches)

Place the water, lemon juice, brown sugar, and spice into a saucepan and bring to a boil. Add the peaches and stir. Reduce heat to medium and continue cooking for about 5 to 6 minutes or until peaches break down. Remove from heat. The compote can be served warm or cold.

"Buttermilk" Buckwheat Pancakes with Mixed Berry Compote

When I began eating a more plant-centered diet a number of years ago, one of the ingredients I missed using was buttermilk. It gives a wonderful, tangy taste to recipes and is an integral part of many baked items: biscuits, corn bread, and of course, pancakes and waffles. Not only does it enhance the flavor of the dish, it reacts with the baking soda in recipes, resulting in a distinctive texture. I finally came upon a way to turn plant-based "milks" into buttermilk. As you can see from the recipe, adding a little apple cider vinegar to the plant milk transforms it into a buttermilk. So, voilà, we can still have our delicious pancakes and waffles while cutting back a scootch on dairy.

Makes about twenty 4-inch pancakes

2 cups whole wheat flour

1 cup white flour

1 cup buckwheat flour

2 tablespoons baking powder

1 teaspoon baking soda

2 tablespoons sugar

1 teaspoon salt

2 eggs, beaten, or 2 tablespoons Ener G egg
replacer mixed with ½ cup warm water

3 cups soy or almond milk mixed with
1 tablespoon apple cider vinegar

2 teaspoons vanilla extract

6 tablespoons vegetable oil, melted butter
(can use melted vegan butter), or half oil
and half applesauce

Mixed Berry Compote (*recipe follows*)

In a bowl, mix the flours, baking powder, baking soda, sugar, and salt. In a larger bowl, whisk the beaten eggs (or egg replacer) with the warm water until frothy. Whisk in the soured soy/almond milk, vanilla, and oil. Mix the dry ingredients into the wet. Do not overbeat.

Cook the cakes on a hot griddle as you would regular pancakes. Serve with Mixed Berry Compote or local maple syrup.

MIXED BERRY COMPOTE

Makes about 2 cups

6   tablespoons brown sugar

2   tablespoons sugar

4   tablespoons water

3   tablespoons lemon juice

4   cups berries (combination of blackberries and blueberries)

Bring the brown sugar, sugar, water, and lemon juice to a boil. Cook for about 3 minutes. Add the berries and gently toss them in the liquid. Simmer for several minutes. Remove from heat. Serve warm, at room temperature, or chilled.

Spelt Waffles with Crystallized Ginger and Chocolate Chips

Sundays were often waffle day at our house and always a special treat. These waffles are outrageously good and bring into play one of the healthiest grains to be found. Farro is all the rage at the trendy restaurants across the country, but truth be told, it is actually spelt. The farro is the whole kernel of the spelt plant, has a nutty taste, and is very nutritious. A number of farmers around the Chesapeake region are once again growing this ancient grain. It does not have the same gluten content as the wheats grown today, so I mix it with other flours. However, you could use all spelt for a delicious, but a bit more dense, waffle.

Makes 12 to 16 large waffles

2   cups spelt flour
1   cup white flour
1   cup whole wheat flour
2   tablespoons baking powder
1   teaspoon baking soda
1   teaspoon salt
3   large local eggs, separated
2   tablespoons sugar
3   cups dairy milk or plant milk
6   tablespoons vegetable oil or melted butter
⅔   cup dark chocolate chips
½   cup finely diced crystallized ginger
Local maple syrup or honey

Preheat the waffle iron.

Sift together the flours, baking powder, baking soda, and salt in a bowl. In a larger bowl, whisk the egg yolks together with the sugar until creamy and pale in color. Slowly whisk in the milk, followed by the vegetable oil or butter.

Stir the dry ingredients into the wet, taking care not to overmix the batter. Beat the egg whites until stiff peaks form. Fold into the batter. Then gently fold in the chocolate chips and pieces of ginger.

Cook in the waffle iron, according to the manufacturer's instructions, until golden brown. Serve with warm maple syrup or honey. If you're feeling festive, a little lightly sweetened whipped topping is nice as well.

Organic or Local—Which Is Better?

Does seeing that "Certified Organic" sticker on your food cause you to mentally conjure up images of misty fields and bucolic farms where the farmer hoes his rows in a tattered straw hat—just like in those old Beatrix Potter books? Does it ensure that your food was grown or raised on a small, independently owned farm with old-fashioned methods, happy cows, and chickens freely running round the barnyard? Not necessarily . . .

I'm sure it's not easy to try to take a broad concept like organic food and precisely codify it into a set of industry-standard regulations; it's even harder to actually enforce them. The US Department of Agriculture (USDA) first took a shot at it in 2002. Since then, pretty much all hell has broken loose as "Big Ag" has muscled its way into the organic market. For instance, early regulations attempted to standardize how organic poultry should be raised by insisting that birds must have access to the outdoors, meaning, as we'd sure like to think, that the chickens spend most of the day happily picking around in the grass. But, no. A large-scale poultry operation can provide "access" by merely opening a small door on a cramped and dank 500-bird chicken house for a portion of the day. If the startled chickens don't wander out—well, they had their "access."

All kinds of legal battles ensue every time the USDA organic standards are revised. Multinational corporations are usually fighting for looser regulations to increase profitability, and small farmers, consumer advocates, and environmental, health, and animal rights organizations are fighting for tighter, more carefully defined regulations.

In a 2001 article, noted food writer Michael Pollan warns:

> There are values that the new corporate—and government—construction of "organic" leaves out, values that once were part and parcel of the word but that have since been abandoned as impractical or unprofitable. I'm thinking of things like locally grown, like the humane treatment of animals, like the value of a shorter and more legible food chain, the preservation of family farms, even the promise of a counter cuisine. To believe that the U.S.D.A. label on a product ensures any of these things is, as I discovered, naive.

What to do? First thing, always read the label. There's a *legal* difference between "100% Organic," and "Organic," which means 95% organic ingredients, and the other 5% just could be something you really don't care to eat. Note too that "Made with Organic Ingredients" means the product may contain as little as 75% organics. Labels such as "All Natural" and "Cage Free," though they mean something, do *not* mean organic.

Know your merchants and vendors—better yet, know your farmer. Invest in your local community-supported agriculture farms that sell subscriptions to their harvest. Shop at your neighborhood farmers' markets, where you can get to know the folks who actually grow and raise what they sell. Many local certified growers, like One Straw Farm in northern Baltimore County, fit our vision of an ideal independently owned and operated organic farm.

So, what is best? Both organic *and* local, if you can possibly find it. But it depends a lot on what you are buying. If you're not sure, ask. Speak directly to the growers and ask how the product was grown or raised. Just because something is not technically "organic" does not mean it is bad by any stretch of the imagination. Some growing habitat is more prone to infestation and requires some type of pest management, which can be done without using highly toxic products. Fruit orchards in our region need minimal spraying for insects and fungus due to the humid climate. Again, developing a relationship with your local farmers and producers is key.

Some things simply aren't produced nearby, such as olive oil, bananas, cocoa, and coffee. I can't imagine living without my morning coffee, which technically is not "local," but I can buy the beans from an independent local coffee roaster. I try to shop carefully, read the labels, and buy local whenever I can. I want the first-hand assurance that the food I'm eating and serving is produced in a way that meets my personal standards. I love to keep my food dollars circulating in the local community, too. Plus, my Saturday mornings at the farmers' market are, for me, one of the best, liveliest, and downright fun social occasions of the week.

Pumpkin Pancakes with Candied Pumpkin Seeds

Pumpkin is not only for lattes, despite what you may have heard. These hotcakes are good any time of the year, but I gravitate toward them in the cooler months. Pumpkin is a staple of every Chesapeake kitchen in the fall and can be steamed, roasted, or even grilled. If you're not inclined to cook a pumpkin just for this recipe, canned will work as well. An easy switch-out for this dish is cooked sweet potatoes or yams, either canned or freshly cooked, in place of the pumpkin.

Makes about twelve 4-inch cakes

1   pound steamed pumpkin flesh, cooled and mashed (about 1 cup mashed pumpkin)

3   eggs, beaten, or egg replacer (1 tablespoon plus 1½ teaspoons Ener G egg replacer whisked with 6 tablespoons warm water)

2   cups dairy milk or plant milk

1   teaspoon vanilla

6   tablespoons melted butter or vegetable oil

2   cups flour

1½ tablespoons baking powder

½   teaspoon baking soda

½   teaspoon salt

1   teaspoon cinnamon

Candied Pumpkin Seeds (optional; *recipe follows*)

Local maple syrup, for serving

Lightly sweetened whipped cream (optional)

Mix the pumpkin, eggs, milk, vanilla, and melted butter or oil together in a bowl. In a larger bowl, sift together the flour, baking powder, baking soda, salt, and cinnamon. Slowly pour the wet ingredients into the dry. Mix well but do not overbeat.

Cook the cakes on a hot griddle as you would regular pancakes. Serve topped with candied pumpkin seeds and warm local maple syrup. A little cinnamon-scented whipped cream wouldn't hurt, either!

CANDIED PUMPKIN SEEDS

2 cups pumpkin seeds

⅓ cup brown sugar

3 tablespoons freshly squeezed orange juice

Pinch of salt

¼ teaspoon ground cinnamon

¼ teaspoon ground coriander

Preheat oven to 325°F.

Toast the pumpkin seeds in a hot cast-iron skillet over medium heat for about 3 minutes or until they puff slightly.

In a small bowl, mix together the sugar, orange juice, salt, cinnamon, and coriander. Add the toasted pumpkin seeds and toss to coat thoroughly. Spread the mixture onto a baking sheet that has been lined with parchment paper. Spread out the seeds so they do not overlap. Bake in the oven until the seeds turn a darkish medium brown, about 12 minutes. Keep a close eye on them as they bake to make sure they don't burn, or you will have to start all over.

Allow to cool slightly on the baking sheet and then transfer to a wire baking rack until cooled completely. Break apart if necessary and store in an airtight container.

Health-Defining Green Smoothies

Many of us grew up watching Popeye eat his spinach and get crazy strong. I tried emulating Popeye, but that canned spinach was just, well, gross. But in our new Chesapeake kitchen, green is the way to go. Smoothies are just the ticket for a quick, nutritious breakfast or midday snack. More and more studies are showing that green leafy vegetables keep us healthy and ward off all sorts of developed-world diseases. Grandma was right about eating your greens, and in our hurried world just sipping down a green smoothie can soothe our jangled nerves. It's a great way to start the day.

Here are the basics on a good smoothie. I'll leave it to you to create your signature smoothie.

Yields about 3 cups

First, the Greens—
2 cups firmly packed greens.

I generally like the younger, baby greens, when possible, as they are more tender. For our standard smoothie batch (about 3 cups), here are some options:

Baby collards

Kale

Spinach

Swiss chard

Arugula (use this as an "accent" green—
 it's spicy, so a little goes a long way)

Mustard greens (use this as an "accent"
 green—it's spicy)

Second, the Liquid—2 cups liquid.

Lots of options here as well, depending on your diet preferences and tastes, but basically you *will* need liquid to make a smoothie.

Water

Soy milk

Almond milk

Coconut milk

Lowfat/nonfat local dairy milk

Yogurt

Kombucha

Fruit juice (be careful, as it tends to be
 very high in sugar)

Third, the Fruit—3 cups cut-up ripe fruit.

The fruit in the smoothie gives sweetness and, most importantly, body and texture. Feel free to mix and match. Smoothies are often quite seasonal and will be influenced by what's available at the farmers' market. Here are a few ideas:

Local in season:

Strawberries

Apples

Grapes

Cherries

Apricots

Plums

Figs

Paw Paw

Persimmon

From warmer climates:

Banana

Pineapple

Orange

Kiwi

Papaya

Mango

Avocado

Optional additions:

Just a tad for extra sweetness if desired.

Honey

Maple syrup

Molasses

Agave

"Superfoods":

Flax seeds

Nutritional yeast

Chia seeds

Hemp seeds

And I suppose you are looking for instructions?
OMG—just put all the ingredients you've chosen
into a blender, process well, and enjoy.

2

APPETIZING BITES

It's party time! Small plates and hand-passed morsels are all the rage for gatherings these days. Many folks are eating lighter, and others just want to get a taste of as many dishes as possible. We've collected an array of dishes from around the Bay, featuring bites from the field, farm, and water. Many of the recipes offer suggestions of how you can adjust ingredients or make variations to create your very own versions. So enjoy and go wild in the kitchen.

Wide Net Blue Catfish Catties

These are a take on the ubiquitous Baltimore "coddie." We use house-made salt-catfish and transform this tasty invasive species into a regional fish cake. My latest obsession is making "salt-cat." I've always been a big fan of salt cod and love the classic dishes made from it, like bacalao and the infamous Baltimore-style coddies. Salting cod was an old-timey preservation technique that is used to this day. It is a staple in Mediterranean cooking and found widely in recipes from New England. The salt cod is usually soaked overnight in water and then soaked a half a day longer, with the soaking water changed often. The same is true of our salt-cat.

Makes 18 to 20 catties

1 pound dried salt-catfish (*see note*)

1½ pounds white potatoes, peeled and cut into quarters

2 tablespoons melted butter, or olive oil

1 small onion, finely diced

3 eggs, beaten

3 tablespoons grain mustard

4 tablespoons minced chives

⅓ cup finely chopped parsley

2 tablespoons chopped dill

Salt and freshly ground pepper, to taste

Oil for frying

Saltine crackers, for serving

Yellow mustard of your choosing, for serving

Soak the salt-catfish in a bowl of cold water for 6 hours, changing the water approximately every 2 hours. When ready to prepare the recipe, place the salt-catfish in a pan and cover it with water. Bring to a boil, reduce the heat, and simmer for 15 minutes. Drain and break up the fish into flakes with a fork. Cool.

Cook the potatoes in lightly salted water until tender; drain and mash well. Let the potatoes cool.

Heat the butter or oil in a pan and gently sauté the onion for 5 minutes, taking care not to brown. Place the catfish, potatoes, and sautéed onion into a bowl and mix together with the mustard, herbs, salt, and pepper. Form the catties into small balls and flatten to about ½-inch thick.

Pour oil into a heavy skillet to a depth of about 1½ inches. Heat the oil and fry the catties a few at a time until golden brown, about 3 minutes on each side. Remove with a slotted utensil and drain on paper towels.

The catties can be served hot, warm, or at room temperature. Serve on crackers with mustard on the side.

Note: To make salt-catfish, place a layer (about ½ inch deep) in the bottom of a large Pyrex dish. Lay out a single layer of catfish and completely cover the catfish with kosher salt. Wrap the tray with plastic wrap and store in the refrigerator for 48 hours. Remove fish from salt and rinse lightly with cold water. Dry the fillets very well. Refrigerate until ready to make the catties.

Prize-Winning Spinach-Wrapped Oysters Casino

Each fall the National Oyster Festival is held in Leonardtown, in St. Mary's County, Maryland, and for many years now I have been fortunate enough to be an invited judge of the National Oyster Cook-Off. Chefs, home cooks, and backyard barbequers from all over the United States come to compete in the contest. Here's a recipe from the 2011 Grand Prize Winner, Loic Jaffres. Hailing from Leonardtown, this guy obviously knows his oysters. The recipe is for twelve oysters, but if you're having company over and serving these as appetizers, trust me, you'll need more than twelve. They go faster than peanuts. Fortunately, the recipe for the Casino Butter is ample, so just keep on shucking!

12 large oysters in the shell
    or 1 pint Chesapeake Bay oysters
12 large spinach leaves
6   slices bacon, julienned
Casino Butter (*recipe follows*)
Rock salt

Preheat broiler to 350°F.

Shuck oysters if using shell oysters. (If you're using shucked oysters, you will need to have some previously shucked oyster shells on hand.) Blanch the spinach leaves very quickly in hot salted water. Lay the spinach leaves out flat, and top each one with an oyster. Fold the spinach leaves up around the oyster. Place the oyster back in a deep oyster shell and top generously with the Casino Butter. Place the oysters on a baking sheet that has a ½-inch layer of rock salt. Nestle the oysters into the rock salt to secure them.

Place the tray under the broiler for about 7 to 8 minutes or until the butter is bubbling. While the oysters are cooking, sauté the strips of bacon in a frying pan until crispy. Remove from frying pan and place on paper towels to absorb the bacon grease. Set aside.

When the oysters are done, top them with the bacon strips and serve immediately.

CASINO BUTTER

1   pound and 1 tablespoon butter, at room temperature

2   shallots, minced

1   small red bell pepper, finely diced

1   small green bell pepper, finely diced

1   cup dry white wine

2   cloves garlic, minced

2   tablespoons chopped parsley

Salt and pepper, to taste

Melt 1 tablespoon of butter in a sauté pan. Add the shallots and bell peppers and sauté until the shallots are translucent, about 5 minutes. Add the white wine and simmer until the wine has almost completely evaporated. Stir in the garlic and parsley, remove from heat, and set aside to cool. When the vegetables are completely cool, whip them into the remaining softened butter. Season with salt and pepper to taste.

Note: This makes a good portion of Casino Butter. If you have some left over, it can be frozen for later use.

Crispy Rockfish Tacos with Lime-Jicama Slaw and Avocado Cream

This is some of the Chesapeake's plant-forward eating at its best. A whole slew of wonderful vegetables coming together, all wrapped in a warm corn tortilla, with crispy pieces of the Bay's favorite finfish, the rock—a.k.a. striped—bass. This dish works well for a party if you set up a taco station with all the ingredients, allowing guests to make their own.

Serves 4

Lime-Jicama Slaw (*recipe follows*)
1   pound rockfish fillet
1   cup flour
2   teaspoons salt
1   teaspoon cumin
1   teaspoon garlic powder
½   teaspoon chipotle powder
½   teaspoon paprika
¼   teaspoon cayenne pepper
¼   teaspoon freshly ground black pepper
Oil for frying
8 fresh small corn tortillas
Avocado Cream (*recipe follows*)
Salsa Fresca (*page 17*)
Julienned radish, to garnish
Lime wedges, to garnish

Prepare the Lime-Jicama Slaw and refrigerate for 1 hour before serving.

Cut the rockfish fillets into 1½-inch chunks. In a bowl, mix the flour with the salt, cumin, garlic powder, chipotle powder, paprika, cayenne, and black pepper and blend well.

Heat oil to a depth of 1½ inches until quite hot. Dust the rockfish pieces with the flour mixture and shake off excess. In batches, fry the fish until golden brown and cooked through. Remove the pieces of fish with a slotted utensil and allow to drain on paper towels.

While cooking fish, heat a dry (not oiled) cast-iron skillet and warm the tortillas for about 30 seconds on each side. Wrap tortillas in a damp towel and keep warm while heating the rest of the tortillas.

To assemble the tacos, place a spoonful of slaw in the center of each tortilla, followed by several pieces of fish and a dollop of Avocado Cream. Garnish with a teaspoon of salsa, plus radish. Serve lime wedges on the side.

LIME-JICAMA SLAW

1   cup shredded cabbage

½   cup shredded jicama

¼   cup chopped green onion

¼   cup julienned carrots

1   tablespoon chopped cilantro

¼   cup mayonnaise

Juice of 1 lime

In a bowl, combine the cabbage, jicama, green onion, carrots, and cilantro. In another small bowl, combine the mayo and lime juice. Pour over the top of the vegetable mixture, tossing to coat well.

AVOCADO CREAM

2   ripe avocados

½   cup sour cream

Juice of ½ lime

Pinch of ground cumin

Salt, to taste

Remove the skin and pit from the avocados and place the flesh in a bowl. Mash the avocado and then add the remaining ingredients.

Lump Crab and Roasted Corn Bruschetta

The combo of freshly roasted Eastern Shore corn paired with the sweet, briny lumps of crabmeat transforms a regular tomato bruschetta into a whole new culinary realm.

Makes about 8 to 10 servings

1½ pounds ripe plum tomatoes, peeled, seeded, and diced

2 teaspoons minced garlic

2 tablespoons extra-virgin olive oil

¼ cup finely chopped fresh basil

1 teaspoon balsamic vinegar

⅓ cup finely diced fresh mozzarella (optional)

2–3 ears roasted or grilled corn (*see note*), kernels cut from cob

Salt and freshly ground black pepper, to taste

½ pound lump crabmeat, picked over for shells

1 baguette

Olive oil for brushing

Preheat oven to 425°F.

In a mixing bowl, combine the tomatoes, garlic, olive oil, basil, and vinegar. Fold in the mozzarella, if using, and the kernels of roasted corn. Season the mixture with salt and pepper to taste. Carefully fold in the crabmeat, taking care not to break up the lumps.

Slice the baguette on a diagonal, about ½-inch thick. Lightly brush each side of the baguette pieces with the olive oil. Place bread pieces on a baking sheet and bake for about 2 to 3 minutes or until the baguette pieces are just lightly browned.

Place the toasted bread on a serving tray and top each piece with a heaping tablespoon or so of the tomato-corn-crab mixture. Serve at once.

Note: To roast corn, place the unhusked corn into a preheated 400°F oven, directly on the rack. Roast for about 20 to 25 minutes. Remove from the oven and allow to cool slightly. Husk the corn and when ready to use, cut the kernels from the cob. To grill corn, husk the ears of corn and place over a medium gas flame on the stovetop burner. With tongs, keep turning the corn, allowing it to just barely char evenly around the cob, about 5 minutes cooking time. Cut kernels from the cob.

Mrs. O'Linder's Crabby (or Not) Deviled Eggs

Mrs. Joanne O'Linder, of Towson, Maryland, is famous for her deviled eggs, which are not so much plant-forward but more like little protein bombs. And what's better than some local, lump crab lacing a dill-infused, old-fashioned deviled egg? Joanne doesn't call for it in this recipe, but I'm sure she wouldn't object to just a light sprinkle of Old Bay atop the eggs before serving. If you are not feeling crabby, this recipe makes awesome deviled eggs, sans crustacean.

Yields 16 pieces

- 8 hard-cooked eggs
- ⅓ cup sour cream, more if necessary
- 3 tablespoons minced chives
- 2 tablespoons white wine vinegar
- ½ teaspoon salt
- Pinch of white pepper
- 2 tablespoons chopped dill
- ½ pound lump crabmeat
- Dill sprigs for garnish (optional)

Slice the hard-cooked eggs in half lengthwise, and place the yolks in a small bowl. Set the whites of the eggs on a tray or platter to await the filling.

Mash the yolks well with a fork. Stir in the sour cream, chives, vinegar, salt, pepper, and dill and mix together thoroughly. Using a rubber spatula, gently fold in half of the lump crabmeat, reserving the larger lumps for garnish.

Spoon the mixture evenly into the egg whites. Top each one with a beautiful lump or two of crabmeat. Garnish with a sprinkle of Old Bay and a small sprig of dill, if desired.

Rumbleway Farm Molasses-Scented Duck Breast with Sweet Potato Crepes

Robin Way, along with her husband, Mark, owns and operates a 62-acre certified organic farm in Cecil County, Maryland. It's a storybook kind of setting, with a stone house dating to the 1800s, rolling hills, lush countryside, and farm animals roaming the fields and wooded areas. Beyond running the farm and an on-premises store, Robin is a first-class chef and cooking instructor. Rumbleway Farm hosts a cooking series each year during the late fall through the winter. It's always a sellout! Here's a delicious recipe from Robin for appetizer crepes, enhanced with sweet potato.

Makes 18 small appetizer crepes

3   duck breast fillets

Salt and freshly ground black pepper

¼   cup olive oil

2   tablespoons freshly squeezed orange juice

1   tablespoon freshly squeezed lime juice

1   teaspoon molasses

½   teaspoon sugar

¼   teaspoon grated orange zest

Sweet Potato Crepes (*recipe follows*)

Preheat the oven to 400°F.

Season the duck breast all over with salt and pepper. Heat the oil and brown the duck in a medium saucepan. Remove from pan and bake in the oven on a wire rack for 20 minutes or until done to your liking—medium rare to medium.

Rest the cooked duck breast in a warm place for 5 minutes. Mix together the orange and lime juices, molasses, sugar, and zest in a bowl; set aside. Discard the duck skin and slice the fillets finely across the grain or shred them into medium pieces. Drizzle the duck with the citrus-molasses mixture. To assemble the crepes, place the drizzled duck inside and fold over. Enjoy!

SWEET POTATO CREPES

Makes 18 crepes

1   cup all-purpose flour

½   teaspoon baking soda

3   eggs

1½ cups whole milk

¼   teaspoon sea salt

1   tablespoon light olive oil

2   teaspoons ground cumin

2   ounces sweet potato, finely grated

Whisk together the flour, soda, eggs, ½ cup milk, sea salt, olive oil, and cumin in a large bowl. Continue whisking until you have a smooth batter. Cover the bowl and place it in the refrigerator to chill the batter for at least 30 minutes or as long as several hours.

Press the grated sweet potato between sheets of paper towel to remove any extra moisture. Stir into the batter.

Heat an 8-inch nonstick skillet or crepe pan over medium heat. Melt a teaspoon of butter in the pan or spray with vegetable spray.

Using a ladle or a measuring cup, pour about ⅛ to ¼ cup of the batter into the pan. Hold the pan with one hand and pour the batter in with the other. Swirl the pan while pouring so that the batter covers the pan thinly and evenly for each crepe. Try not to leave any holes. After the first few crepes, you will know exactly how much batter your pan will hold.

Cook the crepe over medium-high heat until the edges turn brown, about 15 seconds. Flip the crepe using a small spatula and your fingers. Cook on the second side for another 10 to 15 seconds. The second side will not be as evenly browned as the first side. Remove the pan from the heat and invert it over a warm plate to stack the crepes. Keep the crepes warm until ready to use. Continue making crepes with remaining batter, adjusting the heat as needed.

Bison Sliders with Talbot Reserve Cheese and Curry Ketchup

My dear friend Rita Calvert is a culinary icon and one of the leaders in the Chesapeake's farm-to-table efforts. She is the author of the award-winning cookbook *The Grassfed Gourmet Fires It Up!* Rita says this recipe is a novel way to make a slew of sliders all at once. She suggests about 1 ounce per slider, so the meat goes a long way as small bites or hors d'oeuvres. She tops each slider with a rich, cave-aged cheddar from Chapel Country Creamery in Easton, Maryland. You can garnish and build these sliders as you wish: with baguette or slider rolls and with sliced onions, pickles, and lettuce or arugula.

Serves 8

1 pound ground grassfed beef or bison

Kosher salt and freshly ground pepper, to taste

1 French baguette, sliced horizontally, but not through, to open like a book

Freshly grated Talbot Reserve or other full-flavor, aged cheddar cheese, at room temperature

Curry Ketchup (*recipe follows*)

Heat the grill to medium-high.

Place the bison in a bowl and add salt and pepper. Mix with a spoon to keep the meat cold. Form the meat into 2 or 3 long rectangular burgers, which will fit neatly into the baguette.

Grease the grill rack and add the burgers, without crowding. Grill each rectangle on one side until nicely browned, then turn and brown the other side, making sure that the burgers remain rare and juicy. While the second side browns, top the burgers with the cheese to allow it to melt. Toast the opened baguette on the grill until just golden and warm. Then, while still warm, spread one side liberally with Curry Ketchup.

Place the burgers on a cutting board and let rest for a moment. Lay the open baguette on the cutting board. Place each burger on the bottom half of the bread. Close the bread firmly and cut crosswise into 2-inch-thick slices. A toothpick in each slice holds it all together and makes it easy to pick up.

CURRY KETCHUP

12-ounce bottle chili sauce

⅓ cup sweet onion, finely chopped

1 teaspoon curry powder

1 teaspoon balsamic vinegar

Combine all the ingredients in a small bowl. Cover and refrigerate at least several hours before serving.

Oyster Farming

In Greek myth Aphrodite, goddess of love, emerged from a giant oyster shell that rose from the depths of the sea and immediately gave birth to her son Eros. We also know these two as Venus and Cupid, their Roman names, and the terms "aphrodisiac" and "erotic" are still with us. Oysters have long been associated with sexual potency, which is interesting, since they have an ambiguous sexuality. They are hermaphroditic and will normally change sex at least once in their lifetime, usually starting as male and ending up as female. We'll be coming back to this in a bit.

Crassostrea virginica, the native Chesapeake oyster, flourished here for many thousands of years. Huge oyster middens (mounds of shells) left by Native Americans have been dated to as long ago as 2000 BC. The original conditions in the Chesapeake—relatively shallow waters that were rich in nutrients and deeply forested lands bordering the rivers and creeks to deter erosion—were utterly perfect for oysters. Ocean water, mingled with the fresh water from all the rivers flowing into the Chesapeake, created the moderately salty water oysters love. In turn, oysters kept the Bay healthy and clean, removing nutrients as they siphoned water through their gill systems. Biologists estimate that when English settlers reached Virginia and Maryland in the 1600s, there were enough oysters thriving to have filtered the entire Chesapeake Bay once a week, ensuring waters of pristine clarity, even down to a depth of 20 feet.

Astonished at the quantities of oysters here, the early colonists quickly made them an important part of their diet. Still, it wasn't until the 1800s that commercial oystering really took off. Once it did, there was no stopping it. By the mid-1880s, thousands of sailboats plied the Bay, either dredging for oysters or hauling oysters to market. In a little over 100 years, billions upon billions of oysters were taken from the Bay, taken much faster than they could reproduce, with enormous, long-term, negative repercussions for the Bay's ecology. By 2004, a Maryland oyster harvest that reliably yielded sixteen million bushels a year in the 1970s produced only twenty-six thousand bushels.

With oyster harvests plummeting, state officials, conservation and environmental groups, watermen, and seafood packers became worried. Creating reserves or sanctuaries where no dredging could be done; imposing a rotational harvest system, which opens and closes specific oyster bars in rotation; partitioning areas; and creating a leased bottom fishery are some of the efforts made to restore the Bay's oysters. Meanwhile, concerned scientists were searching for a heartier oyster. None was found. Instead, one was created. Here's where the oyster's odd sexual metamorphosis comes into play...

A young graduate student at the time, Standish K. Allen is primarily credited with creating a hybrid (rather than a genetically modified version) of *Crassostrea virginica* that, with careful manipulation of salinity and temperature levels during crucial periods of its life, did not go through its normal sexual changes and remained sterile. This is called a tetraploid oyster, as opposed to the original diploid oyster. Not to go too deep into Genetics 101, but I'll just explain that these tetraploid oysters are now used on a large scale to breed with female diploids to produce "natural" triploid oyster spat, or young, for cultivation.

Instead of expending its energies in spawning, this oyster could grow larger and faster, develop a more protective shell, and become resistant to some of the parasites that plague the diploids. Triploids grew as much as 50 percent larger than normal diploid oysters, and since the sterile triploids were not spawning during the summer months, they were ready to harvest and eat all year 'round.

This was the scientific breakthrough that led to the now-booming business of oyster farming in the Chesapeake, especially in Virginia. Though Maryland has recently been working to update its restrictive leasing laws and laborious application processes, it is still far behind its southern neighbor. In May of 2015, Rona Kobell reported in the *Christian Science Monitor*: "Today, Maryland has 4,000 acres under lease and 474 people working in shellfish aquaculture. Its dockside value for aquaculture in 2014 was more than $3 million." Meanwhile, the value of Virginia farm-raised oysters in 2014 was reported to have topped $17 million.

Modern oyster farmers understand that things change, and that change can sometimes even be for the better. Oysters are usually farmed throughout the year in submerged or floating cages, often near to the shore, whereas the work of cool-season dredging out on the water is dangerous and grueling. Storms, tides, and winter weather can take a toll on your boat, not to mention what they do to your body. Oyster farming brings enormous benefits to our local economy, too, providing steady jobs in many coastal communities where employment levels are often seasonally stunted.

Although oyster aquaculture alone will never recreate the massed oyster beds that once covered the Bay's floor and nurtured so many other aquatic creatures, oyster farming, done right, clearly lessens the stresses on our over-harvested native oysters and will contribute to their gradual restoration. All the while, farmed oysters are contributing to the health of the Bay, filtering the waters of excessive nutrients and encouraging the health of all marine life. Farmers find their cages just brimming with eager little come-alongs, and the waters surrounding oyster farms often sparkle, just like in the days of yore.

Broom's Bloom Cheddar and Sausage Potato Puffs

These little pop-in-your-mouth puffs are not only delicious but actually fun to make. Channel your inner Julia Child, because what we're making is a classic pate a choux, or a cream puff dough. You will need some mini muffin pans for this; otherwise you'll just have some free-form balls baked on a sheet pan. (Not the worst thing in the world.) I enjoy a nice sharp cheddar, like the ones we get from our friends at Broom's Bloom Dairy, in the puffs. But feel free to play around with whatever cheese suits your fancy.

Makes about 4 dozen puffs

1	pound Yukon Gold or Russet potatoes
¼	pound of your favorite sausage, such as turkey, Italian, or kielbasa
1	cup water
¼	cup freshly squeezed orange juice
4	tablespoons butter
2	teaspoons salt
1	cup white flour
5	eggs
½	cup sharp cheddar, or your choice of an in-your-face tangy cheese
2	teaspoons grated orange zest
2	teaspoons finely chopped thyme
1	teaspoon finely chopped oregano
2	egg yolks, beaten, mixed with 2 tablespoons water

Cook the potatoes in ample salted water right in their jackets. This prevents them from getting soggy. When they are just tender, pour out the water and let the potatoes cool down enough that they are not too hot to handle. Mash them well with a potato masher.

While the potatoes are cooking, you could remove the sausage meat from its casings and sauté it in a skillet until the meat is fully cooked. Drain the drippings from the meat and then coarsely crumble the meat and set it aside.

Okay, here comes the pate a choux. In a saucepan, heat the water, orange juice, butter, and salt and bring to a full boil. Remove from heat and, using a wooden spoon, stir in the flour, and continue to beat until well incorporated. Place the pan back over a medium-high heat and stir the mixture vigorously. It will pull away from the side of the pan. Keep cooking for about 3 to 4 minutes, but don't stop stirring, as you don't want it to burn.

I like to use a KitchenAid or similar mixer appliance for this next step. Place the flour mixture into the bowl of the KitchenAid and put on the paddle attachment. Beat at a slow speed, and then add one egg at a time, allowing each egg to incorporate before adding the next. Then add the cheese, orange zest, thyme, and oregano. Stir in the mashed potatoes and the crumbled sausage.

Preheat oven to 400°F. With a small scoop, fill mini muffin pans that have been sprayed with a vegetable oil cooking spray. (In lieu of the mini muffin pans, you could scoop the mixture onto sheet pans that are covered with oiled parchment paper.)

Brush the puffs with just a tad of the egg yolk wash and place into the hot oven. Bake for about 20 minutes or until nicely puffed and golden brown. Let the puffs cool for several minutes and then serve warm.

Tip: You can allow the puffs to cool completely and then wrap well, refrigerate, and reheat later, just before using.

Shady Goat Farm Stuffed Portabella Mushrooms

Artisan goat cheeses are now found throughout the Chesapeake region. Down in Hampton Roads, Virginia, Shannon Rice and her husband, Tim, were pioneers in the local goat cheese movement. Their fine variety of cheeses have been featured at Old Beach Farmers Market in Virginia Beach and are used by Hampton Roads' finest chefs. This recipe is for a veggie bite that pairs herb-infused goat cheese with local cheddar, all nestled in a roasted portabella mushroom cap. It's a perfect appetizer for any occasion.

Serves 4

4 medium-size portabella mushroom caps

Olive oil

4 ounces flavored local chevre (such as garlic and herb-artichoke, garlic, or tarragon-garlic and chive)

4 ounces local cheddar cheese, sliced

Preheat the oven to 450°F.

Brush the mushrooms liberally with the olive oil and place in a baking pan. Cook in the oven for 10 to 12 minutes or until just softened.

Remove the mushrooms from the oven. Divide the chevre evenly among the mushroom caps. Top each mushroom with pieces of sliced cheddar and return to oven. Bake for about 5 minutes or until cheese is melted. Serve hot or warm.

Spicy Sweet Potato Cakes with Apple Fig Chutney "Creme Fraiche"

A great little pass-around appetizer featuring the ubiquitous Chesapeake region's sweet potato. I'm always baking extra sweet potatoes to have around as a snack, and any leftovers you might have on hand will make preparing this dish a breeze. You can play with the "fire" of the chilies however you please, always remembering that the "fire" is in the seeds. If you want less heat, remove some or all of the seeds.

The Apple Fig Chutney "Creme Fraiche" pairs nicely with these spicy little cakes. The sauce is really an easy method for creme fraiche, which normally requires some longer-term fermenting. I substitute a thick Greek yogurt as the base, but should you be at a specialty grocery and find authentic creme fraiche, that would be fabulous.

Serves 4

2 pounds sweet potatoes, roasted, peeled, and mashed

2 cups panko bread crumbs

½ cup flour

⅓ cup roughly chopped cilantro, plus whole leaves for garnish

4 scallions, roughly chopped

2 small red Thai chilies or ½ a serrano chili, minced

1 egg, beaten

Kosher salt and freshly ground black pepper

Canola oil for frying

Apple Fig Chutney "Creme Fraiche" (*recipe follows*)

Mix potatoes, 1 cup of panko, flour, chopped cilantro, scallions, chilies, egg, salt, and pepper in a bowl.

Pour oil into a 12-inch skillet to a depth of about ¼ inch and heat over medium heat, until quite hot but not smoking. Using oiled hands, divide potato mixture into sixteen 2-ounce patties about ½-inch thick. Coat lightly with remaining panko.

Working in batches, fry the cakes, adding more oil if needed. Flip each cake once until golden and crisp on both sides, about 2 to 3 minutes. Drain on paper towels and season with additional salt and pepper as needed. Top each pancake with a dollop of the "creme fraiche" and garnish with cilantro leaves.

APPLE FIG CHUTNEY "CREME FRAICHE"

While I love the Apple Fig Chutney recipe in this book, feel free to use just about any chutney you have available. An apple chutney from an Indian grocery makes an excellent substitute.

Yields 1 cup

½ cup thick plain Greek yogurt

½ cup Apple Fig Chutney (*page 244*)

In a small bowl, whisk the yogurt until smooth. Fold in the chutney, cover the bowl, and refrigerate for at least 1 hour before using.

Sweet Pea and Mint Bruschetta with Chesapeake Chevre

Shoppers at our local farmers' markets go crazy for fresh peas in the spring. Every market I visit has long lines at the resident "pea farmers" stand. Don't try to jump ahead in line—you may get hurt, as our pea aficionados are serious. This dish is unbelievable. Simple, bright, one of the most vibrant small bites imaginable.

I find that a creamy chevre is just the ticket to top off the mint-citrus-scented chunky pea mixture. We are fortunate to have quite the number of award-winning artisan cheese makers in our region. I have worked with FireFly Farms (the granddaddy of Chesapeake goat cheese crafters, creator of the well-known Merry Goat Round), Cherry Glen (producing an extraordinary chevre), and Charlottetown Farm (whose goat ricotta, feta, and chevre are world class). These are just a few of the amazing cheese makers calling the Chesapeake home.

Yields about 2 cups

2 cups shelled fresh sweet English peas (about 2¼ pounds in the pod)

2 teaspoons salt

2 tablespoons extra-virgin olive oil, plus more for brushing

½ teaspoon finely minced lemon zest

2 teaspoons freshly squeezed lemon juice

2 tablespoons minced mint

Salt and freshly ground black pepper, to taste

1 baguette

Chevre goat cheese for garnish

Bring a large saucepan of water and salt to a boil. Add the peas and cook until just tender, 3 to 4 minutes. Remove the peas with a slotted utensil and place in a bowl of cold water. Drain in a colander and transfer to a small food processor. Process until all the peas are broken down but not too smooth. You do not want to purée them—a little texture is just fine.

Transfer the peas to a bowl and add the olive oil, lemon zest, lemon juice, and mint. Season with salt and pepper and mix well.

Slice the baguette on a slight diagonal into ¼-inch pieces. Place the bread on a baking sheet and brush both sides with olive oil. Toast under the broiler until light golden brown.

Spread the pea purée on the toasts and top with a little crumbled goat cheese. Serve immediately.

Say Cheese

You know by now that I often whine about the way things used to be, when it comes to cooking and eating. But one thing I sure don't miss from my childhood is that individually wrapped, gooey, unnaturally vibrant, processed American cheese. You know what I mean—the stuff that was melted over every burger and squashed into every greasy grilled cheese. Luckily, today we have a marvelous array of creative artisanal cheese makers right in our own region who are winning national and international prizes for the top-notch quality of their European-styled offerings. From rich goat chevres to creamy blues, pungent tommes, sharp cheddars, fresh ricottas, and marinated feta, the Chesapeake region's cheese makers have it all covered.

Just north of Baltimore we have Charlottetown Farm in Monkton, creating an exquisite chevre and their own goat cheese fudge and cajeta, a wonderful caramel sauce made with a goat milk reduction. Broom's Bloom Dairy in Bel Air makes a superb cheddar, while just a little east in Darlington, Cedar Hill is building the first real cheese cave in Maryland. Cedar Hill is pushing the envelope on flavored cheeses, too, such as their Cocoa Cayenne, made with crushed red pepper throughout and a rind of honey, cocoa nibs and powder, cayenne pepper, and cinnamon.

Out in northwest Maryland, Frederick's FireFly Farms has been winning important prizes for their goat cheeses, such as their Black and Blue, a longer-aged, complex blue waxed in black, which took the silver medal at the World Cheese Awards in 2015. Cabra LaMancha, an earthy semi-soft, took the Gold in 2008 at the World Cheese Awards and won the Maryland Good Food Award of 2016.

Up in Pennsylvania, Keswick Creamery turns out eighteen different styles of aged Jersey cheeses. Their Tommenator, an edible-rind tomme classic, took the gold medal in 2011 at the North American Jersey awards and their Vermeer, with a Dutch-style natural rind, won the bronze medal in the 2012 World Jersey Cheese Awards.

On the Eastern shore, Chapel's Country Creamery was a pioneer in using raw, or unpasteurized, milk. They made third place with the American Cheese Society in 2012, presenting their Cordova White, a perfectly marinated feta.

Just a little farther south, Cherry Glen in Montgomery County is producing five types of soft-ripened goat cheeses as well as fresh ricotta. Their Monocacy Ash, a tangy, rich goat cheese with an edible, bloomy rind, will knock your socks off.

Down in Virginia Beach, Shady Goat Farm makes, among other delicious things, a dark chocolate–covered goat cheese truffle that utterly defies resistance. Everona Dairy in Rapidan is getting attention with their unpasteurized, aged sheep milk cheeses, like the wonderfully nutty and salty Piedmont.

No matter which way you look, it's all good, as our local cheese artisans are putting the Chesapeake region on the map.

3

SOUPS AND ONE-POTS

We have a whole lot of cooking going on in this chapter. Soups and one-pots are actually the essence of *The New Chesapeake Kitchen* philosophy. This is the way our ancestors have cooked for countless generations and the way most of the developing nations still do.

Throughout humankind's history, there has always been a communal pot on the fire—the centerpiece of community—feeding families and extended families. Most one-pots are full of vegetables—starches, green leafy veggies, tomatoes, and a multitude of herbal combinations, grains, and beans all enhanced by smaller amounts of animal protein.

Here we have a seasonal collection of one-pots highlighting the best ingredients of our region, with a tapestry of flavors from our many ethnic heritages.

Stocks

For extra depth of flavor in your soups and one-pots, a good stock is a valuable resource to have on hand. Stocks are not difficult to make and can be made two to three days ahead. Or, if you want to really stay ahead of the game and cook a lot of soups, they can be made in large batches and frozen. Stock keeps for several months in the freezer. You can also freeze a batch in ice cube trays and store the frozen cubes in plastic ziplock freezer bags—very handy for when a recipe calls for a smaller amount of stock.

Fish Stock

Makes about 8 cups

3½–4 pounds fish heads, bones, and trimmings

10 cups water

2 onions, sliced

3 stalks celery, chopped

2 carrots, peeled and chopped

4 cloves of garlic, unpeeled

2 bay leaves

1 tablespoon whole black peppercorns

2 teaspoons whole dried thyme

½ bunch fresh parsley

In a large pot, combine all the ingredients and bring just to the boil. Reduce the heat to low and simmer for 30 minutes. Skim the foam from the top often.

Strain the stock through a very fine sieve or cheese-cloth. Extra stock freezes well.

Chicken Stock

Makes about 2½ quarts

3-pound chicken, cut into pieces

2   medium onions, sliced

4   stalks celery, chopped

4   whole garlic cloves, unpeeled

4   sprigs fresh thyme or 1 teaspoon
    dried thyme

2   bay leaves

6   sprigs parsley

3   quarts cold water

Rinse the chicken parts well in cold water. Combine chicken and all the other ingredients in a large stockpot. Add 3 quarts of cold water and bring to a boil. Simmer uncovered for 2 to 2½ hours, skimming off the surface foam frequently. Strain the stock through a fine mesh strainer or cheesecloth. Chill and then take the fat off the top of the stock. Stock that will not be used in 2 to 3 days may be frozen for later use.

Note on Chicken Stock: This is a high-end chicken stock and is very rich, with a tremendous amount of flavor. For a lighter—both in taste and on the budget—stock, use chicken backs and wings, to make an excellent, less expensive stock.

Vegetable Stock

Makes about 1½ quarts

2   tablespoons olive oil

2   onions, peeled and sliced

2   carrots, peeled and coarsely chopped

4   celery stalks, coarsely chopped (include a
    little of the leafy tops)

1   bunch green onions, chopped

6   whole cloves garlic, unpeeled and smashed

1   teaspoon whole black peppercorns

½   bunch parsley (about 6 sprigs)

3   bay leaves

1   tablespoon salt, or to taste

2   quarts cold water

Heat the olive oil in a stockpot and add the onions, carrots, celery, green onions, and garlic. Sauté over medium heat for about 5 minutes, stirring often. Add the remaining ingredients and 2 quarts of cold water and bring to a boil. Reduce heat and continue to cook, uncovered, for 30 minutes. Remove stock from heat and let sit for 20 minutes before straining.

Note on Vegetable Stock: This is a basic vegetable stock and the ingredients can be adjusted, depending on the time of the year or what it will be used with. In the summer, you may want to add tomatoes and squash, and in the winter, leeks, mushrooms, and a little celery root. To make a darker stock, continue sautéing the vegetables for about 15 minutes to brown them first, then add the flavorings, 2 tablespoons tomato paste, and the water.

Beef Stock

Makes 2 quarts

5   pounds beef bones, with marrow

4   carrots, peeled and chopped

4   stalks celery, chopped (include a little of the leafy tops)

2   large onions, peeled and sliced

8   cloves garlic, unpeeled and smashed

½   bunch parsley (about 6 sprigs)

6   sprigs fresh thyme or 1 teaspoon dried whole thyme leaves

2   bay leaves

½   teaspoon whole black peppercorns

Preheat oven to 425°F.

Roast the beef bones in a roasting pan until they begin to brown, turning frequently. Add the carrots, celery, onion, and garlic cloves. Continue roasting, turning the veggies and bones frequently, until the vegetables are nicely browned, about 30 to 35 minutes.

Place all the roasted ingredients into a large stockpot and cover with cold water. Using a metal spatula, scrape off all the browned bits in the roasting pan and add to the stockpot. Add the parsley, thyme, bay leaves, and peppercorns. Bring to a boil, reduce the heat to low, and allow to simmer for 3½ to 4 hours. Skim foam and fat from the stock as it cooks.

Strain the stock through a fine mesh strainer or cheesecloth. Chill, then degrease by skimming the fat off the top. Stock that will not be used in 2 to 3 days may be frozen for later use.

Fishing Creek Seafood Chili

Fishing Creek is all about seafood. It's a small town on the upper part of Hoopers Island, in Dorchester County, Maryland, and for generations a seafood mecca, with scores of seafood processing plants and a robust fishing industry. As in most other Bay communities, the seafood business has calmed down quite a bit, and not many of the crab picking houses are still in operation. But most of the folks who live in the area are still involved in fishing and seafood distribution.

During the crabbing season, many of the workers come on temporary visas from Mexico and Central America to work in the seafood processing houses. Quite a number of Latino grocery stores now dot the Eastern Shore of Maryland and Virginia. The flavors and cooking techniques from south of the border are in abundance in local restaurants and homes in small Eastern Shore towns. This recipe is a delicious example of one such dish: slightly thickened with masa harina (ground cornmeal) and spiced with chilies, tomatillos, and a seafood stock. Use any combination of seafood that you like, as a one-pot like this is quite versatile.

Serves 8 to 10

3	tablespoons olive oil
2	cups diced onions (¼-inch dice)
2	tablespoons minced garlic
1	teaspoon hot pepper flakes
½	teaspoon cayenne pepper
2	teaspoons ground cumin
4	teaspoons chili powder
2	tomatillos, papery husks removed, cored, and finely chopped
4	cups fresh or canned chopped, peeled tomatoes
4	cups Fish Stock (*page 58*)
1	teaspoon dried oregano
1	bay leaf
1	teaspoon salt
¾	cup masa harina (*see note*)
2	cups cooked black beans
1	pound claw crabmeat
½	pound shrimp, peeled, deveined, and cut into pieces
¼	pound rockfish fillet, cut into small pieces

In a large, heavy-bottomed pot, heat the olive oil over medium-high heat. Add the onions, garlic, and pepper flakes and sauté for about 5 minutes. Add the cayenne, cumin, chili powder, tomatillos, and tomatoes. Cook for another 5 minutes and then add the stock, oregano, bay leaf, and salt. Bring to a boil, reduce the heat to low, and simmer for 45 minutes, uncovered.

Slowly stir in the masa harina and mix well. Lumps will tend to appear at this point and should be broken up against the side of the pot with the back of a large serving spoon. Smaller lumps will break up as they cook. Simmer for 20 minutes. Stir in the black beans and crabmeat. Heat for 15 minutes and then add the shrimp and rockfish. Cook for about 15 to 20 minutes longer, or until the shrimp and rockfish are just cooked through. Do not overcook.

Top each serving with a dollop of sour cream and a little Salsa Fresca (*see page 17*), if desired.

Note: Masa harina is dehydrated corn dough that has been finely ground for making tortillas and tamales. Look for it in Latino grocery stores and well-stocked supermarkets.

Frogmore Stew

Here's a dish with deep southern culinary roots. It's quite popular in Hampton Roads, Virginia, given the proximity to the Outer Banks of North Carolina. Fueled with a load of fresh summer corn, potatoes, and onions, it is a great example of how to stretch seafood and meat protein while feeding a crowd.

This recipe is based on the Low Country technique shown to me by my friend, the First Lady of Southern Cooking, Ms. Nathalie Dupree of Charleston, South Carolina. You really can use most any sausage of your choosing, depending on how spicy you'd like the dish. This is the perfect menu item for a party out on the patio or backyard.

Serves 8 to 12

2　pounds hot country sausage links, such as Cajun style or andouille

5　quarts water

16　new potatoes (about 1½ inch in circumference), still in their skins but scrubbed

20　whole cloves garlic, peeled

16　medium onions, peeled, halved, or quartered

3　hot peppers, chopped, such as serrano, jalapeño, etc.

8　lemons, halved

2　tablespoons Old Bay seasoning

6　stalks fresh parsley

1¼　cups apple cider vinegar

12　ears fresh corn, husked and broken into 2 pieces

Salt, about 1 tablespoon

Freshly ground black pepper, about 2–3 tablespoons

2 tablespoons Tabasco sauce

5 pounds shrimp in the shell (21/25 size is good, 16/20 even better)

OPTIONAL CONDIMENTS:

Cocktail sauce

Aioli mayonnaise (garlic mayonnaise)

Sour cream

Melted butter seasoned with grated horseradish

In a skillet, cook the sausage over medium heat until almost done and set aside, reserving the drippings.

Fill a 12-quart stockpot or water bath canner with the 5 quarts of water. Bring the water to a boil over high heat. Add the sausage drippings, potatoes, garlic, and onions and return to boil.

Cover and cook for 15 minutes. Add the sausage links, hot peppers, lemons, Old Bay, parsley, and vinegar. Cover and simmer for 15 minutes longer. Then add the corn and bring back to a boil. Add the salt, pepper, and Tabasco. Stir in the shrimp and cook until the shrimp are done, about 5 to 8 minutes. Do not overcook!

Remove and discard the lemons. Strain most of the broth into a bowl and set aside. Pour the shrimp and the rest of the ingredients into a large serving bowl. The cooking liquid can be served on the side for dipping or slurped as a soup.

You can serve the stew with the cocktail sauce and/or other condiments on the side so guests can pick and choose as they like. Provide lots of napkins and perhaps some "wet naps" as well. It is a fun feast, but quite messy.

Community-Supported Fisheries

If it's working so well for farmers, how about taking the community support concept and applying it to our seafood industry? Well, the first community-supported fishery (CSF) was created in Port Clyde, Maine, in 2007, and now there are nearly thirty CSFs in North America. Now this is a great idea, if you ask me. We all need to be committed to providing local, healthful, low-impact seafood via community-supported fisheries and direct marketing arrangements in order to support healthy fisheries and the communities that depend on them.

And it's happening here. A pilot project started in 2015 and made possible through a generous donation from the Ratcliffe Foundation, the Annapolis-based Oyster Recovery Partnership launched the Old Line Fish Company CSF to connect Annapolis residents with seafood harvested by Maryland watermen and seafood farmers. Up-front payment ensures that expenses such as diesel fuel, net repairs, equipment replacements, licenses, etc. can be met without driving our fishermen into debt before they even start their engines. Old Line Fish Company CSF subscribers in Annapolis purchase shares for $225 and receive five bi-weekly deliveries of fresh seafood—Bay favorites such as filleted rockfish, crabmeat, and oysters, and lesser-known fish species as well. OLFC plans to add additional Maryland distribution sites over the next few years, and I'm very excited about this expansion. It's time for the Chesapeake to really get on board with this win-win arrangement.

Mrs. Kitching's EZ Crab Soup

One of my Chesapeake culinary food heroines was the late Frances Kitching of Smith Island, Maryland. She was the acclaimed "first lady" of Smith Island cooking and published an award-winning cookbook with Susan Stiles Dowell, *Mrs. Kitching's Smith Island Cookbook*, which I highly recommend. Many of the vegetable crab soup recipes from our region are somewhat complicated, with all sorts of steps and methods involved to make the soup just so. That's not the case here with Mrs. K's EZ Crab Soup. It is quick, easy, and oh so delicious.

Of course I have futzed a bit with the recipe over the years, but I've kept the basics intact.

Serves 10 to 12

2   (14½-ounce) cans of whole tomatoes (with juice)
2   (10-ounce) packages of frozen mixed vegetables
1   cup diced baked ham
½   cup shredded cabbage
1   teaspoon salt
1   tablespoon Old Bay seasoning
10 cups water
1   cup uncooked egg noodles
1   pound crabmeat, claw or backfin

Place all the ingredients in a heavy-bottomed soup pot, except for the crabmeat. Partially cover and cook over medium heat for about 8 to 10 minutes, or until the vegetables are tender and the noodles are cooked. Stir in the crabmeat and simmer for 5 minutes to heat through.

Serve with biscuits, rolls, or saltine crackers.

Old Line Creole Oyster Stew

Robert "RJ" Johnson of Bushwood, a chef at the Seafarers Harry Lundeberg School of Seamanship, is the creator of this People's Choice Award–winning stew from the 2015 National Oyster Cook-Off in St. Mary's County, Maryland. Chef Johnson has a whole lot of flavor going on here with a potful of oysters that are steeped in a fragrant mix of tomato, red wine, and an ample supply of fresh vegetables. The surprise guest here is just a little fresh crabmeat, stirred in at the end, to keep those succulent oysters company. You'll see why it is a crowd pleaser.

Serves 10 to 12

- 2 tablespoons olive or vegetable oil
- ½ pound andouille sausage, diced small
- ½ cup celery, chopped
- ¼ cup red bell pepper, chopped
- ¼ cup green bell pepper, chopped
- ½ cup onion, chopped
- ½ cup sweet corn, fresh kernels
- 1 tablespoon fresh garlic, minced finely
- 1 quart tomato sauce
- 1 cup water
- 1 cup red wine
- 1½ teaspoons granulated garlic
- ¼ teaspoon freshly ground black pepper
- 2 teaspoons oregano, ground
- 1 teaspoon cumin, ground
- 1½ tablespoons chili powder, ground
- 2 tablespoons brown sugar
- 1 teaspoon hot sauce
- Ground cayenne pepper, to taste
- 1 teaspoon salt, or to taste
- 2 quarts oysters, shucked raw, with liquor
- ½ pound Maryland lump crabmeat, picked over
- Chopped green onions, for garnish
- Chopped Italian parsley, for garnish

Heat the oil in a large heavy-bottomed soup pot. Add the sausage and cook for 5 minutes or until lightly browned. Add the celery, red and green bell peppers, onion, corn, and fresh garlic. Cook for about 10 minutes or until vegetables are tender.

Stir in the tomato sauce, water, red wine, granulated garlic, black pepper, oregano, cumin, chili powder, brown sugar, hot sauce, cayenne, and salt. Simmer for 20 minutes and then add oysters (and oyster liquor) and crab meat. Simmer 10 minutes more or until the oysters just begin to curl.

Remove from heat and serve at once. Serve with hot rice and garnish with chopped green onion and chopped parsley.

Shrimp, Maryland Crab, and Rockfish Seafood Stew

This is essentially a Chesapeake bouillabaisse. It may look like a lot of ingredients and maybe too much work, but it's actually not all that hard to make and well worth every bit of effort. I have been making this soup/stew for nearly thirty years and never cease to be amazed by how satisfying a bowl of well-crafted stew can be. As with most seafood stews, it is easily adapted to different types and amounts of fish. Lobster, mussels, clams, blue catfish fillet—all work well, so feel free to experiment.

Serves 8 to 10

- 4 tablespoons olive oil
- 1 large onion, diced
- 6 cloves garlic, unpeeled
- 2 leeks, well washed, halved, and cut into pieces
- ½ cup chopped fennel bulb or 1 tablespoon fennel seed
- 3 pounds ripe tomatoes, chopped
- 2 tablespoons tomato paste
- 3 small potatoes, peeled and diced
- 2 cups dry white wine
- 3 cups Fish Stock (*page 58*)
- 1 teaspoon dried thyme leaves
- 1 teaspoon dried oregano
- 1 bay leaf
- Grated zest of 1 orange
- 4 threads saffron
- Salt and freshly ground black pepper, to taste
- 8–10 pieces French bread, sliced on the diagonal
- Melted butter and chopped garlic, for toast
- ½ pound rockfish fillets (local)
- 1 pound shrimp, peeled and deveined
- 1 pound fresh lump Maryland crabmeat, picked over for shells
- Rouille, for accompaniment (*recipe follows*)

Heat the oil in a heavy pot and sauté the onion, garlic, leeks, and fennel until slightly softened, about 8 to 10 minutes. Add the tomatoes, tomato paste, potatoes, wine, stock, thyme, oregano, and bay leaf. Bring to a boil, reduce heat, and simmer for 30 minutes. Allow to cool slightly.

Purée the mixture in a blender or food processor. Pour through a fine mesh sieve and return to pot.

Add the orange zest, saffron, salt, and pepper. Cook over medium-low heat, stirring frequently, until somewhat reduced, about 20 to 30 minutes.

Meanwhile, preheat the oven to 375°F.

Brush the bread slices with melted butter and top with garlic. Toast in the oven until browned.

Cut the rockfish into chunks about 2 inches square. Add to the sauce and cook for about 8 to 10 minutes or until the fish is almost done.

Add the shrimp and simmer for 5 minutes. Add the crabmeat and simmer 5 minutes longer. Reserve 1 cup of the liquid for making the Rouille.

Prepare the Rouille (*recipe follows*).

Place 1 piece of garlic bread into each bowl. Then spoon in the fish and add broth. Arrange the shrimp and crabmeat on top. Garnish with parsley. Serve Rouille on the side.

ROUILLE

1	small potato, peeled
1	cup broth from the stew
4	cloves of garlic
4	fresh or dried red chilies
1	teaspoon Tabasco sauce
½	cup olive oil

Kosher salt, to taste

Quarter the potato and cook in the reserved broth until tender. Drain, reserving the liquid.

Finely chop the garlic and chili peppers in a blender or a food processor. Add the potato, Tabasco, and oil.

Process until the mixture forms a paste. Slowly add enough of the reserved liquid to give the mixture the consistency of mayonnaise. Season with the salt.

Wild Shrimp and Sweet Corn Chowder

Recently some folks have undertaken shrimp farming on the Eastern Shore of the Bay with some success, but the overwhelming share of shrimp consumed here is wild-caught American. A couple hundred years ago there was a sizable shrimp industry off the coast, but now the largest catch is running from off the Hampton Roads area into North Carolina and then down the Atlantic coast into the Gulf of Mexico. The wild-caught American product is the best in my book, with a sweet taste and wonderful texture.

Serves 8 to 10

4 tablespoons butter
1 small onion, diced
2 medium carrots, finely diced
2 tablespoons all-purpose flour
6 medium Russet potatoes, peeled and cubed
3 cups milk
1½ cups Fish Stock (*see note and page 58*)
2 cups sweet corn kernels
1 cup half-and-half
1 teaspoon salt
¼ teaspoon pepper
2 cups salted water
1 pound medium wild-caught American shrimp

Crumbled bacon bits, for garnish

Grated sharp cheddar, for garnish

Dill sprigs, for garnish (optional)

In a 4-quart saucepan, melt the butter and sauté the onion and carrots until both are slightly tender, about 5 minutes. Whisk in the flour and cook for 1 minute. Add the potatoes, milk, and stock. Cook over medium heat for 15 minutes or until the potatoes are very soft and some of them have begun to break down. Add the corn, half-and-half, salt, and pepper. Simmer for 10 minutes longer.

In a small saucepan, bring the 2 cups lightly salted water to a boil. Add the shrimp and stir well. Watch the shrimp closely; as soon as they all turn pink, about 2 to 3 minutes, turn off the heat and drain. The shrimp should be slightly undercooked. When they are cool, peel and chop them into big chunks. Add the shrimp to the soup and stir well. Serve the soup sprinkled with bacon bits and grated cheese. Garnish with dill sprigs, if desired.

Note: When making this chowder, I put a handful of shrimp shells in the stock and simmer it for about 5 minutes before straining out the shells and adding the stock to the chowder. It's not absolutely necessary, but I like the extra shrimp flavor it adds.

In the Kitchen with My Culinary Hero, Sydney Meers— I'll Let Him Tell You All about It

With the diminishing supply of fish and crabs in our wonderful area from the Chesapeake Bay to the coastal Atlantic I try to do dishes that use less of the fish but I can still get the bang of flavor from them I always love. In the deep southwest area of Mississippi we did stews a lot because back then we were poor and had a lot of family to feed so you had to figure clever ways of doing this. We made big pots of stews and soups, made sometimes thick and sometimes with a great broth. My grandmother, Winnie Lee Johnson, had a café back in the '40s to '60s and she did this a lot cause most her clients were truckers who stopped by to eat every day. It worked wonderfully and even poor folks got to eat really good food, even though they were footing the bill on their own.

Now with globalization and over-fishing habits we are back to what I call full circle. The difference is we aren't doing it for primarily "expense" reasons.

As a matter of the fact, it's because we now have more money than we've ever had, and we're like the ole Romans, gluttonous. Instead of sharing a pound of steamed shrimp we eat it all by ourselves. So, now we must be clever and allow the fish, crabs, oysters, etc. to rebuild from all our and nature's destruction over the past 50 years and get back to normal.

We have to first be the ones to help lead the way—chefs of every kind of restaurant from all over the world, but most certainly, and most importantly, from right here in the Chesapeake. While we eat a lot of the creatures, guess what lurks below? No, not Jaws, you nut! The red ray, he has a ferocious appetite for crabs and other crustaceans. So we got to now overeat them while still slowing down on the sexy fish we really love. Just in late December, a statement by the fish science people is putting a bigger stop fishing of the rockfish. Damn I love them but we have to cut back or there won't be any in the future. So my friend, I have some dishes for you on using all the sea creatures, but in smaller amounts with tons of flavor, which will feed us in groups of 4 to 6 while we patiently wait for the sea and Bay to replenish itself. The End.
Love . . . Syd

Sydney's Mid-Atlantic Etouffee

I first met Chef Sydney Meers at his legendary Dumbwaiter Bistro in downtown Norfolk, Virginia, back in the 1990s, and it was love at first bite. Sydney now owns and operates Stove, a restaurant/locavore alternative universe in Portsmouth, Virginia, and continues the tradition of his over-the-top culinary prestidigitation, all rooted in solid, classical preparation techniques. He calls his cooking Neo-Southern-Mid-Atlantic cuisine. Syd is so talented, I cannot even begin to explain. He's an artist with food and is also a multidisciplined "outsider" artist. And a craftsman extraordinaire—of gardens, furniture, and prepared foods; of sauces, jams, preserves, hot sauces, smoked hams, and sausages.

We have here Sydney's signature etouffee, which reflects his southern roots (Mississippi), while incorporating the seafood and smoked products from the Chesapeake that he so loves. Syd is a James Beard Award nominee and is recognized as one of the region's most innovative cooks. I have enjoyed this etouffee numerous times and am proud to be able to pass the recipe on.

Now, Syd is one of a kind, as you have probably already gathered, and any effort of mine to simplify this recipe or put it into my "standard recipe" format would be a disservice to the reader and a disservice to Sydney. I think this is a fantastic opportunity for you all to have a visit with Sydney, right in his kitchen, as he leads you through all the steps, twists, and turns of this marvelous regional dish. Sharpen up your knives, get your equipment ready and your cutting boards on the counter—here's Syd and let's cook!

Serves 10 to 12

This dish is so damn good but you'll have to devote a couple of days or one long day to making all the components for it. You'll need a roux, smoked tomatoes, and stock, and the rest can be made the next day but doing it all the same day is best. It's a party, isn't it? Call friends who know how to cook and have them help.

THE HOLY TRINITY

3 medium red onions
4 red bell peppers
4 green bell peppers
2 heads of celery

Chop each veggie to ¼-inch-size chop; when done mix all ingredients together and set aside 'til ready for use.

SMOKED TOMATOES

This dish is great with these smoked tomatoes. I don't recommend not smoking your tomatoes but you can use plain fresh tomatoes (or go buy a good li'l electric smoker and you'll be very happy!).

10 pounds fresh medium-sized tomatoes
8-quart stockpot of water
1 large bowl of ice water

Bring water to a boil. Take tomatoes and put a small "x" on the bottom with a real sharp paring knife and core the top, removing all stem and white part of tomato till you just see red. Pop them into the water for about 10 to 30 seconds, making sure your water is boiling; pull out and place in the ice bath. After all are done you'll then pull off the skins, cut in half horizontally, squeeze out the pulp and seeds and set aside.

Once done, place a mixture of equal parts pecan, hickory, and apple wood chips in the smoker.

Place tomatoes cut side down and place a pan underneath to capture all the smoked tomato water you can get . . . Omgordon—this stuff is great!

Turn on smoker and smoke tomatoes for 20 minutes. Turn off smoker and let stay inside smoker for another 20 minutes; remove and place in sealed containers to allow for more good smoke.

Now, take another 5 pounds of tomatoes and do them the same as for making smoked tomato except once peeled and cleaned you're going to do a rough chop, or as the French call it, "concasse."

After an hour the smoked tomatoes will have good smoke so now take them and chop them the same and mix the non-smoked with smoked tomatoes; this stretches them and allows for the perfect smoke ratio. Place in an airtight container in the fridge till ready for use.

SEAFOOD

5-pound box 10/15-count jumbo
   Carolina shrimp
1 puppy drum or redfish, when running up
   this way, gutted and cleaned—save bones
   for stock
1 dozen fresh oysters (Lynhaven oysters are
   nice and salty, or seaside from the Eastern
   Shore around Chincoteague to central
   Maryland)

Clean shrimp, leaving the tail on the shrimp; save shells for stock for this dish.

If buying the puppy drum from a merchant, it will be fillet so ask for the bones, but if you catch it, clean it and use the bones for your stock. Cut the fillets with skin on in 1-inch cubes, season with coarse sea salt, and set aside in cool box or fridge.

Shuck oysters, saving all the oyster liquor you can, and set aside in the fridge.

MEAT

4 pounds smoked tasso or "Smoochie Bear Ham" (now it's hard to find Smoochie Bear Ham unless you come to my restaurant, Stove, in Portsmouth, Virginia, where I make it. It's like tasso—a spicy ham made in 15 days, cut into small portions, and is from the shoulder of the piggy).

4 pounds of house-made sausage or you can use andouille, but be careful—lots of poorly made andouille out there. If using house-made, roll sausage into 1-ounce balls.

Cut ham into 1/8-inch slices. Roll out all sausage, or if using andouille, slice diagonally 1/8-inch thick. Mix these two together and set in fridge to keep cold.

STOCK

1 gallon filtered water
1 onion
1 lemon
4 bay leaves
6 fresh basil leaves
2 sprigs fresh oregano
2 leaves fresh sage
Shrimp shells, from above
Fish bones
Oyster liquor

Place water in a stockpot with cold filtered water; if you can't filter your water use filtered bottle water.

Rough chop onion and slice lemon; remove seeds and toss these together. Take bay leaf; give it one crush with your hands, then place bay leaf, the onion and lemon, and all the fresh spices in a bag fashioned from cheesecloth and tied firmly. Take the shrimp shells and fish bones and place in another tightly tied cheesecloth bag. Drop the bags into the water.

Add the oyster liquor to the stockpot.

Bring stock to a boil and reduce fast to a high simmer—you don't want a cloudy stock here. Once stock is simmering and has gone for about 30 to 40 minutes, taste and see if the different elements have flavored your stock; if so remove from heat, place in an ice bath, and let cool to 50–60°F.

Carefully remove all the bags so you don't cloud the stock. Once all bags are out, pour the stock through a medium strainer lined with a double layer of cheesecloth or a coffee filter. Pour stock into a container and refrigerate 'til ready.

SPICE MIX

2 ounces cayenne pepper
2 ounces white pepper, fine ground
2 ounces black pepper, fine ground
1 ounce dry thyme
1 ounce dry basil
1 ounce dry oregano
1 ounce Hungarian paprika
1 ounce turmeric
1 ounce ground cumin

Place all ingredients into a food processor and cut it on, letting it run for at least 8 to 10 minutes. Place spices and herbs in a shaker so you can shake the spice to taste.

ROUX

2 pounds high-gluten flour (all-purpose flour can be used if you don't have access to high-gluten flour)

1½ pounds liquid fat—you can use lard, butter, veggie oil, or a combination of any, but remember it's the flavor—for here we'll use ½ pound fresh lard (or cook down a pork belly and save the liquid; pour off liquid and place in a container for a day and lard will float to top and gelee will stay on bottom; it can be used for all kinds of flavoring in other dishes) and 1 pound of clarified butter.

Mix the butter and lard together, set in a heavy-bottomed saucier pan, and cook on low flame to get the fat just hot. Add the flour a little at a time 'til all is blended well. Stir constantly, and keep on watching your roux to be sure it does not scorch. Cook till you get a dark brown color and a smell and taste between a nut flavor and an almost coffee taste. Remove from heat and stir till cool. Roux will settle over time, but just stir it back together and you're good to go.

RICE

I use a good grade of short-grain rice which when cooked will become sticky—divine! California and Mississippi, to name a few, make good rice, and even South Carolina has finally gotten a commercial crop of Carolina Gold rice, but I don't recommend it here; it's so good on its own or with a simple preparation that it's wasted in this dish. Short-grain rice here is a component to carry the flavors, otherwise the rice on its own is bland.

4   cups uncooked rice (2 pounds)

8   cups water

Sea salt to taste

Bring water to a boil, rain in the rice, and stir constantly 'til you blend well and have no lumps. Reduce flame to a low boil and set timer for 12 minutes and let boil on low. After 12 minutes remove from fire and place a lid on the rice and let finish off for another 15 minutes. Adjust seasoning if needed.

BRINGING IT ALL TOGETHER—TO MAKE THE FINISHED ETOUFFEE

All the above, plus:

2   jalapeños, sliced in thin strips from top to bottom with bitter white ribs and seeds removed

Scant 1 ounce filé powder

Fresh scallions, chopped, for garnish (optional)

Note: This dish can also be made for 1 to 6 people with same procedure, but I'd use a large sauté pan when making a large batch if you're making it for 10 or more. You will want to use a low-sided but large stockpot, as long as you can get your arms in there to work it—girl you'll be fine! A 12-gallon stockpot with about a ¼-inch-thick wall is best. With thin walls you'll have to be very careful not to burn the roux-stock combo or you're done!

Place ¼ of the roux in the pot and add all the Holy Trinity, stirring well to get it going. Look for onions and pepper to sweat.

Add one-fourth of the stock and stir well, increasing the fire to a medium boil.

Add the tomatoes and stir again, adding a little more stock and taking notice of the thickness. You want a nice thickness like you'll find in a boiled custard, so if it doesn't thicken up with more of the ingredients you'll need to add a little more roux. Be patient, it will thicken, but if you overdo the roux—good news. It will enhance the flavor and you can thin it with more stock. We may not use all the roux or all the stock. The idea here is to alternately add small amounts of each to balance the roux and the stock until you achieve the desired consistency.

Once you have gotten the volume and viscosity you're looking for, now it is time to season. Shake the spices and herbs about 6 to 8 times, stirring and allowing for the flavors to meld. You can always add more spice but you can't take it away. I shoot for an 8 to 10 on a scale of 10; hello, it's spicy but full of flavor!

Once you've gotten the spice and viscosity correct then, just before serving, add the jalapeños to the stew. You'll need to season with sea salt to taste, and all that's left is once you're within 20 minutes of serving, add the sausage and ham, stirring well, and just before serving add all the fish, oysters, and shrimp, giving them only enough time to just get done—I leave the seafood at medium rare. Remember, the seafood continues to cook after you take it off the heat, and there's nothing worse than a good gumbo or etouffee with overcooked seafood. The last thing to do is stir in some filé powder, maybe about an ounce or less. It's a great flavor but be sure to stir briefly.

Now you're done, ready to plate up. Get bowls and place some rice in the bottom, stir the pot with the ladle, and scoop up some of the etouffee, pouring it over the rice. If you want, you can garnish with some fine-chopped fresh scallions out of the garden—voilà, now you have an incredible dish for all your friends. If any is left it will intensify with flavor for your next meal. As we say here in the Mid-Atlantic area: "Bon-boe-tee-toe!" Shut up! Not really, LOL.

Caribbean Vegetable Stew

During the dark days of slavery many of the slaves came from the Caribbean. There are generations of Caribbeans who still call the Chesapeake home, with new arrivals coming all the time. The cooking styles of these islands work perfectly with the bountiful fresh produce of the region as well as the abundance of fish and shellfish. That said, many of the dishes of the Caribbean are plant-based by nature, and this stew is a great example. It can be served as is, or you may, as I do, serve it over steamed rice.

Serves 8 to 10

2   cups chopped onions
½   cup vegetable broth for sautéing
3   cups chopped cabbage
1   fresh serrano or other hot chili, minced (and seeded for a milder "hot")
1   tablespoon grated fresh ginger root
2   cups water or Vegetable Stock (*page 59*)
3   cups sweet potatoes, cut in ½-inch cubes
Salt, to taste
2   cups chopped fresh or canned tomatoes
2   cups fresh or frozen okra, sliced
3   tablespoons freshly squeezed lime juice
2   tablespoons cilantro, chopped
Chopped peanuts, for topping
Sprigs of fresh cilantro for garnish (optional)

In a heavy-bottomed pot, sauté the onions in the broth on medium heat for 4 or 5 minutes. Add the cabbage and the chili and continue to sauté, stirring often, until the onions are translucent, about 8 minutes.

Add the grated ginger and the water or stock and cover the pot, bringing to a boil. Stir in the sweet potatoes, sprinkle with salt, and simmer for 5 or 6 minutes, until the potatoes are barely tender. Add the tomatoes, okra, and lime juice. Simmer until all of the vegetables are tender, about 15 minutes. Just before serving, stir in the cilantro and add more salt to taste.

When serving, sprinkle the stew with chopped peanuts and top with a few sprigs of cilantro for garnish.

Invasive Species

Sound like something from a sci-fi movie, don't they? Well, they're kinda like that, actually. Invasive species are plants or animals that have been introduced, whether accidentally or on purpose, into a place where they did not naturally evolve. They become "invasive" when they have no natural predators in this new environment, creating an unnatural imbalance in the local ecology. They cause enormous harm by encroaching on the food or habitat of native plants or animals, over-establishing themselves at their expense. Dealing with them is a big problem, since once an invasive is well established, it can be almost impossible to eradicate.

The Chesapeake suffers from some particularly troubling invasives—such as the northern snakehead, a long fish with a mottled, snake-like pattern and lots of teeth. Native to China, they were first discovered in a pond in Crofton, Maryland, in 2000. Now they have spread to the Potomac River, its tributaries, and the Rappahannock River. In Maryland and Virginia, anglers who catch the fish are required to kill it. Both the Virginia and Maryland Department of Natural Resources have asked local chefs to consider the fish for their menus. It really is a tasty piece of seafood, but availability is spotty, and it hasn't caught on.

Another big problem is the blue catfish. It's native to the Mississippi, Missouri, and Ohio River basins, where it evolved naturally and was not considered invasive. It was artificially introduced in Virginia for sport fishing in the 1970s—probably not such a good idea. Turns out that "blue cats," with their few natural predators in our region, are devouring important natives such as shad, menhaden, blue crab, and river herring. They can grow to 150 pounds and live up to 20 years. Luckily, the smaller-size blue cat is also delicious, and inspiring efforts such as the Wide Net Project (*see page 108*) are making some real headway against this critter by reconsidering it as an easily harvestable species.

The zebra mussel is a tiny bivalve with zebra-like stripes and a triangular shell. It was introduced to the Great Lakes region in the 1980s, most likely in ballast water from a European ship, and has since spread throughout the United States. The zebra mussel attaches itself to hard surfaces and can produce millions of offspring annually, competing with native bivalves, fish, and invertebrates for plankton, a type of algae. They are responsible for the drastic decline of native clam, mussel, and oyster populations in many areas of the Chesapeake. I love steamed mussels, but unfortunately this type of mussel is not suitable for eating, so we will not be able to eat ourselves out of this one.

And here's a relatively new one you may not have heard of—the Chinese mitten crab, a light-brown crustacean with a distinctive pair of hairy, white-tipped claws. Native to East Asia, it has recently been discovered here in the Chesapeake. This guy damages fishing nets and equipment and feeds on fish in the nets. Its other destructive habit, burrowing into soft sediment banks, dykes, and coastal protection systems, results in the serious erosion of vulnerable areas. Yes, the Chesapeake means "crab" to people, but this is one crustacean that will not serve a crab cake well.

Huge efforts are under way by our local governments and community organizations to combat these dangerous invasives, but is there anything we can do as individuals? Well, some simple precautionary actions can have a big positive impact on our Bay. Taking the time to clean the hull of your boat and your gear after each and every trip can help protect the waters from aquatic hitchhikers. Keeping bait, and especially aquarium species, out of storm drains and waterways is also important. We all need to take care and do our part to protect the Bay.

South Mountain Creamery Cheddar Cheese and Blackwing Lager Soup

Here is the perfect marriage in this rich, flavorful soup. We're taking two regional Chesapeake favorites and tying the knot: a vibrant cheddar from South Mountain Creamery near Catoctin Mountain with a full-flavored lager crafted by the nationally renowned Union Craft Brewing of Baltimore, Maryland.

Serves 4

- 4 tablespoons butter
- 4 tablespoons flour
- 3 cups milk, or 1½ cups milk and 1½ cups vegetable broth (for a lighter soup)
- 1 tablespoon garlic, minced

Salt and pepper, to taste

- ½ teaspoon crushed red chilies, chopped
- 2 cups extra-sharp cheddar cheese, shredded
- 1 cup dark beer (a lager is preferable)

Heat butter in a heavy-bottomed pot. Add flour and cook on low heat, whisking constantly, for several minutes, until it starts to bubble. Do not allow it to brown. Remove from heat and set aside.

Heat milk, garlic, salt, pepper, and chilies in a saucepan and bring the mixture almost to the boil.

Whisking slowly, gradually stir the hot milk into the flour-butter mixture to achieve a smooth consistency. Stir constantly to avoid burning. Turn down the heat and add cheese and beer. Stir to allow cheese to melt. The soup should have a smooth, consistent texture. May be reheated at a low temperature, but do not boil.

Moroccan Chickpea Vegetable Tagine

I know this sounds kind of exotic, especially because it's called a "tagine," but it really is a simple vegetable stew. An authentic tagine is prepared in a cylindrical, cone-shaped pot that slow-cooks meats and vegetables. It works especially well for meats and chicken, as the shape of the pot funnels the steam back into the pot and makes the meat very moist and tender. But this recipe is all-veggie and could almost be called a Farmers' Market Tagine. I have just used a few vegetables here as an example, but go crazy with this. The fragrant sauce works magic on just about any vegetable imaginable. I adapted this recipe from one of my favorite websites and the documentary *Forks Over Knives,* where you can find plenty of plant-based and plant-forward recipes.

Of course, you could use this basic recipe and add some chicken. In that case, I would braise the chicken in the spiced tomato sauce until done, and then add all the assorted veggies at the end. In either case, it's a veggie-lover's dream come true.

Serves 8 to 10

Spice Mix

2 teaspoons ginger powder
2 teaspoons cumin
2 teaspoons paprika
½ teaspoon turmeric
½ teaspoon cayenne
1 teaspoon cinnamon

3 tablespoons olive oil, for sautéing
1 large onion, chopped
1 red bell pepper, chopped
1 green bell pepper, chopped
1 yellow bell pepper, chopped
2 tablespoons minced garlic
4 cups cooked chickpeas, rinsed well with cold water
6 roasted tomatoes, peeled and chopped
1 cup chopped diced tomatoes
¾ cup raisins
¾ cup chopped dates
7 cups Vegetable Stock (*page 59*)
1 bunch asparagus, stems removed, and cut into 1½-inch pieces
3 zucchini squash, cut into chunks
3 yellow squash, cut into chunks
Salt and freshly ground black pepper, to taste
Cooked quinoa, couscous, or rice, for accompaniment
Chopped toasted almonds, for topping (optional)
Chopped fresh cilantro, for topping

In a small bowl, combine the spices to make the spice mix.

Heat the olive oil in a pot and sauté the spice mixture for about 2 to 3 minutes. Add the onions, bell peppers, and garlic and continue to sauté for about 8 minutes more. Add the chickpeas, tomatoes, raisins, dates, and stock. Bring almost to a boil, reduce the heat, and simmer partially covered for 20 minutes. Cover completely and simmer for 20 minutes longer. (The sauce can be made ahead of time and put aside until you are ready to serve the meal.)

When ready to serve, heat the sauce, add the cut-up asparagus, and cook over medium heat for about 3 minutes. Add the zucchini and yellow squash and continue to cook for about 8 minutes or until the vegetables are tender. Season with salt and freshly ground pepper to taste.

Serve over the quinoa or couscous and top each serving with some toasted almonds and chopped cilantro.

African-Inspired Sweet Potato and Peanut Soup

Our regional Chesapeake cuisine owes much of its heritage to the cooking of Africa. The spice blends of the Afro-Caribbean cultures, with a touch of heat, take the humble sweet potato and peanut and transform them into a complex, hearty soup. To make this dish a complete meal, I often add a couple of extra sweet potatoes for a thicker, more stew-like consistency and serve it over brown rice or whatever grain I may have on hand.

Serves 8 to 10

2   tablespoons olive oil
1   large onion, diced
½   teaspoon hot pepper flakes
4   cloves garlic, minced
3   tablespoons fresh minced ginger
2   teaspoons ground cumin
2   teaspoons ground cinnamon
1½ teaspoons ground coriander
¼   teaspoon ground cloves
4   ripe medium tomatoes, cored and diced, or one 14½-ounce can diced tomatoes
2   pounds sweet potatoes, peeled and coarsely chopped
2   medium carrots, peeled and diced
5   cups water or Vegetable Stock (*page 59*)
2   tablespoons local honey
1   teaspoon salt
½   cup chopped, unsalted, roasted peanuts
¼   cup creamy peanut butter
Chopped cilantro, for topping
Chopped toasted peanuts, for topping

Heat the olive oil in a large pot and sauté onions until lightly browned, about 6 to 8 minutes. Add the hot pepper flakes, garlic, ginger, cumin, cinnamon, coriander, and cloves. Sauté for 5 minutes longer.

Stir in the tomatoes, sweet potatoes, and carrots. Pour in the water or stock, honey, and salt. Bring to a boil, reduce the heat, and simmer for about 40 minutes or until the sweet potatoes are tender.

Remove from heat and stir in the chopped peanuts. Take out half of the soup and set aside. Purée the remaining soup and then pour the reserved soup back in. Reheat the soup, whisk in the peanut butter, and adjust seasonings.

Serve in bowls and top with cilantro and chopped peanuts.

Trash Fish

We also call it "by-catch," which refers to miscellaneous not-so-popular fish, cartilaginous rays, gnarled whelks, and other currently unmarketable critters that fishermen scoop up while in pursuit of the more popular edibles in the waters and seas. Key word there is *popular*, which I also refer to as the "sexy" fish—grouper, Chilean sea bass, salmon, sword, mahi-mahi, etc. They are found on menus all around the globe and are the stars of the seafood world. But while those fishing industries are endangered, there is still quite an abundance of the lesser-known so-called trash fish in local coastal regions, including the Chesapeake.

It might be hard to imagine today, but not all that long ago, lobster was considered a trash fish. At least, the respectable members of society wouldn't touch it. Lobster was fed to the financially destitute, criminals, indentured servants, and even to livestock. It was ground up for fertilizer. According to the nineteenth-century politician and social observer John Rowan, "Lobster shells about a house are looked upon as signs of poverty and degradation." And believe it or not, blue crab had the same trash-fish status until the late nineteenth or early twentieth century.

With currently popular species such as swordfish, cod, and wild salmon suffering from habitat destruction and overfishing, it's time to reconsider what we have been labeling "trash." In that vein, the important and influential organization Chefs Collaborative has been hosting Trash Fish Dinners around the county since 2013 and promoting what's become a serious trend in the culinary world—though it may be time to reconsider that attention-grabbing name.

Here in the Chesapeake region, we have many underutilized species, such as pollock, hake, and dogfish, which all have flesh that matches the flaky, mild profile of dwindling cod. The Atlantic croaker, or hardhead, is another relatively unused species that is lean, flavorful, and slightly sweet when cooked. Smaller fish like porgies, crappies, perch, and spot are also delicious to eat. One hundred years ago, these were "popular," before airline shipping became commonplace and seafood lovers became enamored with more "luxurious" species from far away. Pretty quickly, some fish that were the mainstay of local fishermen were suddenly "trash." But yes, that "trash" just might be our "treasure" for the twenty-first century.

Roasted Carrot and Beet Soup

Root vegetables are my favorites, and if you haven't tried the combo before, carrots and beets go together like bread and butter. Roasting the vegetables first truly brings out the flavors and natural sugars. It really is worth the bit of extra time and effort.

Serves 6

1   pound golden beets, trimmed and peeled

1   pound carrots, trimmed and peeled

3   tablespoons extra-virgin olive oil

1   teaspoon salt

1   teaspoon freshly ground black pepper

1   cup onion, diced

2–3 tablespoons red curry paste

4   cups vegetable broth

1   can (13.5 ounces) coconut milk

Preheat oven to 400°F.

Roughly chop the beets and carrots into 1- to 1½-inch pieces. Toss on a rimmed baking sheet with 2 tablespoons of the olive oil and ½ teaspoon each of the salt and black pepper. Roast for 35 to 45 minutes or until the vegetables are softened, stirring about halfway through the time. Remove from the oven and set aside.

In a large, heavy-bottomed pot over medium-high heat, sauté the chopped onion in the remaining olive oil until slightly softened, about 5 minutes. Add the red curry paste (2 tablespoons will give you a pleasantly warm spice level) and cook, stirring constantly, for another 1 to 2 minutes.

Add the vegetable broth, the roasted vegetables, and the remaining ½ teaspoon each of the salt and black pepper. Bring to a boil and then turn down to a slow simmer. Simmer uncovered for about 30 minutes or until all the vegetables are soft.

Remove the pot from the heat and allow soup to cool slightly. Purée using an immersion blender—or carefully transfer to a food processor or blender, working in batches if necessary. Purée until smooth. Return the soup to the stovetop over medium-low heat to re-warm. Stir in the coconut milk, reserving 1 to 2 tablespoons for garnish.

To serve, ladle the soup into bowls and drizzle with the reserved coconut milk. Soup can be stored in an airtight container in the refrigerator for up to 3 days.

Schillinger Farm Watermelon Gazpacho

Yolanda Johnson is the Soup Queen of Charm City (a.k.a. Baltimore), and her much-beloved soups have brightened the days and satisfied the bellies of many locals over the years. Every summer, patrons of our restaurant, Gertrude's, clamor for this wonderful, refreshing soup. Yolanda prefers the Sugar Baby variety of watermelon, but any sweet watermelon will work. Optional—topping each bowl with a few lumps of crab, as we've done here, makes a gorgeous garnish.

Serves 6 to 8

½   Sugar Baby watermelon, peeled and seeded

3   slices Pullman white bread, crust off

½   cup blanched almonds

1½ cups orange juice

2   tablespoons freshly squeezed lime juice

1   small serrano chili, seeds removed, minced

½   teaspoon chopped garlic

2   tablespoons chopped cilantro

Mix and purée all the ingredients listed above.

Then fold in:

½   small seedless watermelon, rind cut off and inside cut into chunks

1   seedless cucumber, diced

½   yellow bell pepper, finely diced

½   red onion, finely diced

Chill well before serving.

Spring Pea Soup with Tarragon Truffle Oil

My mother would call this an "uptown" soup, something she considered highfalutin, to be served on special occasions. There's nothing like spring peas in season, and all their glorious flavor comes shining through in this relatively simple soup. This version is vegan, if you use oil instead of butter in the sautéing process. However, if you want a richer soup, add ¼ cup of heavy cream just before serving. A little advance planning in buying extra peas when they are in season and freezing them ensures that this soup can be made year-round.

Serves 4 to 5

2   teaspoons butter or olive oil
2   teaspoons minced shallot
½   cup thinly sliced green onion
2   cups freshly shelled peas (frozen will work
     if fresh not available)
4   cups Sweet Pea Stock (*recipe follows*)
1   teaspoon kosher salt
½   teaspoon sugar
Salt and freshly ground black pepper, to taste
Tarragon Truffle Oil for garnish (*recipe follows*)
Green onions for garnish, thinly sliced

In a soup pot, melt the butter. Add the shallot and green onion and sauté over low heat for about 3 minutes or until softened. Add the peas, stock, salt, and sugar. Bring to a boil and then simmer for 5 minutes.

In batches, transfer the soup to a blender and purée. Return to the pot and season with salt and pepper to taste. Serve immediately in bowls and drizzle with a touch of Tarragon Truffle Oil. Garnish with green onions.

SWEET PEA STOCK

1 bunch scallions, washed and chopped

1 stalk celery, chopped

3 cups cleaned pea pods

½ teaspoon kosher salt

In a 2-quart stockpot, combine all the ingredients with 5 cups of cold water. Bring to a boil, reduce the heat, and simmer covered for 20 minutes, then strain.

TARRAGON TRUFFLE OIL

4 sprigs fresh tarragon, leaves removed and stems discarded

¼ cup parsley

Pinch of kosher salt

2 tablespoons truffle oil

4 tablespoons olive oil

Blanch the tarragon leaves in boiling water for 2 seconds. Remove with slotted spoon and place into a blender. Add the parsley and salt. Purée well. With the blender running, slowly drizzle in the truffle oil and olive oil. Place mixture in a container and set aside.

Winter Root Vegetable Stew

This hearty winter vegetable stew is inspired by Deborah Madison, cookbook author and founding chef of Greens restaurant in San Francisco. A simple salad along with a loaf of crusty whole-grain bread is the perfect accompaniment to the stew. It may seem like a lot of stew, but it holds up well for days, and the flavor just gets better and better.

Serves 8 to 10

2   tablespoons olive oil
2   medium onions
2   leeks
2   cloves garlic, minced
½-inch piece fresh ginger, peeled and minced
10–12 cups (peeled and cut into attractive chunks) root vegetables (*see note*)
2   cups carrot chunks
10   or more cups Vegetable Stock (*page 59*) or broth
1   teaspoon dried thyme
2   bay leaves
Salt and freshly ground black pepper, to taste

In a large heavy-bottomed pot or in a stockpot, cook the onion, leeks, garlic, and ginger in the olive oil over medium heat until the onions and leeks are translucent and sweet, about 8 to 10 minutes. Add the root vegetables and carrots and cook for 5 minutes, stirring frequently. Add 10 cups of the stock or broth, thyme, and bay leaves. Bring to a boil, then lower the heat to medium and cook until the vegetables are just tender, 30 to 40 minutes.

For a lovely, creamy stew, put about half of the soup into a bowl and set aside. Then purée the remaining stew that is in the pot with an immersion blender, or alternatively in batches in a blender with a tight-fitting lid.

Return the unblended portion of the stew to the pot, mix well, and season with salt and pepper to taste. Reheat before serving.

Note on root vegetable combination: Choose a number of root veggies for the stew, such as rutabagas, potatoes, celery stalks, celery root, parsnips, and turnips. At least one or two parsnips are a must, as they give a fantastic sweet dimension to the stew.

Bavarian Hunter's Stew

Some of the first early arrivals to the Chesapeake were from England and Africa, but not long thereafter, hordes of Germans began to arrive in the port cities of the Bay. During the late nineteenth century the German community was among the largest immigrant populations in the region. My grandmother Gertie's parents were from Prussia, and their home was filled with the aromas and flavors of the Old Country. Soups and stews were a staple of the Wissman household.

This is a great winter meal, with most of the ingredients available at a farmers' market. It makes smart use of the beef, with a little going a long way. The small amount of fat from the beef does a first-rate job of flavoring this wonderful assortment of vegetables. Keep an eye on the consistency of the stew as it cooks, adding a little more stock or wine if necessary. The Kitchen Garden Rye bread (*see page 202*) is the perfect accompaniment to the stew.

Serves 6

3 tablespoons butter, divided
3 tablespoons oil, divided
1½ pounds beef bottom round, cut into ¾-inch cubes
2 onions, chopped
2 medium carrots, peeled and coarsely cubed
3 tablespoons minced fresh chives
4 tablespoons coarsely chopped parsley
1 pound fresh mushrooms, trimmed and sliced
4–5 medium potatoes, peeled and cubed
⅓ cup dry German white wine
1 cup Beef Stock (*page 60*)
1 teaspoon imported sweet paprika
1 teaspoon salt
⅛ teaspoon freshly ground black pepper
Generous pinch of nutmeg
⅓ cup sour cream

In a Dutch oven or heavy-bottomed casserole, heat 2 tablespoons of butter and 2 tablespoons of oil. Brown the beef on all sides and remove with a slotted spoon. Add the onions, carrots, chives, and 2 tablespoons of the parsley. Sauté for about 4 to 5 minutes. Add the reserved meat to the Dutch oven.

Melt 1 tablespoon butter with 1 tablespoon oil in a skillet. Add the mushrooms and cook for about 4 to 5 minutes. Add to the meat in the Dutch oven. Stir in the cubed potatoes.

In a small bowl, combine the wine and stock with the paprika, salt, pepper, and nutmeg. Pour over the meat mixture and bring to a boil over medium heat. Reduce the heat to low, partially cover, and simmer for about 1 hour and 15 minutes, adding a little more wine if necessary if the stew becomes too thick. Remove pot from heat, stir in sour cream, and adjust seasonings.

Garnish with the remaining fresh parsley.

Kevin's Hearty Crock Pot Venison and Chevre Stew

Kevin Neibuhr is a man for all seasons. He is a fixture at the Saturday Waverly farmers' market in Baltimore, positioned at the Charlottetown Farm stand selling crafted goat cheeses to his regular customers. He is also a master furniture maker and can build out a new kitchen or remodel a room quicker than who-struck-John. One would think those are more than enough talents to be given a person in one lifetime, but no, Kevin is also a self-taught, intuitive cook. As this recipe testifies, Kevin has a great sense of flavors, showcased in this hearty stew. Nice crusty bread to accompany the stew is essential, according to Kevin.

Serves 6

12 ounces sliced mushrooms

1-pound package baby carrots

4 medium potatoes, cubed

1 white onion, diced

1–2 pounds cubed venison stewing meat

1 (28-ounce) can of tomatoes (Kevin suggests Furmano brand with basil, garlic, and oregano)

1 cup beef broth

3 tablespoons extra-virgin olive oil

1 tablespoon onion powder

1 tablespoon garlic powder

1 tablespoon sweet paprika

1 cup dry red wine, such as Merlot, Malbec, or Carmenére

Salt and freshly ground black pepper, to taste

4–8 ounces of Charlottetown Plain chevre (depending on how rich you like your stew)

Put all the mushrooms, carrots, potatoes, and onion into a 6-quart crock pot. Place the meat over the vegetables and pour the tomatoes, beef broth, and olive oil over the top. Add the onion powder, garlic powder, paprika, and red wine. Season with salt and pepper to taste. Mix thoroughly.

Cook on a high setting for 6 hours, stirring every hour. Turn the heat to a low setting and add the chevre. Cook 2 more hours or until carrots and potatoes are tender, continuing to stir every hour.

Springfield Farm Brunswick Stew

This is as authentically American as you can get for a recipe. It harkens back to the eighteenth century, when early American subsistence cookery would often use squirrel or rabbit in the one-pot dishes. Many families around the region have their own variations on this dish, but very few still call for squirrel as the primary ingredient. The recipe nowadays almost exclusively calls for cut-up chicken. I'm sure the squirrels are breathing sighs of relief.

This is an awesome plant-forward-style recipe, as it's almost a succotash-like stew—full of lima beans and corn that are accentuated with tomato and herbs. Some friends of mine omit the potatoes and serve the not-as-thick stew over steamed rice, but as an Irishman in exile, I'm partial to the spuds.

Serves 4 to 6

All-purpose flour seasoned with salt and freshly ground black pepper

1   frying chicken (about 3 pounds), cut into serving pieces

2   tablespoons butter

2   tablespoons bacon drippings (optional)

2½ quarts boiling water or Chicken Stock (*page 59*)

1½ cups dried lima beans, soaked in cold water overnight

1   large onion, coarsely chopped

4   large ripe tomatoes, chopped

1   cup canned tomato sauce

1½ cups fresh corn kernels (3 ears)

4   potatoes, peeled and cut into quarters

1   teaspoon dried thyme leaves

1   bay leaf

Salt and freshly ground black pepper, to taste

Lightly flour the chicken pieces. Melt the butter and bacon drippings (if not using the bacon drippings, substitute canola oil) in a heavy-bottomed pot and brown the chicken well on all sides. Pour in the water or stock and bring to a boil. Cover, reduce the heat, and simmer for 1 hour.

Drain the lima beans. Add lima beans and all the remaining ingredients to the pot. Cover and continue to simmer over a very low heat for another hour or until the meat is tender.

4

OVEN FIRED

One might imagine the oven as the original, prehistoric crock pot. The original ovens were more like what we know as Dutch ovens and were buried in ashes and hot embers to slowly cook food. As humankind progressed, the ovens were made more front-loading, with the Greeks credited for this advance. Of course, they had other motives besides looking for a patent, as these devices were used to make the first yeasted breads. And so it progressed, to where nowadays the oven is one of the centerpieces of the home kitchen. Ovens made the casseroles and braised dishes that we so love possible and opened up a whole new realm of cookery.

We have here an eclectic array of recipes for fish, crab, meat, poultry, and lots of veggies. They run the gamut, from colonial recipes to a pan-Asian treatment for an invasive species to traditional Eastern Shore fare and a few more down-home comfort dishes. Ovens have made cooking a little more simple and for generations have been providing delicious aromas of lovingly crafted meals to our homes.

Wide Net Blue Catfish in Banana Leaves

Wendy Stuart, cofounder of the brilliantly innovative Wide Net Project (*see page 108*), provided this very nifty (and tasty) recipe. You are creating packets of beautifully marinated fish fillets that make their own "sauce" while baking.

Serves 4

3 garlic cloves

2 inches peeled ginger root, roughly chopped

¼ cup lime juice

2 Thai chilies or 1 serrano (optional)

2 shallots, roughly chopped

3 kaffir lime leaves, crushed

4 stalks lemongrass, white portions only, sliced thin

1 teaspoon brown sugar

3 tablespoons fish sauce

1 tablespoon cumin seeds, toasted and ground

½ teaspoon coriander seeds, toasted and ground

½ teaspoon mustard seeds, toasted and ground

½ cup cilantro leaves

4 (6-ounce) Wide Net blue catfish fillets

2 banana leaves, thawed (available in the frozen section of Latin and larger grocery stores)

2 tablespoons chopped cilantro leaves, for garnish

2 limes, halved, for garnish

Place the garlic, ginger, lime juice, chilies, shallots, lime leaves, lemongrass, brown sugar, fish sauce, cumin seeds, coriander seeds, mustard seeds, and cilantro into a food processor and blend to a thick paste.

Using a sharp knife, score the fish fillets once every inch or so (there should be 2 to 3 cuts). This is to let the marinade penetrate the fillet. Spread paste on both sides of the fillets. Wrap each fillet in half of a banana leaf, folding the ends over to keep steam in each packet. Keep closed with toothpicks, if necessary.

Place wrapped fish pieces in a baking dish, in one layer. Marinate in the refrigerator for 1 to 2 hours, then bring to room temperature.

Preheat oven to 400°F.

Bake the fish in the banana leaves for 22 minutes.

To serve, place fish packets over cooked brown or white rice. Open the packets, letting the juices from the wrapped fish drizzle into the rice. Garnish each with cilantro and half of a fresh lime.

Bluefish with Tomatoes and Capers

Most watermen and sports fishermen I know go crazy for the blues—bluefish, that is. I think it has a marvelous flavor, with a beautifully moist and meaty texture. The thing about bluefish is that it needs to be fresh, with a capital F. If it has been sitting too long, it can take on a slightly metallic flavor. So trust your fishmonger or a fishing friend to steer you to a just-out-of-the-water bluefish. It can be enjoyed simply grilled, with a squeeze of lemon, or baked in a nice tangy sauce, like the one that follows. I've been enjoying this dish for years.

Serves 4

¼ cup olive oil

1 medium onion, diced

2 stalks celery, diced

1 rounded tablespoon minced garlic

⅓ cup finely chopped green onions

1½ pounds tomatoes, peeled and chopped, with juice (about 3 cups)

1 cup dry white wine

3 tablespoons capers, drained and coarsely chopped

½ teaspoon dried (or 1 teaspoon fresh) thyme

1 bay leaf

Juice of 1 lemon

Salt and freshly ground black pepper, to taste

4 bluefish fillets (5–6 ounces each)

Preheat the oven to 375°F.

Heat the oil in a heavy pot and sauté the onion, celery, garlic, and green onions until limp. Add the tomatoes, wine, capers, thyme, bay leaf, and lemon juice. Simmer over low heat for 45 minutes. Season with salt and pepper to taste.

Spread half of the tomato sauce in the bottom of a 13 x 9 x 2 inch glass baking dish. Arrange the fillets on top. Spoon the remaining sauce over the fish. Butter one side of a sheet of wax paper large enough to cover the dish. Cover the dish with the wax paper, buttered side down. Bake for 20 to 25 minutes or until the fish flakes at the touch of a fork.

Remove the fish fillets to a heated platter. Remove and discard the bay leaf and spoon the tomato sauce over the fish. Serve at once.

Smith Island Rockfish with Potatoes

Here is some more fine eating from the Chesapeake's Eastern Shore region. Mrs. Frances Kitching is the inspiration for this dish, with a simple bake of rockfish with potatoes and onions that is moistened with water or seafood stock. By whisking some flour into the liquid before the baking process, the fish makes its own gravy as it cooks. And a delicious gravy it is.

Serves 3 to 4

5 medium potatoes, peeled
1 large onion, diced
Salt and freshly ground black pepper
2 cloves garlic, minced
1 teaspoon whole dried thyme
1 rockfish, 2–3 pounds, scaled, head and tail removed, and boned
3 tablespoons bacon grease or olive oil
2 tablespoons flour
1½ cups water or Fish Stock (*page 58*)

Preheat oven to 350°F.

Cut the potatoes into ½-inch rounds. Place half of the potatoes in a greased baking dish. Sprinkle half of the onion pieces over the top. Repeat with another layer of potatoes and onions. Season well with salt and pepper. Sprinkle the garlic and thyme on top of the vegetables.

Place the rockfish atop the vegetables and drizzle with bacon grease or olive oil. Season again with salt and pepper.

Place the flour in a small bowl and slowly whisk in the water or stock to achieve a smooth consistency. Pour evenly over the fish and vegetables and cover the baking dish tightly with aluminum foil or a tight-fitting lid. Place in the oven and bake for about 1 hour or until the fish is cooked through.

To serve, cut the fish into serving portions, place on top of the potatoes, and drizzle with the pan juices (gravy). A seasonal green vegetable or garden salad is a perfect accompaniment.

Aunt Bessie's Crab Pudding

Boy, I love this crab pudding! It's one of my favorite Chesapeake dishes and a great way to stretch that precious crabmeat. With crab cakes, I could feed only three people with 1 pound of blue crab, but my Aunt Bessie magically turned 1 pound of crab into a dish that can feed a crowd.

Serves 6 to 8

6 tablespoons butter or bacon drippings

½ cup minced onion

½ cup diced celery

2 cups coarsely chopped mushrooms

½ cup finely diced green bell pepper

1 pound lump or backfin crabmeat, fresh or pasteurized, picked over for shells

8 slices white bread, crust removed, cubed

4 eggs, lightly beaten

2 cups milk

2 cups heavy whipping cream

1 teaspoon salt

½ teaspoon ground black pepper

1 teaspoon Worcestershire sauce

Dash of Tabasco sauce

1 cup finely shredded sharp Cheddar cheese

Butter a 9 x 9 inch casserole or baking dish.

In a skillet, melt the butter or bacon drippings over medium heat. Add the onion, celery, mushrooms, and bell pepper. Sauté for about 5 minutes or until soft. Remove from heat, gently fold in the crabmeat, and set aside.

Place half of the diced bread in the bottom of the prepared baking dish. Spread the crabmeat vegetable mixture over the top. Place the remaining diced bread on top.

In a mixing bowl, combine the eggs, milk, cream, salt, pepper, Worcestershire sauce, and Tabasco. Mix well and pour evenly over casserole. Cover with aluminum foil and chill in the refrigerator for an hour or more.

Preheat the oven to 350°F. Place casserole in the oven and bake for 20 minutes. Reduce heat to 325°F. Remove the foil and distribute the cheese evenly over the top. Continue baking until set, about 40 minutes. Serve hot.

Asparagus and Crab Tart

Crabs start "running" in the Bay just a few weeks before the asparagus of the Eastern Shore is at the market. So, in no time at all, there is plenty of both crab and asparagus to be found. And they go together perfectly. This is a lovely recipe for a luncheon or dinner and, when served with a side salad, a complete meal.

Serves 6 to 8

Pastry Dough for a Single-Crust Pie
(*recipe follows*)

3   eggs, slightly beaten

½   cup mayonnaise

2   tablespoons flour

1   teaspoon chopped fresh thyme

Freshly ground black pepper

8   ounces Swiss cheese, finely shredded (about 2 cups)

½   small onion, thinly sliced

½   pound fresh asparagus, tough ends trimmed, blanched, and chopped into 1-inch pieces

1   pound lump crabmeat, picked over for shells

Sprigs of thyme and sliced fresh fruit for garnish

Prepare the pastry dough and line a 9-inch pie pan.

Preheat the oven to 350°F.

Combine the eggs, mayonnaise, flour, thyme, and black pepper in a bowl and mix well. Gently stir in the cheese, onion, asparagus, and crabmeat. Pour mixture into the pastry shell. Bake until a knife inserted into the center comes out clean, about 40 minutes. Garnish each serving with a sprig of fresh thyme and sliced fresh fruit.

PASTRY DOUGH FOR A SINGLE-CRUST PIE

1½   cups all-purpose flour

¾   teaspoon salt

½   cup solid vegetable shortening

3–4   tablespoons cold water

Sift together the flour and salt into a mixing bowl. Use a pastry blender or your fingers to work the shortening into the flour mixture until it is the consistency of coarse meal. Add the water 1 tablespoon at a time, mixing with a fork after each addition. Add only enough water to make the dough stick together. When you can form it into a ball, wrap it in plastic wrap and refrigerate for at least 15 to 30 minutes before using.

Emily's Hungarian Brisket

Who would have thought that the best brisket I've ever eaten would be made by the woman who grows all the apples, peaches, pears, and every other fruit imaginable that we use at our restaurant? But it is the truth, and this is the brisket that Emily Zaas, of Black Rock Orchard, prepared for us one evening up in the farmhouse. On recounting the history of this dish Emily remembered, "The reason I started making the brisket is that David (my husband) likes gravy. It was the only thing I knew how to make with gravy when we got married except wiener goulash." Well, I haven't had the pleasure of tasting the wiener goulash, but I can attest that this brisket is a winner.

When Emily serves the brisket at the long farmhouse table, there are, as may be expected, many bowls and platters of side dishes. She suggests rice pilaf, potato kugel, and some potato pancakes with applesauce.

Serves 10 to 12

Salt (about 2–3 teaspoons)

Freshly ground black pepper

4 tablespoons or more Hungarian paprika

3 cloves garlic, crushed

1 tablespoon olive oil

6–10 pounds brisket

3 large onions, chopped

2 large (20-ounce) cans crushed or diced tomatoes

1½ cups apple cider

Preheat the oven to 400°F.

Place salt, pepper, and a lot of paprika together in a bowl and mix well. Stir in the garlic and olive oil and mix together to form a paste-like rub. Rub this mixture over both sides of the brisket.

Roast uncovered for about 20 minutes per side, turning the brisket as necessary to brown it nicely on both sides. Remove the pan from the oven and add the onions, tomatoes, and apple cider.

Reduce heat to 275°F.

Return the brisket to the oven and cook uncovered for 1 hour. Remove the roasting pan, cover tightly with aluminum foil, and continue to bake for about 3 hours or until very tender.

Pour off all the cooking liquids and reserve. Allow the brisket to cool before carving. For the best results, refrigerate the brisket overnight. It really makes it much easier to slice. When ready to serve the next day, slice the brisket against the grain, and reheat the slices in the reserved cooking liquid.

Note: The cooking liquid can be blended and reduced to make the sauce a little thicker. Adjust seasonings at that time.

Chicken Pot Pie with Sweet Potato Crust

This is a true "from scratch" recipe—it includes poaching the chicken whole, simmering chunks of vegetables in the resulting broth, and preparing a very homemade pie pastry enhanced with baked sweet potato. This is real home cooking and the epitome of comfort food.

Serves 6 to 8

Salt

1   large chicken (about 4 pounds)

1   large onion, sliced

2   whole cloves

Sweet Potato Crust (*recipe follows*)

16 pearl onions, peeled

1   cup medium-diced carrots

1   cup medium-diced celery

1   cup corn kernels

1   cup fresh peas

8   tablespoons (1 stick) butter

½   cup all-purpose flour

1   cup heavy whipping cream

Freshly ground black pepper and ground nutmeg, to taste

Bring a large pot filled with salted water to a boil and add the chicken, sliced onion, and cloves. Reduce the heat and simmer until the chicken is tender, 1 to 1½ hours. While the chicken is cooking, cook and chill the sweet potato for the pastry. Remove the chicken from the pot and when somewhat cooled, pick off the meat. Set aside. Strain and reserve the liquid from the cooking pot. Skim off the fat.

Combine the pearl onions, carrots, celery, corn, and peas in a saucepan. Pour in only enough of the strained cooking liquid to cover. Simmer until tender. Drain, and reserve this cooking liquid, adding additional chicken cooking liquid to make 3 cups.

Preheat the oven to 350°F.

Arrange the reserved chicken meat and the vegetables in a greased 4-quart baking dish.

To make the sauce, melt the butter in a saucepan and whisk in the flour. Cook, stirring constantly for 2 to 3 minutes. Gradually whisk in the 3 cups of the combined cooking liquids and the cream. Bring to a boil, reduce heat, and continue to simmer for 3 minutes. Season well with salt, pepper, and nutmeg. Pour over the top of the chicken and vegetables. Finish making the pastry crust and fit it on the top of the baking dish. Crimp the edges of the pastry with a fork or your fingers.

Bake the pot pie for about 45 minutes or until the top is nicely browned and the filling is piping hot. Remove from oven and let stand for 5 to 10 minutes before serving.

SWEET POTATO CRUST

1–2 sweet potatoes (enough to yield 1½ cups mashed)

1¾–2 cups all-purpose flour

1½ teaspoons salt

2 teaspoons baking powder

½ cup solid vegetable shortening

2 eggs, beaten together with 1 teaspoon honey

Preheat the oven to 400°F.

Bake the sweet potatoes until soft, 45 to 60 minutes, depending on the size. (I like to wrap the potatoes in foil, as they cook more quickly and don't ooze out all over the oven or tray.) When cool enough to handle, scoop out the flesh and mash. Chill (the potatoes, not you).

Sift together the flour, salt, and baking powder in a large bowl. Add the chilled sweet potatoes, shortening, and eggs. With a pastry blender, two knives, or fingertips, work in the flour, adding more as necessary to achieve a rollable dough. Turn the dough out onto a lightly floured surface and roll it to a size that will cover the baking dish.

Big Chicken, Little Chicken

According to the National Chicken Council, in 2014, the United States produced over thirty-eight billion pounds of broiler chicken. A typical large-scale chicken farm, registered with the USDA as a Concentrated Animal Farming Operation (CAFO) measuring 490 feet by 45 feet, can hold at least thirty thousand chickens. Each full-grown chicken must be allotted an amount of space equivalent to an 8.5 x 11 inch piece of paper. That sounds like a lot of chickens crammed into a relatively tiny space.

CAFO chickens are typically fed genetically modified (GM) corn and soy beans. Processing by-products, such as chicken feathers and other animal parts, can also be added to the feed. To prevent the inevitable spread of disease from stress, overcrowding, lack of vitamin D (as CAFO chickens may never see the light of day), and an unnatural diet, the animals are fed regular doses of antibiotics. Cheap CAFO chicken and eggs may be taking a hidden toll on your health when you eat them.

The Delmarva Peninsula is already one of the most concentrated areas for poultry CAFOs in the country. From Virginia's Accomack County to Delaware's Kent, more than two hundred new large chicken houses are in the pipeline, according to an Environmental Integrity Project report released in September 2015. Some of the new houses are built to hold as many as sixty thousand birds. Farmers and investors often cluster big chicken houses in groups of a half-dozen or more on one plot of land. Nearby residents complain of illnesses, unbearable stench, and unbreathable air.

Over two hundred thousand tons of excess chicken manure already seeps into nearby waterways every year, and from there it washes into the nearby Chesapeake Bay. This pollution, with its high levels of nitrogen and phosphorus, can stimulate spectacular algae blooms that suck oxygen from the water, creating an environment in which fish can't breathe—zones where everything dies. Feeling a little queasy?

Compare that with raising a reasonable amount of poultry within an integrated farming system, like we see at Rumbleway Farm in Cecil County, where the birds are free to roam in the fresh air and sunlight. Chickens and turkeys are the best natural "pesticide" imaginable when it comes to dealing with bugs and slugs in the garden, too. Rumbleway uses portable fences, known as "chicken tractors," to move the flocks around the farm. They keep the area bug free; birds are out in the fresh air and happily scratching around for the natural and healthy diet that they like best. Do Rumbleway's poultry products cost more? Sure they do. But are those cheap chicken nuggets really worth the damage CAFO operations are causing to our health and to the health of our Bay?

Beef Brisket with Tangy Peaches

This is a sweet-and-sour braised brisket chock full of local peaches. Make sure the peaches you choose are not too mushy-ripe—if they are, they will disintegrate while cooking in the finished sauce. The braised brisket is step one in the overall dish. The tender beef is best served with or over potatoes or, as I have suggested here, cheesy grits. Slow braising is key, so don't try to rush this dish. I like to let the meat rest for at least an hour before serving while the flavor of the sauce deepens. If you have leftovers, fantastic—it's even better the next day!

Serves 8

3 tablespoons rendered beef fat or vegetable oil

4 pounds (1 piece) beef brisket

2 onions, chopped

2 carrots, peeled and chopped

3 cloves garlic, minced

3 cups Beef Stock (*page 60*)

4 tablespoons brown sugar

4 tablespoons apple cider vinegar

6 cups peeled, sliced fresh peaches

2 bay leaves

1 teaspoon ground cinnamon

½ teaspoon ground cloves

Salt and pepper, to taste

Boiled, mashed, or roasted potatoes for serving, or Broom's Bloom Cheddar Hominy (*page 134*)

In a heavy pot or Dutch oven, heat the oil and brown the brisket well on both sides. Remove brisket and set aside. Add the onions, carrots, and garlic. Sauté for about 10 minutes over medium heat.

Return the brisket to the pot and add the stock. Bring to a boil and add the brown sugar, vinegar, and 3 cups of the sliced peaches. Stir in the bay leaves, cinnamon, and cloves. Season with a little salt and pepper.

Bring the pot back to a boil and then cover with lid. Reduce the heat to a simmer and cook for approximately 2½ to 3 hours. Turn the brisket several times during this period. When brisket is tender to the fork, place the meat on a platter and cover to keep warm.

Push the braising liquid through a coarse strainer into a saucepan. Bring sauce to a gentle boil and reduce by about one-third. Add the remaining sliced peaches and warm gently. Adjust seasoning.

Slice the brisket and place on a warm platter for serving. Serve the peach gravy on the side. For a nice change from the usual brisket-and-potato combo, try serving the brisket with some Broom's Bloom Cheddar Hominy (*see page 134*) or your favorite cheese grits recipe.

Charlottetown Farm Swiss Chard and Goat Cheese Gratin

My favorite "goat cheese lady" is Ms. Pam Miller, creator and animator of the wonderful array of cheeses that are Charlottetown Farm. You can feel the passion and joy emanating from Pam at her farmers' market stand as she tells the weekly tales of the cheese-making process. She always includes stories of her "girls," from whom the milk flows, their unique antics, and how they are doing. This gratin is flavored with Pam's creamy chevre and enhanced with just a tad of pungent grain mustard. And did I mention it's loaded with leafy greens?

Serves 6

5   tablespoons unsalted butter
1   cup panko bread crumbs

1   clove garlic, chopped
2   tablespoons finely chopped fresh herbs (Pam suggests sage, thyme, and chives)
⅛   teaspoon freshly grated nutmeg
Salt and pepper, to taste
1   cup Chicken Stock (*page 59*)
½   cup heavy cream
1   tablespoon grain mustard
5   ounces Charlottetown Farm chevre
1   tablespoon flour
½   small onion, finely chopped
3   pounds Swiss chard leaves and stems, separated and cut into 1-inch pieces
1   pound spinach, coarse stems discarded, leaves coarsely chopped

Preheat oven to 400°F.

Melt 2 tablespoons butter and toss with panko, garlic, herbs, nutmeg, and salt and pepper to taste. Set aside.

Simmer the stock in a saucepan until reduced by half. Add the cream, grain mustard, and chevre, whisking until smooth.

Melt 1 tablespoon butter in heavy-bottomed saucepan over moderate heat, and stir in flour. Cook the roux, whisking constantly for 2 minutes; remove from heat, and season sauce with salt and pepper.

Cook the onion in the remaining 2 tablespoons butter in a large pot until softened. Add Swiss chard stems and nutmeg, salt, and pepper to taste. Cook, stirring until the stems are tender but not browned, about 8 minutes. Then increase the heat to moderately high and add the Swiss chard leaves and spinach. Stir until all the greens are wilted.

Transfer the vegetables to a colander and drain well, pressing out excess liquid with the back of a spoon. Toss the vegetables with the cream sauce and transfer to a shallow, buttered 2-quart baking dish. Top with panko-herb mixture and bake until it's bubbling and topping is golden, about 20 minutes.

Small-Scale Animal Husbandry

Tending to farm animals such as pigs, cows, poultry, sheep, and goats requires a much different skill set than growing crops for harvest. You don't get a day off. Good animal husbandry takes a year-round commitment to housing, feeding, tending, birthing, and genuinely caring about your herds and flocks. Diseases, predators, and nasty weather can all take a tremendous toll. Luckily, we have many small farmers in our region who are successfully rising to the challenges.

Our marvelous artisanal cheeses all come from smaller operations like Shady Goat Farm, the Hampton Roads area's first licensed cheese-making farm. Shannon Rice got her start as a hobby farmer after taking a goat farming class back in 2010. Two years later, she quit a career in nonprofit fundraising and marketing and began goat farming full time. Her herd includes Saanens, Alpines, LaMancha Crosses, and Nubians, and she knows each goat by name.

On Maryland's Eastern Shore, Marilyn and Lew Dodd raise a mixed herd of grass-fed beef, some hogs, chickens, and turkeys at their 92 acres on Cedar Run Farm, where the animals graze, forage, and do all the things they naturally love to do. Out in the Frederick Valley in Buckeystown, Maryland, at

Nick's Organic Farm, an integrated farming system minimizes off-farm inputs by combining intensive grazing and an 8- to 12-year crop rotation to raise vegetables, hay, pastures, grains, seed, and livestock. They grow their own organic grain and grind their own poultry feed.

Also in Buckeystown is Hedgeapple Farm, a combined beef research and educational effort launched by the Jorgensen Family Foundation. Hedgeapple focuses on the development and feasibility of production and marketing strategies to help make the region's smaller beef operations more viable. Their 310-plus acres are in permanent grassland and are utilized as pasture and hay for the farm's herd of Black Angus cattle. All the calves born on the farm are retained for pasture finishing and are direct-marketed through their on-farm retail market.

In Harford County at Maryland's largest organic produce operation, One Straw Farm, Joan and Drew Norman have added heritage breeds of hogs to the mix and are offering pasture-raised pork in their farm store. Robin Way, at Rumbleway Farm in Cecil County, has always incorporated livestock, with beef cattle, sheep, poultry, and rabbits fully integrated into her farming system. Her meat products are also available at her farm store or by subscription.

The farms highlighted above are just a fraction of all the operations currently utilizing small-scale production techniques. Humane, organic, small-scale animal husbandry in the farming systems of the Chesapeake region makes good economic and ecological sense.

The Wide Net Project

The Wide Net Project's goal is to get as much fish out of the water as possible and feed our neighbors in need, while also supporting the local economy and conservation.

One nasty fish—and the perfect solution.

The big blue catfish, a powerful, aggressive invasive predator, had been wreaking havoc on the Chesapeake, devouring important natives such as shad and herring—even threatening our precious blue crabs and striking a severe blow to the health of our fishing industries. Then came the Wide Net Project (WNP), started by Sharon Feuer Gruber and Wendy Stuart.

Sharon's experience and efforts revolved around promoting healthy food access for all, through urban gardening and sustainability-focused food distribution systems. She worked with Bread for the City of Washington, DC, spearheading their farm-to-food pantry program and starting their nutrition education campaign. Wendy has experience working with industry leaders in the development of Seafood Smart, a regional, scalable certification program directed by the National Aquarium in Baltimore; she brought her expertise as an economist to the WNP. Together they developed a financially sound approach that would address the problem and move beyond it toward a creative solution providing real, tangible economic and social benefits to everyone involved.

Recognizing that the blue catfish is an edible species, Sharon and Wendy sought to structure a system for harvesting and marketing it that would also support the healthy food access issues they both found so important. Building a strong coalition of industry partners, concerned environmental organizations, and community activists dealing with hunger and nutrition issues, they have created a business model that will surely be replicated far and wide.

While successfully creating a healthy demand for blue catfish, for every pound of fish sold through regular seafood markets, Wide Net donates a portion to feed neighbors in communities of need. They provide fish for free or below cost to efforts such as Miriam's Kitchen (a community soup kitchen that serves 150 to 175 guests in their dining room every weeknight), the Arcadia Center for Sustainable Food and Agriculture, the N Street Village, and other community-based hunger-relief organizations.

Creating a thriving market for an underutilized food source has bolstered the economic vitality of the fishery industries and greatly eased the environmental stresses caused by this super-predator. Beyond that, by partnering with existing community efforts aimed at addressing serious issues of health and nutrition, Wide Net supports hunger relief and the betterment of life for everyone in the community.

"There are too few projects that are connecting environmentalism and the various segments of the disparate food system, and the Wide Net Project does just that."

—Barton Seaver, chef, author, and director of Harvard's Healthy and Sustainable Food Program

Lentil Shepherd's Pie with Potato-Parsnip Topping

Here's a satisfying casserole dish for those Meatless Mondays suppers. It can be vegan and low fat, depending on how much oil, if any, you use and whether you use cow's milk. It's another of those fun dishes where you can play around with the ingredients. Sometimes I use half the amount of lentils and substitute half with store-bought "meat" substitutes, such as Smart Ground or Boca Crumbles. And you can add more or fewer veggies and even use sweet potatoes in place of the parsnips in the mash.

Serves 6 to 8

4   large Russet potatoes, peeled and quartered

3   medium parsnips, peeled and cut into chunks

⅔   cup unsweetened plant milk or dairy milk

2   tablespoons vegan butter, olive oil, or sweet butter

Salt and pepper, to taste

¼   cup minced chives

1½ cups lentils, green or brown

3   tablespoons olive oil

2   small onions, diced

3   medium carrots, peeled and diced

3   ribs of celery, diced

½   pound mushrooms, sliced or cut into chunks

1   teaspoon tomato paste

1   cup Vegetable Stock (*page 59*)

1   teaspoon whole dried thyme leaves

½   teaspoon dried basil

½   teaspoon dried rosemary

2   cups peas, fresh or frozen

2   cups corn kernels, fresh or frozen

In a large pot of salted water, cook the potatoes and parsnips until tender, about 25 to 30 minutes. Drain in a colander and return to the pot. Add the milk and butter. Mash well with a potato masher or hand mixer. Season to taste with salt and pepper. Fold in the minced chives and set aside.

To cook the lentils, first soak them for about 30 minutes in cold water. Drain in a strainer and rinse well. Put the lentils and 3 cups of water in a pot and bring to a boil; reduce the heat and allow to simmer until all the liquid is absorbed. Set aside. Preheat oven to 350°F.

In a large sauté pan, heat the olive oil and sauté the onion for about 5 minutes or until softened. Add the carrots and celery and sauté for about 10 minutes or until the carrots have softened a bit. Add the mushrooms and sauté for 5 minutes longer. Add the lentils, tomato paste, ⅔ cup stock, thyme, basil, and rosemary. Fold in the peas and corn. Should the mixture be too thick, add more stock, a little at a time, until a good, non-runny consistency is reached. Readjust the seasoning with salt and pepper as necessary.

Pour the mixture into a greased 9 x 13 inch baking dish, and top evenly with the potato-parsnip mash. Bake for about 45 to 50 minutes, or until nicely browned and bubbling.

Colonial Mushroom Tart

I found this recipe years ago when I was researching Maryland colonial cooking for my first cookbook. Many of the recipes I discovered called for baking veggies, fish, meat, and/or game in some sort of pastry or crust, sometimes topped, other times open faced. It was an old-world technique to make an oven-fired, one-pot dish that could feed a number of people. This is an excellent "base" recipe that could accommodate added meat or poultry, should you have any leftovers in the fridge.

Serves 4

1   Flaky Pastry Crust for 8- or 9-inch tart shell (*recipe follows*)

2   slices bacon, small dice

4   tablespoons butter

½   small onion, minced

1   small shallot, minced

1   pound mushrooms, chopped

1   tablespoon flour

3   tablespoons dry sherry

3   tablespoons heavy cream

Pinch of cloves

Salt and freshly ground black pepper, to taste

2   tablespoons chopped parsley

⅓   cup grated Swiss cheese

¼   cup dried breadcrumbs

Preheat oven to 375°F.

Heat a large pan and cook the bacon until crisp. Remove the bacon pieces and set aside. Add the butter to the bacon drippings and, when melted, add the onion and shallot. Sauté for about 3 minutes, stirring often. Add the mushrooms and cook over a low heat for about 15 to 20 minutes or until very soft. Increase the heat to medium and add the flour.

Cook for 1 minute, stirring constantly. Add the dry sherry, heavy cream, cloves, salt, and pepper. Continue cooking until almost all of the pan liquid has evaporated, but mixture is still moist, not dried out.

Remove from heat and fold in the parsley and bacon pieces. Place the mixture into an 8- or 9-inch tart pan lined with thinly rolled (about ⅛-inch thick) pastry. Spread the filling evenly in the tart shell. Sprinkle with cheese and breadcrumbs.

Place in the oven and bake for 30 minutes or until set. Remove from the oven and allow to rest for about 10 minutes before serving.

FLAKY PASTRY CRUST

2   cups all-purpose flour

1   teaspoon salt

8   tablespoons (1 stick) butter, cut into very small pieces

2   tablespoons vegetable shortening

¼   cup ice water

Sift the flour and salt together in a mixing bowl. Use a pastry cutter or your fingers to work the butter and shortening into the flour mixture until it is the consistency of coarse meal. Add the water, 1 tablespoon at a time, mixing with a fork after each addition. Add only enough water to make the dough stick together. When you can form it into a ball, wrap it in plastic wrap and refrigerate for at least 1 hour before using.

Champagne Cabbage and Apples

Not that I really understand the concept, but some people just do not like sauerkraut—go figure. But I found a solution—a little devious, but a solution nevertheless. And here it is: a braised champagne "kraut," with ginger, caraway, and a goodly amount of tart apples. The secret is rinsing the sauerkraut well under cold water, and then the kraut naysayers will enjoy a plateful extolling the virtues of cabbage and, of course, champagne. Honestly, whether you like kraut or not, this dish is a crowd pleaser.

Serves 8

6   tablespoons butter or olive oil

2   slices bacon, cut into ½-inch pieces (optional)

1   small onion, thinly sliced

2   tablespoons minced fresh ginger

1   teaspoon minced garlic

3   tart apples, peeled, cored, and thinly sliced

2   jars (2 pounds each) sauerkraut, rinsed in cold water several times and drained

2   cups dry champagne

1   teaspoon caraway seed (optional)

Salt and black pepper, to taste

Preheat oven to 350°F.

In a heavy ovenproof pot, melt the butter, and if using, render the bacon for a few minutes. Add the onion, ginger, and garlic. Sauté for 4 minutes. Add the apples and sauté for 2 minutes longer.

Place the rinsed sauerkraut into the pot. Pour in the champagne, caraway seed, salt, and pepper. Toss together and bring to a boil.

Cover tightly and bake in the oven for 1 hour.

5

PASTA AND FLATBREAD

Preparing a satisfying pasta or a freshly baked flatbread pizza is perfect for stretching protein and incorporating those veggies and grains into a meal. In this section we have recipes for a variety of whole-grain pastas, all of which are quite versatile and can be made with just about any pasta type of your choosing.

Flatbread pizzas are really just small "pizzettas" that will feed two to four persons, or they can be made individually. The crust is normally a little thinner than on a proper pizza, and lately I have seen quite a number of high-quality, premade flatbread shells in grocery stores. Some are even made with ancient grains or whole grains, and others are gluten-free. So even if you don't have time to make a dough from scratch, there can still be flatbread on the table in a jiffy.

Doug's Crab Dip Flatbread

Chef Doug Wetzel knows his way around a batch of dough, be it enriched egg bread, homemade donut, or foccacia. Here he creates a dough that is a hybrid between a pizza dough and a foccacia. To give the dough a different profile, you could substitute half whole-grain or spelt flour for half of the white flour. Since not everyone has a pizza stone in their kitchen, this recipe calls for baking sheets, but should you have a stone, by all means use the preheated stone to bake the flatbread.

Pizzas and flatbreads are kind of interchangeable, but in general, a flatbread is smaller than a traditional pizza and formed into small rectangles or ovals. Crab dips are ubiquitous to the Chesapeake, and this flatbread takes the dip one step further. Get all the pleasure of a delicious crab dip, but no dipping is necessary. Just grab a piece of this flatbread and enjoy a truly Chesapeake, no-dipping experience.

Serves 4 to 8

2 cups mayonnaise

1 tablespoon Dijon mustard

2 teaspoons Worcestershire sauce

1 tablespoon lemon juice

1 teaspoon Old Bay seasoning

Pinch of cayenne pepper

¼ cup fresh chopped parsley

8 ounces cheddar cheese, shredded

1 small jar (6–7 ounce) artichoke hearts, drained and cut into bite-size pieces

1 pound backfin or lump crabmeat, picked over for shells

1 batch Flatbread Dough (*recipe follows*)

Cornmeal for dusting baking pan

In a large mixing bowl, combine the mayonnaise, mustard, Worcestershire, lemon juice, Old Bay, cayenne, and parsley. Stir in the cheddar cheese and the artichoke hearts. Mix well. Gently fold in the crabmeat, taking care not to break up the lumps of crab. Cover the bowl and refrigerate until ready to use.

Prepare the Flatbread Dough.

Preheat oven to 400°F.

To bake, place the rectangles of dough onto a sheet pan that has been dusted with cornmeal and thickly spread the crab dip mixture on top of each piece of dough. Place sheet pan in the oven and bake for about 15 minutes or until it is nicely browned and dough has firmly baked. Serve immediately.

FLATBREAD DOUGH

2½ cups bread flour

¼ ounce yeast (1 envelope)

1   teaspoon salt

1   teaspoon sugar

2   tablespoons extra-virgin olive oil

About 1+ cup very warm (120–130°F) water

Place the flour, undissolved yeast, salt, and sugar in a mixing bowl. Add the olive oil and ¾ cup of the warm water. Mix until well blended, about 2 minutes, adding more water or flour as needed.

Turn the dough out onto a floured board and knead until smooth and elastic, about 5 minutes. Divide the dough into 8 equal portions. Cover rounds with a clean dish towel and allow to rest for 10 minutes. Roll each piece into a thin rectangle or oval, about 12 x 4 inches, and cover with a towel.

Fig, Arugula, and Goat Cheese Flatbread

This flatbread is a hit at our restaurant, Gertrude's, at the Baltimore Museum of Art, and flies out of the kitchen whenever we run it as a special. If you like a cheesier flatbread/pizza you could substitute ricotta for the chevre or mix ricotta and chevre together. Another variation takes some very thin slices of prosciutto, or country ham, that have been julienned and places them just under the arugula when assembling the flatbread.

Serves 4 to 6

1   batch Fig Spread (*recipe follows*)
1   batch Flatbread Dough (*page 117*), rolled into 8 rectangles
4   cups arugula
Extra-virgin olive oil
Salt and freshly grated black pepper, to taste
1   cup crumbled chevre goat cheese
Cornmeal for coating pans

Preheat oven to 425°F.

Prepare the Fig Spread and the Flatbread Dough. Roll the dough as described in the Flatbread Dough recipe.

Place the arugula in a mixing bowl, lightly drizzle with just a touch of olive oil, and toss. Season with salt and pepper.

Place the rectangles of dough onto a sheet pan that has been dusted with cornmeal and generously smear the Fig Spread mixture on top of each piece of dough. Scatter about ½ cup of the dressed arugula over each flatbread. Sprinkle crumbled goat cheese evenly over the flatbreads. Place sheet pan in the oven and bake for about 10 to 12 minutes or until it is nicely browned and dough has firmly baked. Serve immediately.

Note: Since not everyone has a pizza stone in their kitchen this recipe calls for baking sheets, but should you have a stone, by all means use the preheated stone to bake the flatbread.

FIG SPREAD

Yields about 1½ cups

10- to 12-ounce package dried figs, such as Turkish, calimyrna, or black mission

2 tablespoons sugar

2 tablespoons freshly squeezed lemon juice

Water, as needed

Place the figs, sugar, and about 1¼ cups water in a saucepan. Bring to a boil, reduce the heat, and simmer covered for about 15 to 20 minutes, or until the figs are tender. Place the figs and remaining liquid from the pan into a food processor and blend until fairly smooth. Add the lemon juice and a little more water as necessary to achieve a nice, thick yet spreadable paste.

Farfalle with Pea Tendril and Mint Pesto and Roasted Asparagus

For many years we've been conducting gardening and cooking classes at the historic Evergreen Museum and Library on North Charles Street in Baltimore. In the late spring when the peas are going strong, there are pea tendrils aplenty, and we were never sure just what to do with all of them. Here is a nifty idea that came from our Edible Evergreen series.

Serves 4 to 6

1　pound local asparagus, with tough bottom stalks trimmed off

Extra-virgin olive oil, as needed

Kosher salt

Freshly ground black pepper

1　pound farfalle pasta (regular or whole wheat), cooked al dente, rinsed, drained, and cooled

1　red bell pepper, seeded and diced

½　cup minced chives or green onions

Pea Tendril and Mint Pesto (*recipe follows*)

Salt and freshly ground pepper, if needed

Preheat oven to 400°F. Coat the spears of asparagus with olive oil and dust with salt and pepper. Lay the asparagus on sheet trays, making sure they do not overlap. Roast for about 20 to 25 minutes, until tender but still a little crisp. Set aside and when cool enough to handle, cut into 1½-inch pieces. While the asparagus is roasting, cook the pasta and cool.

To assemble, place the pasta in a large mixing bowl and toss with the bell pepper, chives, and asparagus. Fold in pesto, a little at a time, until just nicely coated. Season the pasta salad with additional salt and pepper if necessary.

PEA TENDRIL AND MINT PESTO

3–4 cups pea tendrils

1　cup mint leaves

½　cup toasted pine nuts

4　cloves minced garlic

1　lemon, zested and juiced

½　cup grated parmesan (optional)

4　tablespoons extra-virgin olive oil

Salt and freshly ground pepper, to taste

Place the pea tendrils, mint leaves, pine nuts, garlic, lemon zest, lemon juice, and parmesan, if using, into a blender or food processor. Process the mixture until smooth. With the blender running, slowly add the olive oil. Season the pesto with salt and pepper to taste.

Farmer Joan's Pasta and Greens

When approaching the One Straw Farm stall at the local farmers' markets, you will always find a line. Yes, their produce is amazing and beautiful, and did I mention organic? They are the largest organic farm in Maryland. The line is not always about the greens or radishes or broccoli, but rather to speak with Farmer Joan.

Joan is the grand dame of the local farmers' movement, and she holds court at market. She is amazing to behold. Joan rattles off rapid-fire recipes for just about everything she grows and sells. Better bring a notepad, because it's all verbal. She loves this recipe for families with small children who often struggle with getting their kids to eat their greens. Joan says this is a sure-fire dish, and she has used it on her own, now-grown, brood.

You can use all types of greens in this dish, like spinach or beet greens or chard. Joan suggests that if you'd like some meat or seafood in the pasta, just cook a little sausage or shrimp when sautéing the olive oil and garlic. Another friend told me she adds some wedges of tomatoes to the pasta water and greens, along with some sliced black olives and pecans, when tossing the pasta. As you can see, this is another easy, basic recipe on which you can build.

Serves 4 to 6

1	large bunch kale (about 1½–2 pounds)
1	pound good-quality dry pasta
2	tablespoons minced garlic
¼	cup extra-virgin olive oil
½	cup freshly grated Parmigiano-Reggiano or 1 cup crumbled feta

Wash kale well in cold water and remove the leaves from the stems. Tear the leaves into small pieces and set aside.

Bring a large pot of generously salted water to a boil and begin cooking the pasta. While the pasta is cooking, heat a pan with the olive oil and gently sauté the garlic for about a minute, taking care not to burn. Remove from heat. When the pasta is approaching the al dente stage, add the pieces of kale. Cook for several minutes until the pasta is just done and still a bit firm; do not overcook.

Drain the pasta and kale in a colander and place in a large serving bowl. Pour the olive oil evenly over the pasta and sprinkle in the grated cheese or the crumbled feta. Toss all together well and serve immediately, with extra cheese on the side.

Ratatouille with Spelt Penne

I love ratatouille. Yeah, of course the movie, but beyond that, I love this classic French dish that brings together some of the finest summer vegetables imaginable. I've adapted this recipe from an old *Gourmet* magazine version and like to pair it with a whole-grain pasta. Spelt is an ancient grain grown throughout the Middle East and Europe from antiquity through the Middle Ages, and now it is making a big comeback. It has a high protein and vitamin content and is low in gluten, making it a better choice for gluten-sensitive individuals. But please note— it is not gluten-free and not appropriate for those with celiac disease. That said, it has a lovely nutty flavor that I adore, and it pairs well with the ratatouille.

Serves 6

2   eggplants (1½ pounds), cut into 1-inch cubes

2   large onions, chopped

½   cup olive oil

Kosher salt, to taste

4   yellow squash (1½ pounds), cut into 1-inch cubes

2   large red bell peppers, cut into 1-inch cubes

8   ripe plum tomatoes, peeled, seeded, and chopped

8   cloves garlic, minced

1   teaspoon fresh thyme

1½ pounds spelt penne rigate or other whole-grain pasta of your choice

½   cup finely chopped flat-leaf parsley (Italian parsley)

½   cup finely chopped fresh basil

Grated Parmigiano-Reggiano for serving

Preheat the oven to 450°F.

Stir together the eggplant, onions, ¼ cup olive oil, and kosher salt in a large roasting pan. Bake for 15 minutes, stirring occasionally. Stir in the squash, bell peppers, 2 tablespoons olive oil, and more salt. Roast for about 25 to 30 minutes, stirring occasionally, until bell peppers are tender.

While the vegetables are roasting, simmer the tomatoes, garlic, thyme, remaining 2 tablespoons oil, and salt in a heavy saucepan until thickened, about 15 minutes, stirring often. Stir tomato sauce into the roasted vegetables and season with salt and pepper to taste.

Cook the penne in a 6-quart pot of boiling, salted water until al dente, and drain. While the pasta is cooking, stir the parsley and basil into the ratatouille. Toss the penne with one-third of the ratatouille and serve topped with the remainder. Serve the grated cheese on the side.

Roasted Cauliflower Linguine

The beautiful heads of cauliflower piled high at the stands of the farmers' market always set my mind racing trying to figure out what to make. Soups and gratins are the first ideas that come to mind. But I remembered that years ago, when living in Baltimore's Little Italy neighborhood, local ladies would make a delicious, somewhat sweet, Italian pasta dish with cauliflower. After some research and playing around with the recipe, here is the dish I remember.

Serves 4 to 5

2   tablespoons extra-virgin olive oil

2   small onions, peeled and thinly sliced

4   teaspoons minced garlic

Pinch of red pepper flakes

1   tablespoon tomato paste

¼   cup heavy cream

½   cup golden raisins, steeped in ⅓ cup hot water

Pinch of saffron threads, soaked in ¼ cup hot water

1   large head cauliflower, cut into florets and roasted (*see note*)

Salt and freshly ground black pepper

1   pound whole-grain pasta (reserve 1 cup of cooking liquid)

½   cup freshly grated Parmesan cheese

¼   cup toasted pine nuts

Chopped flat-leaf parsley, for topping

In a large pan, heat the olive oil and sauté the onions, garlic, and red pepper flakes for 5 minutes or until the onions have softened. Whisk in the tomato paste and cook for 5 minutes, stirring frequently. Whisk in the cream, the raisins and their soaking water, and the saffron and its water. Stir in the roasted cauliflower and season with salt and pepper.

Cook the pasta in a large pot of boiling, salted water until the al dente stage. Drain in a colander and place in a large pasta or mixing bowl. Add the cauliflower mixture and grated cheese. Toss well with the pasta, then top with toasted pine nuts and parsley and serve immediately.

Note: To roast cauliflower, preheat oven to 400°F. Cut the head of cauliflower into florets and place in a mixing bowl. Drizzle with a little extra-virgin olive oil and season with kosher salt and freshly ground pepper. Toss well. Place the cauliflower on a baking sheet and roast in the oven for about 25 to 30 minutes.

Spaghetti with Cantaloupe

I first heard of this dish from Dr. Michael Stang, a friend who frequently visits our restaurant. He had been to a writers' seminar in Italy where they were served this pasta, and he fell in love with it. After a number of unsuccessful attempts to procure the recipe from the seminar's organizers, he did some sleuthing. He came upon a video/recipe from Giuliano Hazan, a chef and cooking instructor, and was finally able to reconstruct the recipe he so longed to have.

When he told me about it, I was immediately intrigued, as it uses one of my favorite fruits, cantaloupe. In my opinion, the Eastern Shore of the Chesapeake region grows some of the finest melons to be found. Must have something to do with the sandy soil, high humidity, and hot, sunny summer temperatures. So, a spaghetti with cantaloupe? You gotta be pulling my leg. We got busy in the kitchen and worked on the recipe and folks, the doctor was right—outstanding pasta dish. So when summer rolls around and the melons are at the height of flavor, do yourself a favor and check this out.

Serves 4 to 5

1 medium cantaloupe (about 3–4 pounds)

4 tablespoons butter

Salt and freshly ground black pepper

Juice of ½ lemon

2 teaspoons tomato paste

½ cup heavy cream

1 pound spaghetti

½ cup freshly grated Parmigiano-Reggiano, plus more for serving

Remove the skin and any green from the flesh of the melon. Remove the seeds and cut the melon into small chunks.

In a large skillet, melt the butter and add the cantaloupe pieces, seasoning well with salt and pepper. I know that sounds weird, but trust me. Cook the melon on a medium-high heat for about 10 minutes, stirring often. The melon will cook down, but you may have some larger pieces still in the sauce. Use the back of a large serving spoon and mash the remaining chunks. Whisk in the lemon juice and tomato paste and sauté for 5 minutes. Whisk in the heavy cream and simmer for 5 to 8 minutes, or until the sauce has reduced a bit.

While the sauce is cooking, prepare the pasta. Cook it in a large pot of salted, boiling water for about 8 to 10 minutes, until the al dente stage is reached. Drain the pasta in a colander. Place the hot pasta in a large serving bowl and pour the sauce directly over it. Add the grated cheese and toss well with the spaghetti. Serve additional grated cheese on the side.

Mama Lan's Tangy Noodles

Okay, okay, I heard you. I can't tell you how many of our regular guests at Gertrude's have asked me for this recipe. We use it as a side dish for a number of five-spice chicken dishes and at other times with bits of grilled garlic shrimp folded in. The late Mama Lan was my "other mother" when I lived on the West Coast and operated Gertie's Chesapeake Bay Cafe in Berkeley, California. She had been resettled from Vietnam after the war and became my right-hand chef at Gertie's. Lan had restaurants in Saigon before the war and was one of the best cooks I've ever known. This is her recipe and, with every bite I take, I remember my Mama.

Serves 6 to 8 as a side dish

1–pound package udon noodles

3   tablespoons sesame oil

3   tablespoons double black soy sauce (*see note*)

3   tablespoons black vinegar (*see note*)

2   tablespoons sugar

2   teaspoons hot chili oil

½   teaspoon salt

Juice of 1 orange

Zest of one orange

4   scallions, chopped

Cook the noodles in a large pot of salted, boiling water for 3 to 5 minutes, until soft but not mushy. Drain in a colander and immediately rinse with plenty of cold water to cool the noodles. Set aside.

In a mixing bowl, whisk together the sesame oil, soy sauce, black vinegar, sugar, chili oil, salt, orange juice, and orange zest. Toss the noodles with the marinade to coat well. Add the scallions and toss well. It is best if you let the noodles rest for at least 20 minutes before serving.

Note: Both double black soy sauce and Asian-style black vinegar can be found at Asian markets or in the international section of most grocery stores. The double black soy sauce is enriched with molasses and is quite different from generic soy sauce. Asian-style black vinegar is traditionally barrel aged and has a malty, smoky flavor.

A Plant-Based Diet

When talking about Bay- and body-friendly food, the concept of "plant-based" is central. Does that mean we need to become strict vegetarians? No, that's not necessarily what I'm suggesting. Rather, I *am* suggesting that we take the advice of food writer Michael Pollan: "Eat [real-whole] food. Not too much. Mostly plants." A plant-based diet is one that is centered on whole, unrefined, or minimally refined plants. It's a diet based on fruits, vegetables, tubers, whole grains, and legumes; it minimizes meat (including chicken and fish), dairy products, and eggs, as well as highly refined foods such as bleached flour, refined sugar, and hydrogenated oils. (Michael Pollan also warns: "Don't eat anything with ingredients your grandmother wouldn't recognize!") Why? Well, there's a whole lot of reasons.

Evidence clearly suggests that plant-based diets could help prevent some of the top killer diseases in the Western world—such as Alzheimer's, cancer, diabetes, heart disease, high cholesterol, high blood pressure, Parkinson's disease, age-related macular degeneration, cataracts, Crohn's disease, gallstones, kidney stones, diverticulitis, rheumatoid arthritis, and ulcerative colitis.

Raising enough animals to keep the current taste for burgers and chicken nuggets supplied requires massive amounts of land, food, energy, and water. A staggering 51 percent or more of global greenhouse-gas emissions are caused by animal agriculture, according to a report published by the Worldwatch Institute. According to the magazine *Scientific American*, a 2009 study found that four-fifths of the deforestation across the Amazon rainforest could be linked to cattle ranching. And the water pollution from factory farms can produce as much sewage waste as a small city, according to the Natural Resources Defense Council. Furthermore, the widespread use of antibiotics to keep livestock healthy in those overcrowded conditions has led to the development of antibiotic-resistant strains of bacteria that directly threaten our own health.

You can experiment by making your favorite recipes more plant-based. For example, just reduce the amount of meat, or replace the meat, in your favorite chili with some extra beans, make veggie burgers instead of meat burgers, or make that stir-fry with tofu instead of chicken. Or substitute half the amount of chicken called for in the stir-fry with the tofu. Many of our new recipes here offer ideas on how to stretch the animal protein to create delicious Bay- and body-friendly food.

Whole grains, potatoes, and beans are some of the most affordable bulk foods you can buy. Create meals around these staple items and you will spend less than you did on a meat-heavy diet. Vegetable and fruit smoothies are a delicious alternative to heavy, egg-centered breakfasts. To get a healthy measure of good fats and oils, just occasionally snack on a handful of seeds and nuts such as pumpkin, hemp, and flax seeds, walnuts, almonds, and cashews. Eat nut butters and avocados. Look for exciting new recipes for dishes that stretch meat protein in dishes like soups and stews that incorporate lots of good fresh vegetables.

You just might be surprised at how great you feel and how much more you can do once you're feeling healthier.

Bison Ragu with Pappardelle

For over a decade, Gunpowder Bison & Trading Company, in Monkton, Maryland, has been raising top-quality bison and selling a variety of products and cuts of meat. Their bison are grazed in the rolling hills of northern Baltimore County where owner Tre Lewis runs an excellent locally owned operation serving the metropolitan Baltimore region.

This is an adapted recipe originally for braised beef, but it works beautifully with the slightly sweet flavor of the grass-fed bison. It is paired with broad, flat pasta, which soaks up the savory, garlic-tomato braising juices. Obviously, if you can't get ahold of bison, a beef roast is perfect, but you would need to cook it about a half-hour or so longer.

Serves 5 to 6

2   pounds boneless bison chuck roast, in 2-inch cubes

Salt and freshly ground black pepper

1   tablespoon extra-virgin olive oil

2   tablespoons chopped rosemary

1   tablespoon chopped sage leaves

1   small red onion, diced

2   cloves garlic, finely chopped

1   carrot, peeled and diced

1   celery stalk, diced

2   cups dry red wine

1   28-ounce can peeled whole cherry or plum tomatoes

1   pound pappardelle

3   tablespoons butter, softened

1   tablespoon finely grated orange zest

½   cup freshly grated Parmigiano-Reggiano, plus extra for serving

Preheat oven to 300°F.

Season the bison with salt and pepper. Heat an ovenproof Dutch oven over medium heat and add the olive oil. When oil is hot, add the bison and sear until it is well browned on all sides, about 5 to 7 minutes. Add the rosemary, sage, onion, garlic, carrot, and celery. Reduce heat to medium-low and sauté until vegetables are softened, about 5 minutes.

Add the red wine and continue to simmer until liquid has reduced by half, about 15 minutes. Add the tomatoes and their juices. Bake, covered, for 3 hours.

When ready to serve, place a large pot of lightly salted water over high heat and bring to a boil. Cook the pappardelle until al dente, about 7 to 10 minutes. Drain and place in a mixing bowl or large serving bowl. Toss the pasta with the softened butter, orange zest, and ½ cup of grated cheese. Top with the stewed bison and sauce. Serve additional cheese on the side for topping if desired.

Ziti with Sauerkraut and Kielbasa

Krautfest is an annual event held at our restaurant celebrating all things kraut, complete with a polka band and beer hall. This recipe is a Krautfest favorite and can easily be made vegan by substituting a vegan kielbasa (the Tofurky brand of kielbasa is awesome) and Vegetable Stock (*see page 59*) for the cream. Either way, it'll make you want to polka, trust me!

Serves 6

- 3 tablespoons extra-virgin olive oil
- 1 medium onion, finely chopped
- 1 medium-size red bell pepper, thinly sliced
- 1 pound kielbasa sausage or smoked sausage, cut into ¼-inch-thick slices
- 12 ounces sauerkraut (about 3 cups), rinsed, well drained
- 3 tablespoons Dijon mustard
- ½ cup heavy whipping cream
- ¼ cup dry white wine
- 1 teaspoon caraway seeds
- Pinch of cayenne pepper
- 1 pound ziti pasta
- 3 tablespoons chopped flat-leaf parsley

Heat the olive oil in a large, heavy skillet over medium heat. Add the onion and red bell pepper and sauté for about 8 to 10 minutes or until softened. Add the sausage and sauté until beginning to brown, about 8 minutes. Mix in the sauerkraut, mustard, whipping cream, white wine, caraway seeds, and cayenne pepper. Bring to a boil, reduce the heat, and then gently simmer for about 8 to 10 minutes.

While the kraut mixture is simmering, cook the ziti in a large pot of boiling, salted water for about 8 minutes, until al dente. Do not overcook. Drain the pasta in a colander and then return it to the pot, adding the kraut-sausage mixture and parsley to the ziti. Toss to coat the ziti well and season with salt and pepper to taste.

6

BEANS AND GRAINS

In this chapter, we celebrate the often unsung ingredients that nourish us. I'm talking about the grains and legumes that are the foundation of humankind's nutritional life. They are the building blocks of our meals, providing numerous vitamins, protein, and fiber. They are what make us feel *full*. Enhance with a little meat or a touch of seafood and miraculously, a complete meal, feeding a whole family, appears. Be it ground dried corn transformed into hominy by reverse osmosis or fashioned into cornmeal masa harina for tamales, polenta, or porridge "mush," or the array of beans that satisfy and warm our bellies, these recipes have been handed down from one generation to the next and heralded in lore and song.

That's a big responsibility to lay on these lowly ingredients but, as they say, the proof is in the pudding, or in this case, the plate of beans. We have tasty dishes from south of the border and others that we might classify as "country" or "southern" cooking. Don't be put off by the need to soak the beans or the long cooking process, because it is well worth the time and effort. And, it really makes the house smell incredible. So get out the crock pots and Dutch ovens and let's get cooking.

Mama Maria's Seafood Tamales

Maria Cruz is the "kitchen mother" of our restaurant. Every year she makes large batches of tamales around the Christmas holiday, and we eagerly await their arrival. The recipe is from Maria's village in El Salvador, but it is an oral recipe, passed down for generations. Once, while eating her famous chicken tamale, I wondered, "What would this taste like with seafood?" I think Mama may have thought I'd lost my mind. But we kept at it and decided to give it a go. Instead of wetting the masa harina with chicken stock, we substituted a fish stock, and instead of pulled chicken we made a seafood mixture of crab and shrimp. We held our breath as the tamales steamed but, lo and behold, a scrumptious seafood tamale was born.

If you are not familiar with tamales and find the assembly instructions confusing, you are not alone. Almost everyone I know (myself included) was at a loss during our inaugural attempt. I suggest doing a YouTube search for "making tamales" to come up with a fantastic selection of videos that show the rolling technique. Really helpful!

Yields about 24 tamales

Tamale Seafood Filling (*recipe follows*)

½ onion, peeled and chopped

1 tomato, cored and chopped

½ green bell pepper, chopped

1 teaspoon minced garlic

1 teaspoon ground cumin

4 cups masa harina (*see note*)

1 teaspoon salt

1 teaspoon Old Bay seasoning

1½ teaspoons baking powder

Warm water, as needed

1½ cups lard or solid vegetable shortening

2 cups (plus or minus) Fish Stock (*see note and page 58*)

1 (8-ounce) package large, dried corn husks, soaked in warm water for several hours

Prepare the seafood filling.

Place the onion, tomato, bell pepper, garlic, and cumin in a blender or food processor. Blend into a smooth mixture, place in a bowl, and set aside.

In a bowl, mix the masa harina, salt, Old Bay seasoning, and baking powder together. Slowly stir in some warm water until the mixture is somewhat crumbly.

Place the lard or shortening in a mixer and beat until somewhat smooth. Then little by little, add the masa harina mixture to the shortening. Add stock ¼ cup at a time until a nice soft dough is formed. You don't want it wet and runny. It should be similar to a cake batter and should drip very slowly from a spoon. Again, not runny!

Make the tamales one husk at a time. Drain the husk and pat dry, place it on a work board, and then spread about 3 tablespoons of the masa mixture in the center of the bottom end of the husk (the straight-edged side), spreading it into a rectangle along the bottom half of the husk, about ½-inch thick. Leave about ¼ inch empty around the sides of the husk. Put 3 tablespoons or so of the seafood mixture down the center of the masa rectangle. Wrap by folding the rectangle in half and bringing the right side of the dough over the filling. Roll the tamales up tightly. Pull the top half of the husk down over the filling to make a packet. Tie the husks with kitchen string or cut-off strips of husk.

In a steamer or a large Dutch oven with a steamer rack, pour boiling water up to the top of the rack. Place a couple of unfilled husks on top of the rack. Stack the tamales, seam side down. Cover the pot and steam at a constant heat for 1 hour and 15 minutes. Turn off heat and let the tamales rest in the steamer for 10 minutes. Serve warm or at room temperature. An option is to serve with a chili sauce of your choosing, mixed with a little sour cream, on the side for dipping.

TAMALE SEAFOOD FILLING

2   cups diced steamed or grilled shrimp

1   pound backfin or claw crabmeat, picked over for shells

4   tablespoons melted butter

1   teaspoon Old Bay seasoning

3   tablespoons minced chives

Place the shrimp and crabmeat in a mixing bowl. In a small bowl, mix the melted butter and Old Bay together. Pour over the seafood and toss. Stir in the chives. Refrigerate until ready to assemble the tamales.

Note: Masa harina is the traditional flour used to make tortillas, tamales, and other Hispanic dishes. Translated from Spanish, it means "dough flour," because the flour is made from dried masa, a dough made from specially treated corn that is dried again and then ground into a flour meal. It can be found at most supermarkets and in Latin grocery stores. You can also buy a "coarse-ground corn masa for tamale," which does not require moistening with warm water.

Note on stock: We used a little trick when developing this recipe. We took several shrimp shells, simmered them in the stock for about 10 minutes, and then strained the stock. It gives the masa a wonderful shrimpy flavor.

Broom's Bloom Cheddar Hominy

We love working with local dairies and local cheese makers for the products we use at our restaurant. Broom's Bloom Dairy in Harford County, Maryland, is one of my favorites, and they produce several excellent cheddars. The sharp cheddar works splendidly with the chewy kernels of hominy.

A reminder: Whole kernels of hominy are not grits. Grits are milled from dried hominy, but what we use here in the Chesapeake is the whole kernels, also known in Hispanic and southwestern cooking as *posole*. Manning's Hominy makes a fine canned version if you are in a hurry, but I really like the firm texture you get with dried hominy prepared from scratch. This recipe feeds a crowd and keeps well, but you could always just make half.

Serves 8 to 10

1	pound hominy (about 3 cups); if using canned hominy, 3 (29-ounce) cans
2	teaspoons salt
8	tablespoons butter
½	cup all-purpose flour
3	cups milk
2	cups local white or yellow cheddar, grated

Salt and freshly ground pepper, to taste

Soak the hominy in cold water overnight. In the morning, drain the hominy in a colander. Place the hominy in a heavy-bottomed pot and cover with cold water by about 1 inch. Bring to a boil, reduce heat to medium, and cook for about 1½ to 2 hours, until hominy is tender but not mushy. When the hominy is just about done, add the 2 teaspoons of salt.

While the hominy is cooking, prepare the cheese sauce. Heat a saucepan and melt the butter. Whisk in the flour a little at a time, stirring all the while. Cook over medium heat for about 3 minutes, taking care not to brown the flour. Remove from heat and slowly whisk in the milk, a little at a time, to make a smooth sauce. Return to heat and bring almost to the boil. Reduce heat to low and add the grated cheese. Stir for several minutes or until the cheese has melted. Remove from heat and season with salt and pepper to taste.

Drain any excess water from the cooked hominy in a colander and return the hominy to the pot. Add the cheese sauce and stir together thoroughly with the hominy. Reheat gently and serve hot.

The hominy can be served as a side dish with any meal or in place of home fries on a breakfast plate.

Polenta with Stewed Tomatoes and Okra

You've got your fair share of corn and tomatoes here in this recipe. This is an old-timey dish that utilizes the legendary corn meal mush. Makes you think of the Great Depression, doesn't it? But when I tell you this is a lovely polenta, things are sounding much better. Yes, the "mush" is just a creamy polenta that serves as a bed for one of the Chesapeake's favorites—stewed tomatoes.

Serves 6 to 8

3 cups Vegetable Stock (*page 59*) or Chicken Stock (*page 59*)

3 cups milk or plant milk

2 cups medium-grind stone-ground cornmeal

2 teaspoons salt

Stewed Tomatoes and Okra (*recipe follows*)

Pour the stock and milk into a pot and bring to a boil. In a very slow, steady stream, whisk or stir the cornmeal into the boiling liquid. Add the salt and continue cooking, stirring all the while, for about 15 to 20 minutes. You have to be careful not to burn or scorch the cornmeal. Another method would be to add cornmeal to the boiling water as described above, but then transfer the liquid to the top pot of a double boiler and cook for 30 minutes, stirring often.

Place the hot cornmeal mush in the center of a plate or shallow bowl, and make a well in the center with the back of a spoon. Ladle the hot stewed tomatoes and okra over the mush and serve.

Another idea for serving is to pour the cornmeal mush into greased loaf pans when it has just finished cooking. Let it cool and then turn out the loaves. Slice the loaves in the desired thickness and then fry in a pan, with either a little oil or bacon fat. Place the slices on a plate and top with hot stewed tomatoes and okra.

STEWED TOMATOES AND OKRA

10 large ripe tomatoes, cored

6 tablespoons butter

½ white onion, diced

1 small green bell pepper, small dice

3 cups sliced okra, fresh or frozen

2 teaspoons tomato paste

⅓ cup brown sugar

⅛ teaspoon nutmeg

Salt and freshly ground black pepper

Drop the cored tomatoes into a pot of boiling water. Count to 10 and remove tomatoes with a slotted utensil and place in a bowl of ice water to cool. Peel, halve, and seed the tomatoes. Set aside.

Heat a pan and sauté the onion in the butter for 3 minutes. Add the bell pepper and sauté for 5 minutes longer. Stir in the okra and cook for 5 minutes, stirring often. Add the tomatoes and tomato paste. Bring to a boil, reduce the heat, and slow-simmer, partially covered, for 1 hour. Add the sugar and nutmeg and cook for 10 minutes more. Add salt and pepper to taste.

New Earth Farm's Savory Oats "Risoatto"

This recipe is from Kevin Jamison at the New Earth Farm in Virginia Beach, who clearly knows his way around the kitchen as well as the garden. It's a perfect example of the type of flexible recipe I love. He dares us to be creative, to make it our very own—and shows us just how to approach that challenge. Have fun, use the ingredients that you love, that are in season—or even just what you happen to have on hand.

Kevin explains the approach to the dish: "In this particular recipe (usually made in the summer) that we often prepare at one of our cooking classes, we top the 'risoatto' with fresh crumbled farmers cheese, sun-dried tomato crisps, chopped basil and a cornmeal crusted egg yolk that was very lightly sautéed as well as a couple slices of pickled okra for the acidity. We cut the Surryano into long thin slices and crisp lightly in olive oil in a pan, putting several of the slices on top of each serving to add a nice smoky saltiness to the dish."

Serves 4 to 6

8   tablespoons unsalted butter, divided
1   bunch of green onions, chopped
2   cloves garlic, minced
2   cups field peas
1   pound thick-cut rolled oats (about 5 cups)
6   cups Vegetable Stock (*page 59*)
1½–2 cups whole milk
½   cup chopped basil

In a large pan, melt 4 tablespoons of the butter and sauté the green onions and garlic for 5 minutes. Add the field peas and continue gently cooking until they are tender but keeping their color and texture intact. Remove from heat and set aside.

In another pan, lightly sauté the oats in the remaining butter until they begin to turn a golden brown. Gradually add the stock to just barely cover the oats and stir. When the oats have absorbed most of the liquid, but before all the liquid at the very bottom is absorbed, add more stock to just cover the oats again. Taste for firmness. The oats should have a slight firmness left to them. Stir in about 1½ cups of the milk and simmer briefly, stirring often, for about 5 to 7 minutes. If the mixture appears too thick, add a little more milk. Fold in the sautéed onion, garlic, peas, and chopped basil. Remove from heat.

To serve, spoon about 1½ to 2 cups of the oats onto each plate. You can either add topping to each plate or have bowls of the toppings on the dining table and allow guests to "build their own."

Optional toppings:

Farmers cheese (can also use Cotija, feta, or any crumbly cheese) to crumble on top

Pickled okra—several pods per serving

Chopped sun-dried tomatoes

Several very thin slices of cured ham, such as Edwards and Sons Surryano

Note: This recipe (like many) is very adaptable to any season, so feel free to experiment with other ingredients as per what is in season in your area.

Patsy's Veggie Rice Pilaf

My sister, Patricia Shields-Davis, strongly believes in using organic and non-GM ingredients whenever possible. "People say they cost more, but they're cheaper than copays at the doctor's office."

Patsy loves this recipe, as it goes with the seasons, and she says, "You can add ¼ cup diced tomato, diced zucchini or yellow squash, in the summer, and diced butternut squash and apples and pears in the fall—whatever the bounty offers!" Patricia uses a generous amount of turmeric in the rice, which gives it a beautiful color and adds a lovely fragrance to the dish. Turmeric is used widely to reduce inflammation, so as the saying goes, "Let your food be your medicine."

Makes about 4 servings

- 1 tablespoon olive oil (or use oil spritzer to coat pot—*see note*)
- ¼ cup chopped onion
- ½ cup chopped carrot
- ½ cup chopped mushrooms
- ¼ cup diced red or green bell pepper
- 1 tablespoon turmeric
- 1 teaspoon grated fresh ginger
- ¼ cup chopped Italian parsley
- 1 teaspoon dried basil
- 1 teaspoon dried thyme
- 1 cup basmati, jasmine, or other white rice
- 2 cups water or low-sodium Vegetable Stock (*page 59*) or Chicken Stock (*page 59*)
- 1 handful fresh spinach or Swiss chard leaves, chopped
- ¼ cup shredded cheddar cheese (or 2 tablespoons nutritional yeast to keep it vegan)

Pour (or spritz) oil in a saucepan and heat briefly on medium-low heat. Add the onion, carrot, mushrooms, pepper, turmeric, ginger, parsley, basil, and thyme and cook for 1 to 2 minutes, just to soften the onion. Add rice and increase heat to medium/high. Sauté the rice-veggie mix for 1 to 2 minutes to make the rice a bit golden, then add the water or stock. Bring just to the boil, reduce heat to medium-low, cover, and cook for 15 minutes. Lift lid, add spinach leaves and cheese or nutritional yeast to the top, replace lid, and remove from heat.

Let sit 5 minutes, stir, and enjoy.

Note: If you restrict fats from your diet, an oil spritzer allows a minimal amount yet still adds the rich flavor of the olive oil. When using this method, add a teaspoon of water if the sauce appears a bit dry, to keep the mixture moist.

HEX Miso Kimchi Bowl with Crispy Green Onions

HEX Ferments, in North Baltimore, is a welcome addition and an innovator in the Chesapeake local food economy. Fermentation is one of the oldest forms of food preservation known to humankind. Husband-and-wife team Meaghan and Shane Carpenter use traditional fermentation processes to transform local, organic products into nourishing food teeming with beneficial bacteria. Good for the gut, these products protect and support our immune systems. HEX Ferments's sauerkraut, kimchi, and kombucha are simply amazing.

Here we have a versatile sauce that goes well with rice noodles, wheat pasta, brown rice, and whole grains like quinoa and farro. The combo also pairs well with sautéed chicken or tofu and is delicious over steamed vegetables. You can prepare the sauce ahead of time and store in the refrigerator to use as needed.

Serves 4 to 6

- 1 tablespoon unrefined toasted sesame oil
- 1 bunch green onions, washed, root ends trimmed, sliced into ¼-inch-thick rings, green stalk and all
- 1 pound whole-grain pasta or 6 cups cooked brown rice or other grain
- 1 teaspoon or so unrefined toasted sesame oil (if using pasta)

HEX Miso Kimchi Nut Butter Sauce (*recipe follows*)

Heat the oil over medium heat in a large sauté pan. You want the oil very hot. Test by tossing in some onion to see whether it sizzles. If it does, quickly add the rest and fry until golden brown and a bit crispy, about 3 to 5 minutes.

If using pasta for the dish: Cook pasta al dente or according to package instructions. Drain the pasta and rinse with cool water. Then put it back in the pot and stir in a teaspoon of toasted sesame oil, or just enough to coat the noodles. Pour the Miso Kimchi Nut Butter Sauce over the noodles and mix well.

To serve, top with a generous portion of HEX vegan miso kimchi and crispy green onions, and add a side of steamed greens and tamari.

HEX MISO KIMCHI NUT BUTTER SAUCE

⅔ cup smooth unsalted peanut butter or other unsalted nut butter of your choice (cashew and almond work really well)

1 tablespoon tamari

2 tablespoons apple cider vinegar

½ cup yellow onion, roughly chopped

1 large clove fresh garlic, sliced thin (roughly 2 teaspoons)

1 teaspoon fresh grated ginger (skin removed)

⅛ teaspoon chili flakes (or more!)

¼ cup HEX miso kimchi, plus more for serving

1 cup low-sodium Vegetable Stock (*page 59*) or Chicken Stock (*page 59*) or quick dashi (*see note*), cold or slightly cooled (if making fresh)

Combine all the ingredients in a blender, or use an immersion blender. Blend on high until smooth. Taste and add sea salt or more chili flakes if needed. Note: by adding cold or cooled broth you keep the kimchi's beneficial bacteria alive! If you can comfortably sip the broth, it's ok to add to the sauce. Or take its temperature—at or below 110°F is good. The sauce keeps well for 4 days.

Note on how to make a quick dashi: Soak a 2 x 4 inch piece of kombu seaweed and a generous pinch of bonito flakes in 1 cup of hot water for half an hour. Strain out the kombu or bonito flakes and add ⅛ teaspoon of sea salt. Serve the kombu on the side. For a vegan dashi, add 3 to 4 fresh, sliced shiitake mushrooms instead of bonito. Serve these on the side, too!

Hot Butter Beans Come to Supper

When envisioning a new Chesapeake kitchen, I kept recalling a phrase from a Benedictine nun, Sister Joan Chittister, that we need to keep one foot in the ancient to see our way to the future. Pretty heady stuff when we're just talking beans. But I am reminded of the old-timers who I used to sit and visit with in their kitchens; as they grew up, a staple on all of their tables were beans, in all their many ways, shapes, and forms. It was a common table memory for all.

I remember playing the childhood game Hot Butter Beans Come to Supper, a sort of hide-and-seek with a hidden object, played by a bunch of friends, in which the person who found said object would holler—you guessed it, "HBBCTS." My grandmother Gertie would often make "butter beans," which are actually the large, dried lima beans that are beige in color. I always adored them and loaded up my plate, much to the dismay of Miss Alma, who was a boarder at my grandmother's house. Gertie would announce dinner with reference to the bean dish as "HBBCTS," and it would get me running to the dinner table damn fast. Gertie knew the beans would fill you up and were good for you as well.

The butter beans, when slow-cooked, actually make their own buttery sauce. There's not much to the dish except good eating. Some people add just a touch of heavy cream to jazz up the beans, and I'll leave that to your discretion. You can easily make these vegetarian by omitting the bacon, or fatback, and adding just a couple drops of Liquid Smoke to the simmering beans.

Serves 6 to 8 as a side dish

1 pound large lima beans, a.k.a. hot butter beans

4 ounces bacon, cut into pieces, or salt pork, cut into small pieces

2 tablespoons bacon fat

½ cup heavy whipping cream (optional)

Salt and pepper, to taste (Gertie used just a little white pepper, as she didn't want black flecks in the beans)

Place the beans in a pot and cover with ample cold water. Allow to soak overnight. The next day, drain the beans and return them to the pot. Barely cover with cold water. Bring the beans to a boil, reduce heat to low, and let them simmer.

Heat a heavy skillet and cook the bacon or salt pork until it begins to crisp up a bit. Put the bacon and 2 tablespoons of the reserved bacon fat into the pot of butter beans. Give it a stir and continue to slow-cook for about an hour. Add a teaspoon of salt and the heavy cream, if using, and allow to cook for another hour or until the beans are tender. The beans should be very soft but not mushy. Don't mess with the beans too much as they cook, since you don't want them to fall apart. A soft stir every now and then will do. You'll need to add a touch more water from time to time as they cook, but never more than to just barely cover the top of the beans. When the beans are tender and done, adjust the seasoning with salt and pepper to taste.

Good Grains

So many folks I know feel they are gluten intolerant. Yet humans have been eating grains since prehistory without such distress. What is going on? Some evidence seems to point to the fact that the modern versions of our favored grains have become over-hybridized or that it's really the residues of pesticides, herbicides, and other nasties making us ill. It didn't used to be this way—that's one thing we can be sure of.

The American Midwest is called the "breadbasket of the world," and most of our grain products come from enormous farms spreading over thousands of acres, growing only grain, year after year. However, in the past, farms were smaller, and growing grain was just one part of an integrated farming operation. Preindustrial wheat was very tall, its straw as valuable as the grain for fodder, thatch, biomatter for healthy fields, fuel, livestock bedding, and dozens of other uses.

Only a few generations ago, grains were grown abundantly in the Chesapeake region and ground at independent mills. Huge crop yields and durability in milling and storage were low priorities, since milling and flour distribution were local. In 1810, Pennsylvania had over 2,000 mills. Virginia had 441 mills, and even Baltimore City proper had 22 mills in the 1850s—you can see what remains of some of them in the Woodberry neighborhood, west of Hampden.

With short stalks and roots, modern hybridized wheat has been developed to put all its energy into producing big kernels that are easily harvested by machine. This wheat will grow in extremely dense mono-cropped conditions—conditions that deplete the soil, encourage insects, funguses, and other diseases; conditions that require enormous amounts of irrigation and lots of chemical fertilizers and pesticides to meet the demands of the crop. No wonder we don't feel so good. And scientific studies have found that many of the older grain varieties do *not* cause an adverse gluten response in sensitive people, despite having just as much gluten as modern grains.

Fortunately, as of late, there's been a lot of interest from local Chesapeake farming communities in reviving heritage grains. In 2010, Next Step Produce in Charles County, Maryland, began offering organic whole barley, oats, rye, and wheat at the Dupont Circle farmers' market. Now they are milling as well as growing their heritage Turkey Red flour, and it's what you'll find at Baltimore's Atwater's Bakery in their popular Turkey Red Loaf.

Atwater's has set a goal of using at least 25 percent local flours in their bakery, and they also buy from McGeary Organics up in Lancaster, Pennsylvania. Selling under the brand name of Daisy Flour, McGeary mills their wheat at the historic Annville Mill. Built in 1740, it's the oldest continuously working mill in the United States. Working with the Rodale Institute, Daisy Flour is now producing their heirloom Lancaster Red Reserve Series of heritage wheat flours. On the Eastern Shore, permaculturist Vint Lawrence is constantly experimenting with heritage grains at his Lands End Farm. Doug Rae at the highly regarded Evergrain Bread Company in Chestertown gets much of his specialty flour from Lands End.

Creative and community-conscious bakers like Ned Atwater and Doug Rae are bringing the wonderful old-fashioned tastes and textures of these nearly forgotten strains of wheat to the marketplace, with good results. Tim McGuire, the operations manager at Atwater's, remarks, "Hopefully we're big enough and present enough to show people what can be done with local flour."

Robin's Mushroom Risotto with Turkey Schnitzel and Shredded Confit

Farmer and chef Robin Way of Rumbleway Farm knows how to stretch some turkey and chicken to make a meal go a long way. Here Robin prepares a flavorful mushroom risotto and tops it with lightly fried fillets of turkey and an incredibly moist turkey confit. There are actually three recipes in one here, and you could use any on their own, should you so choose. But together—exquisite!

Serves 8 to 10

1   small turkey (10–12 pounds)

Olive oil and/or fat from chicken, duck, or turkey

Salt and pepper

3–4 whole garlic cloves

Flour for dredging

2   eggs, beaten

Panko or bread crumbs

Oil for frying

Salt and pepper (optional)

½   onion or shallot, diced

½   pound mushrooms, chopped

2   cups Arborio rice

4   ounces white wine

6–8 cups Chicken Stock (*page 59*) or turkey stock, hot

For the confit, remove legs, wings, and breasts from turkey. Reserve the backbone and excess fat. Place wings, legs, and backbone in a pot and cover with oil. Make sure all the pieces are submerged. Add salt and pepper and whole garlic cloves. Bring to a low simmer (lowest setting possible) and cook for 1 hour. Make sure the oil is not boiling. Once the meat is very tender, pour the mixture through a strainer and reserve the oil for next time (it freezes well). Once the meat has cooled, remove the meat from the bones and roughly chop. Set aside. For long-term storage, place meat in a container, add enough reserved oil to cover the meat, and place in refrigerator or freezer.

For the schnitzel, cut the turkey breasts into several pieces and pound until thin. Place the flour, beaten eggs, and panko in separate containers. Flour the breasts, then place in egg wash, then lightly coat with panko. You can add any spices or seasonings you like to the panko before breading. Place on a sheet pan. Heat the oil in a frying pan and once it is hot, brown breast pieces on both sides. Remove to tray lined with parchment or paper towel. Sprinkle with salt and pepper if desired.

For the risotto, heat a small amount of oil in a large skillet and cook onion and mushrooms until tender. Add rice and sauté until all the grains are coated. Add the wine and cook until evaporated. Next, turn the heat down to low and start adding stock, 1 cup at a time, allowing the stock to be absorbed between additions. Stir often. This step may take 30 to 45 minutes. Cook until risotto is tender. Add salt and pepper to taste.

To serve, spoon risotto onto plate and place schnitzel on top; put the chopped confit on the top and serve with your favorite vegetable or salad.

Succotash

I know, I know, this is supposed to be a fancy cookbook, and this recipe is just way too simple. Well, sometimes simple is best. I cannot think of any other side dish that screams summertime and Chesapeake more than this traditional recipe. Another way to enjoy the dish is cold, as a summer salad on a bed of leafy greens with some vine-ripe tomatoes. Alright, one more tip. If you are a fan of cream of crab soup, try folding a batch of this succotash into the pot of soup. Just heat thoroughly, and you are in for a treat.

Serves 4

1   cup young (baby) lima beans, fresh or frozen
Salt
1   cup fresh sweet corn kernels
3   tablespoons butter
Juice of ½ lemon
Salt and freshly ground black pepper, to taste

Place the lima beans in a saucepan and add cold water, just enough to barely cover the beans. Bring to a boil, lower the heat, and cook partially covered for about 15 to 20 minutes or until just tender. Add the salt and the corn and simmer on a low heat for 10 minutes. Drain off any water and season with butter, lemon juice, and salt and pepper to taste. Serve at once.

Warm Lentil Salad with Medallions of Liberty Farm Tenderloin and Cherry Balsamic Reduction

This is an amazing warm and earthy dinner or luncheon dish. Chef Steve Balcer, who prepared and arranged all the beautiful recipes for the food photographs in this book, designed this dish. It's a lovely blend of flavors, tastes, and textures. He uses a beef from Liberty Delight Farms, located in Reisterstown, Maryland, and glazes the finished product with an easy-to-make cherry balsamic. Here is another great example of a "plant-forward" plate.

Serves 4

1   cup green or brown lentils

Chicken Stock (*page 59*) or water

6   tablespoons extra-virgin olive oil

¼   cup finely diced onions

¼   cup finely diced celery

¼   cup finely diced carrots

1   teaspoon minced garlic

½   green bell pepper, finely diced

½   red bell pepper, finely diced

3   tablespoons aged sherry wine vinegar

⅓   cup sliced green onions

Salt and freshly ground black pepper

6   ounces arugula, chopped

6   ounces local goat cheese

Cherry Balsamic Reduction (*recipe follows*)

1½ pounds center-cut tenderloin of beef, roasted (*see note*)

Rinse the lentils in cold water in a strainer. Place in a pot and cover with water or stock or a combination of both. Bring to a boil, reduce heat, and simmer until tender, about 20 minutes.

While the lentils are cooking, heat 3 tablespoons of the olive oil in a sauté pan and add the onions. Sauté for 3 minutes and then add the celery, carrots, and garlic. Sauté gently for 5 minutes. Add the bell peppers and sauté 5 minutes longer. Turn off the heat and add the remaining olive oil and sherry wine vinegar.

Drain the lentils and place them in a bowl. Pour the olive oil–vegetable mixture over the top and mix well. Stir in the green onions and season the mixture with salt and pepper to taste. Fold in the arugula and crumbled goat cheese.

Divide the lentils among 4 dinner plates, mounding in the center of each plate. Arrange 4 tenderloin medallions around each mound of lentils. Drizzle the meat with some Cherry Balsamic Reduction and serve at once.

CHERRY BALSAMIC REDUCTION

Yields about 1 cup

- 2 cups balsamic vinegar
- 3 tablespoons brown sugar
- ½ cup chopped pitted cherries and their juice (fresh or frozen—no canned cherries)

Place all the ingredients into a pan and bring to a boil. Reduce heat to medium-high and allow to reduce by half. Pour the reduction through a fine strainer. If it's not as thick as you may like, return to heat and reduce just a little more. Remove from heat and let stand until ready to use.

Note on roasting tenderloin: Place on a rack and rub the tenderloin with a little olive oil, salt, pepper, and sugar. Roast in a preheated 425°F oven for about 35 to 40 minutes. For medium-rare, a meat thermometer should read 135–140°F when you take it out. Let meat rest 15 minutes before slicing.

Beans and Bacon with Grilled Goat

Here's another recipe from my buddy Rita Calvert, author of *The Grassfed Gourmet Fires It Up!* and advocate of the locally pastured, grassfed animal movement. Many folks in America are not terribly familiar with cooking, or even eating, goat meat. That's rather surprising, considering that goat meat is the most consumed meat in the world, eaten more than beef, pork, or chicken. It takes much less acreage to raise goats, and their meat is quite lean compared to beef or pork. That said, this really is a bean-centric dish and any type of grilled—or even braised, for that matter—meat or poultry will work beautifully.

Lima beans are a staple of the Chesapeake region, starring in succotash, salads, and Brunswick stew. Limas are a great source of fiber and are high in protein. From late summer into the fall, fresh lima beans can be found at the farmers' markets. They do not require presoaking, and they cook more quickly than a dried lima. But most of the year, what you'll find is the dried variety. An overnight soak in water and then cooking for less than an hour is all that's required. Always remember when cooking beans to not season or salt them during the cooking process. It makes them tough, so season after they have finished cooking.

Serves 6

6   ounces thick, nitrate-free sliced bacon, diced

1   large sweet onion, diced

1   cup fresh poblano chili peppers, diced

2   cups goat meat, grilled and shredded (*see note*)

4   cups cooked large limas or 2 (16-ounce) cans butter beans, rinsed and drained

¼   cup dark molasses

¼   cup brown sugar

Few dashes hot sauce such as Tabasco; more if desired

3   medium cloves garlic, minced

Kosher salt and freshly ground pepper, to taste

Preheat the oven to 350°F.

Heat a medium-sized sauté pan over medium-high. When hot, add the bacon and sauté for 2 minutes to release some of the fat. Add the onion and poblano, and continue cooking for about 10 minutes. Drain any extra fat from the sautéed mixture.

In a large bowl, combine the shredded goat meat with the remaining ingredients. Finally, stir in the sautéed mixture and pour into a baking dish.

Bake uncovered at 350°F for 1 hour, stirring once after 30 minutes. Serve immediately or, equally as good, at room temperature.

Note: Leg or ribs of goat are a good choice for grilling. But Rita cautions that goat meat, as it is lean, will dry out and toughen when cooked at high heats. So, slow-cooking is the way to go. But just about any other meat will work in this recipe as well. If using chicken, I would suggest chicken thighs, as they are quite moist. Another idea, instead of grilling, would be to use your favorite braised, pulled pork recipe.

Big Pot o' Beans and Greens with Ham Hocks

This is soul-satisfying, down-home comfort food at its best. The recipe can be made a day ahead, because the beans just get more flavorful by resting for a night. For a complete meal, serve with a garden salad and—need I say?—lots of corn bread and butter.

Serves 8 to 10

2 cups small white beans (great northern), about 1 pound

4 tablespoons olive oil or bacon drippings

2 onions, diced

1 cup diced celery

3 tablespoons minced garlic

6 cups water, Chicken Stock (*page 59*), or Vegetable Stock (*page 59*)

2 medium smoked ham hocks

½ teaspoon cayenne pepper

1 bay leaf

2 pounds collard greens or kale

3 tablespoons apple cider vinegar

Salt and freshly ground pepper, to taste

Soak the beans in cold water overnight. The next morning, drain the beans in a colander and rinse well. Set aside.

In a large pot, heat the olive oil or bacon drippings and sauté the onions for 5 minutes. Add the celery and garlic and cook for 5 minutes longer. Add the beans, water or stock, and ham hocks. Bring to a boil, reduce heat to medium, and add the cayenne pepper and bay leaf. Cook for 3 hours, adding more water or stock as necessary. When the ham hocks are tender and the meat is falling from the bones, remove them from the pot and set aside in a bowl. As soon as the ham hocks are cool enough to handle, pull the meat from the bones and return meat to pot.

While the soup is cooking, wash the greens in cold water and drain. Pull the leaves from the stems and tear the leaves into small pieces. After the beans have cooked for 3 hours, add the greens to the pot and allow to cook for 1 hour longer, adding water if necessary to thin the pot of beans. Remove from heat and add the apple cider vinegar. Taste soup and then adjust for seasoning if necessary with salt and pepper. I like to let the beans rest at least an hour before serving so all the flavors can come together. Depending on consistency, serve the beans on a plate or in a bowl.

7

SALAD BOWL

Salads and salad bowls conjure a myriad of images for people. To some it can only mean a big wooden bowl overflowing with freshly picked garden lettuces, lightly dressed with a simple vinaigrette. To others the image is a stoneware, crock-like salad bowl that is the vessel for composed salads, made from root vegetables or shredded cabbage. Other folks, maybe with Eastern European roots, will think of salads as fish and meat, dressed with mayonnaise, sour cream, vegetable oil, or a combination of all. Actually, the salads in this chapter are *all* of the above, pulling together the traditions of our ancestors who came from around the globe and settled on the shores of the Chesapeake Bay. The salad bowl reminds me of the great tapestry of Chesapeake cookery.

Sweet Corn, Red Bell Pepper, and Lump Crab Salad

Instead of feeding three people a meal of crab cakes with this 1 pound of succulent lump Chesapeake Bay crabmeat, we're now able to have a feast of crab and corn that stretches the meal to feed six. I love this recipe and make it often during the summer. A fun variation is to grill the corn over charcoal and, when cool enough to handle, cut the kernels off the cob and use it in the salad. Gives the whole dish a dreamy, smoky flavor. Ah, gotta love summer!

Serves 6

3   tablespoons extra-virgin olive oil

1   tablespoon sherry vinegar

1   large garlic clove, peeled and mashed

Juice of 1 lime

1   small red onion, peeled and finely minced

1   pound lump crabmeat, picked over
    for shells

1   large red bell pepper, cored, seeded, and
    finely diced

4   cups fresh sweet corn kernels

3   tablespoons fresh cilantro leaves, chopped

½   teaspoon Old Bay seasoning

Salt and freshly ground black pepper

Combine oil, vinegar, garlic, lime juice, and onion and whisk thoroughly. Add crab, red pepper, corn, and cilantro. Season with Old Bay and salt and pepper and toss gently to coat. Take care not to break up the lumps of crab. Cover and chill for about 2 hours before serving.

Minted Crab and Shrimp Salad

A number of years ago, at the "Cooking for Solutions" event at the Monterey Bay Aquarium, I was blown away by a rendition of this amazing dish. Bursting with flavor, texture, and heat, this salad engages all your senses, and it's a dish that will impress your guests for sure. Originally designed for calamari by the Two Hot Tamales, Susan Feniger and Mary Sue Milliken of Food Network fame, I took the liberty of revamping it a bit and giving it a Chesapeake twist. Susan and Mary Sue served the salad in martini glasses at the fundraiser, making for quite the festive appetizer.

Serves 8 to 10

¼ cup Thai fish sauce

3 tablespoons fresh lime juice

2 tablespoons white vinegar

1 teaspoon Old Bay seasoning

⅓ cup Fish Stock (*page 58*) or clam juice, chilled

¼ cup extra-virgin olive oil

1 small red onion, finely diced

3 serrano chilies, finely minced, with seeds

2 large tomatoes, peeled, seeded, and diced

2 Euro-style cucumbers or Kirbies, diced, with skins

1 jicama, peeled and diced

1 bunch fresh mint, chopped

1 bunch fresh cilantro, chopped

1 pound medium wild-caught US shrimp, steamed, cleaned, and diced

1 pound lump crabmeat

Tabasco, salt, and freshly ground black pepper, to taste

Romaine or endive spears to garnish

In a bowl, whisk together the fish sauce, lime juice, vinegar, Old Bay, chilled stock, and olive oil. Add the onion, serrano chilies, tomatoes, cucumbers, jicama, mint, and cilantro, and toss well with chilled shrimp and crabmeat. Season to taste with Tabasco, salt, and pepper.

Serve the salad chilled in a martini glass, with romaine or endive spears for garnish.

The Svelte Crab and Veggie Salad

Perfect for summertime, when we are trying to fit into that swimsuit from last season. This is a most basic salad that is wide open for improvisation. A little avocado, toasted sunflower seeds, and crumbled lowfat cottage cheese are just a few ingredients that come to mind. The star of the recipe is, of course, the crab, but what keeps the pounds off is the dressing. The hot water added to the dressing recipe, along with a goodly amount of vinegar and less olive oil, do the trick.

Serves 6

Romaine lettuce

Mesclun salad mix

1   pound lump crab

6   hard-boiled eggs, cut into wedges

3   carrots, shredded

12 radishes, sliced

2   cucumbers, sliced

18 or so grape tomatoes

2   small red onions, sliced

Lemon wedges

Skinny Balsamic Dressing (*recipe follows*)

On a plate, make a bed of the lettuces and place a line of crab down the center. Arrange the eggs, carrots, radishes, cucumbers, tomatoes, and red onion around the plate. When serving, drizzle some of the dressing over the vegetables. Squeeze a lemon wedge over each serving of crab.

SKINNY BALSAMIC DRESSING

Yields about 1 cup

1   teaspoon minced garlic

½   teaspoon prepared horseradish

2   teaspoons Dijon mustard

½   cup balsamic vinegar

3   tablespoons hot water

2   teaspoons sugar

3   tablespoons extra-virgin olive oil

1   tablespoon minced herbs, such as basil, thyme, and flat parsley

Salt and freshly ground black pepper, to taste

Place the garlic, horseradish, Dijon, and vinegar in a blender or food processor. Blend together. Add the hot water and sugar and blend well. With the machine running, drizzle in the olive oil very slowly. Add the herbs and salt and pepper to taste.

Herring, Apple, and Red Onion Salad

Many of the streams and tributaries around the Chesapeake region make reference to herring in their names. This small fish was plentiful and found in neighborhood fish markets. With the large German and Eastern European population that came to work in the factories and canneries along the Bay, there was a big demand for the herring, which would be pickled, brined, or creamed. Most folks would pickle their own herring and enjoy it as a snack with some pumpernickel or rye bread and a cold glass of local beer.

I've used "pickled" herring for this recipe, but if you have access to salt herring, it is a great choice as well. You will need to remove the skin from the fillets and soak them in cold water overnight, changing the water a couple of times.

2	cups pickled herring
1	cup boiled potatoes, peeled and diced
1	cup diced beets
1	large tart apple, peeled, cored, and diced
1	small red onion, minced
1	small dill pickle, minced
1	tablespoon sugar
1	teaspoon vinegar
1	teaspoon Dijon mustard
2	tablespoons olive oil
1	cup sour cream
½	cup toasted walnuts

Salt and freshly ground black pepper

Bibb lettuce

Rinse the pickled herring in cold water, pat dry, and cut into approximately ½-inch pieces. Place in a large mixing bowl. Add the potatoes, beets, apple, onion, and pickle. In a small mixing bowl, combine the sugar, vinegar, and Dijon mustard, mixing well. Slowly whisk in the olive oil. Stir in the sour cream and mix well.

Pour the dressing over the herring mixture and add the walnuts. Toss everything together and season with salt and pepper to taste. Chill for at least 1 hour before serving. To serve, place a piece of Bibb lettuce on a plate and mound the salad on top of the lettuce.

Baltimore's Early City Markets

Here in Baltimore, our network of municipal markets began in the 1700s and was the first of its kind in the country. The produce, dairy, meats, seafood, fruits, cheeses, and bakery goods sold in these markets came solely from the surrounding fields, forests, waters, gardens, and ovens—and were eaten in the city. It was that simple. Talk about farm to table!

At their inception, our municipal markets were genuine farmers' markets, open air and street side, just as our new community markets are today. As time went on, the city covered most of the markets to protect the vendors and their products from the elements and to ensure that food would be available all year 'round, every day.

These markets were like the town squares of old. Many of my relatives had stalls and sold their goods at the markets for generations. They developed relationships over the years and their customers became their friends—even sometimes their family, since romance tends to bloom wherever friendship is strong and real.

As something we naively called "progress" raised its head, the markets began to seem passé; there were prepackaged and processed food, shopping malls, and a "modern" lifestyle. I remember being somewhat perplexed by my grandmother's insistence on having everything fresh from the field, the Bay, or from her city duplex backyard garden during the 1960s and '70s. In our house in the suburbs, the pantry was stocked full of canned vegetables and meats, and the freezer overflowed with frozen food, designed to be cooked in plastic packets dunked into boiling water. I figured maybe my grandmother was poor and couldn't afford the newfangled processed food. The only thing that I knew for sure was that the food she served at her dining room table was definitely more tasty than the food at our house in the 'burbs.

How the pendulum continues to swing . . . now, many urbanites wouldn't think of missing their own neighborhood's farmers' market day—I know I wouldn't!

Arugula, Tomato, and Tabbouleh Salad

The principles of this dish, arugula, Italian parsley, and green onions, can be easily grown right in your own backyard. That said, these late spring and early fall ingredients are in good supply at the farmers' market, so not to worry if the gardening isn't going full speed ahead.

This recipe was inspired by one of my favorite cookbook authors, Madhur Jaffrey. Traditional tabbouleh, a Middle Eastern dish, is based on flat-leaf parsley and mint. The wonderful peppery taste of the arugula is a welcomed addition and pairs perfectly with a slightly tangy Chesapeake-crafted goat cheese. To keep the dish even more "local," use chopped, toasted, black walnuts or pecans in place of the pine nuts.

Serves 6

2   cups water

1½ teaspoons salt

1   cup bulgur wheat (fine grain)

2   medium tomatoes, seeded and very finely chopped

1½ cups finely chopped arugula

1½ cups finely chopped Italian parsley

10 green onions, thinly sliced crosswise

¼   cup extra-virgin olive oil

¼   cup fresh lemon juice

Freshly ground black pepper

For topping:

Approximately 1 cup crumbled goat cheese

6   tablespoons toasted pine nuts

In a bowl, combine 2 cups water, 1 teaspoon salt, and the bulgur. Set aside to soak for 1 hour.

Place a colander in the sink and line with a clean dish towel. Place the bulgur into the colander. Gather up the ends of the towel and twist, squeezing out as much water as possible.

Place the bulgur in a large bowl and fluff it with a fork. Add the remaining ingredients plus another ½ teaspoon of salt. Mix thoroughly and serve at room temperature or chilled.

Just before serving, sprinkle each portion of salad with the crumbled goat cheese and toasted pine nuts.

Shaved Brussels Sprout Salad with Spring Onions, Orange, and Toasted Black Walnuts

We don't often think of Brussels sprouts as a choice for a salad. We love them roasted, fried, creamed, or even Buffaloed, but this dish is a light, refreshing change of pace. The brown butter–enriched vinaigrette gives the dish a rich dimension, and the addition of the Chesapeake's black walnuts brings it all together.

Black walnuts have a bold, distinctive flavor. Throughout our region, they are found mostly in the fall and winter and do not have a long shelf life, since the nut has a high oil content and will turn rancid. If you have extras, they can be frozen. English walnuts can be substituted nicely.

Serves 4 to 5

1   pound Brussels sprouts, trimmed
1   tart apple
4   teaspoons lemon juice, divided
4   tablespoons butter
1   tablespoon sherry wine vinegar
2   tablespoons olive oil
Salt and freshly ground black pepper, to taste
1   orange, peeled and sectioned
2   spring onions, cut into small rings
½   cup black walnuts, toasted

Using a mandoline or the slicing blade of a food processor, thinly slice the Brussels sprouts and transfer to a mixing bowl. Set aside.

Peel and core the apple and cut it into matchstick slices or thin slices. Place in a bowl of cold water with a teaspoon of lemon juice added.

In a saucepan, melt the butter and continue to cook until it just begins to color and is turning a light brown. Remove from heat to cool.

In a mixing bowl, combine the vinegar and remaining 3 teaspoons of lemon juice. Slowly whisk in the brown butter, followed by the olive oil. Season to taste with salt and pepper.

Pour the vinaigrette over the sliced Brussels sprouts and toss well to coat. Add the orange sections, spring onions, and walnuts and toss again. Adjust the seasoning. Cover the bowl and refrigerate at least 1 hour before serving. This dish will hold nicely for several hours.

Asparagus, Fennel, and Roasted Beet Salad with Walnuts and FireFly Farms MountainTop Blue Vinaigrette

Two decades ago, the first Chesapeake cheese makers I worked with were the guys from FireFly Farms in the rolling hills and mountains of Garrett County, in western Maryland. Pablo Solanet and his partner Mick Koch are award-winning cheese makers, and their MountainTop Blue is a fantastic "young blue" cheese, with a luscious, silky-creamy texture. They were at the forefront of the local food movement here in the Chesapeake and continue to produce some of the finest cheeses in the United States.

Serves 4 to 6

1 pound beets, cooked, peeled, and cut in small wedges

¼ cup olive oil

Salt and pepper, to taste

½ pound fresh asparagus, trimmed and blanched

1 medium fennel bulb, thinly sliced

1 small head butter lettuce, torn into bite-sized pieces

½ pound spinach

1 bunch arugula

½ cup toasted black walnuts, chopped (English walnuts can be used, although they won't have as distinctive a flavor)

FireFly Farms' MountainTop Blue Vinaigrette (*recipe follows*)

Preheat oven to 400°F. Grease a cookie sheet or baking pan.

Toss the cooked beets with olive oil, salt, and pepper and spread in a layer on greased pan. Roast for 25 minutes and allow to cool.

Combine the beets, asparagus, fennel, lettuce, spinach, arugula, and walnuts in a salad bowl. Toss with MountainTop Blue Vinaigrette and serve.

Note: To toast walnuts, heat oven to 400°F. Spread walnuts on a cookie sheet and toast until fragrant, 3 to 5 minutes. Watch to make sure nuts don't burn.

FIREFLY FARM'S MOUNTAINTOP BLUE VINAIGRETTE

1   shallot, minced

2   tablespoons white wine vinegar

1   tablespoon lemon juice

1   teaspoon Dijon mustard

3   ounces MountainTop Blue cheese, crumbled

¼   cup olive oil

Salt and pepper, to taste

With a fork, whisk the shallot, vinegar, lemon juice, mustard, and cheese together. Continuing to whisk, slowly drizzle with olive oil. Season to taste with salt and pepper.

Cybee's Radish and Sweet Corn Salad

It's the salt and the honey that make this marvelous salad "pop." We always use local honey in our recipes, and our favorite is Cybil Preston's Cybee's Honey from up in Harford County, Maryland. I have to admit that growing up, the only way I ever ate radishes was off the Thanksgiving and Christmas relish trays. I really enjoyed them, but figured that was all they were good for. Boy oh boy, years later I developed a whole new appreciation for radishes, and after trying this salad, you may agree.

Serves 6 to 8

Juice of 1 large lemon

2   teaspoons of local honey, or maple syrup for vegans

Pinch of cinnamon

¼   cup extra-virgin olive oil

8–10 medium radishes (mix 'n match varieties and colors if you like), trimmed and thinly sliced

3   cups fresh corn kernels (about 4 ears)

¼   cup finely minced red onion

¼   cup finely chopped mint

¼   cup finely chopped flat-leaf parsley

Salt and freshly ground pepper, to taste

In a bowl, mix the lemon juice, honey, and cinnamon together. While whisking vigorously, slowly add the olive oil.

In a large bowl, mix the radishes and corn together. Add the dressing and toss well. Add the red onion, mint, and parsley, mixing well. Season the salad with salt and pepper. I like to use kosher or sea salt if it's available whenever making a radish salad. The salt is an integral part of the "taste profile" (chef lingo).

Place the salad in the fridge for at least an hour before serving.

Teach Your Children

For several years, I've been working with the Institute of Wine and Food's National Days of Taste program, which introduces third-graders in several Baltimore inner-city schools to the tastes of fresh local food. Volunteer chefs spend two days in the classroom with the kids, and on a third day, the kids travel by bus to a local farm to see where their food really comes from. Volunteer Riva Khan, a genuine super-heroine who makes this daunting job look easy, coordinates Days of Taste.

On the first day of the class, Riva starts off by showing each group a carrot—a whole carrot with the greens attached. Most of them (not all, however) will recognize it as a carrot. But when she asks them which part of the carrot grows beneath the ground and which part grows above the ground, they are usually completely stumped. Now, to me, that is a bit frightening, but I guess not surprising, given how disconnected we've become from agrarian life. We need to do a much better job of teaching our children what food actually is, where it comes from, and how it grows. Many ongoing efforts try to address this need—and boy, they all deserve your support. Here are just a few:

In the BUGS program (that's Baltimore Urban Gardening with Students), after-school and summer-school classes are offered at the Living Classroom's East Harbor campus, where the students have planted vegetable and flower gardens. Many of the children enrolled live in areas where there is almost no green space whatsoever, and few extracurricular activities are available to them.

As part of the Baltimore City public school system, Great Kids Farm in Catonsville belongs to all Baltimore City school children, their families, and their communities. The 33-acre campus is host to a diverse number of living things, from vegetable gardens and fruit trees to composting worms, honeybees, mushrooms, goats, and chickens. During a visit to the farm, students participate in garden activities and work together to strengthen their understanding of nutrition, agriculture, and our precious natural resources.

In Washington, DC, City Blossoms is a nonprofit dedicated to fostering healthy communities by developing creative, kid-driven green spaces. Using their gardens as the focal point for science education, art, healthy living, and community building, they "blossom" in neighborhoods where kids, their families, and neighbors may not otherwise have access to green spaces. Their Garden Fiesta each summer is a full-blown garden Mardi Gras!

This year the Washington Youth Garden celebrated its forty-fifth anniversary. It's a program of the Friends of the National Arboretum and primarily serves low-income schools and families northeast of the Capitol. The garden serves as a hands-on learning experience to enrich science learning, inspire environmental stewardship, and cultivate healthy food choices in youth and families.

Envisioning the garden as an interactive classroom that fosters an environment for engaged and project-based learning spanning all academic subjects, the Norfolk School Garden Collective is working to build, maintain, and support outdoor learning classrooms and productive food gardens at every school in Norfolk, Virginia.

I fervently believe *every* school needs a garden. The lessons of the garden are too important to be left out of the curriculum, and every child deserves to understand where their food really comes from and how it grows. As the famous chef Alice Waters has proclaimed: *"If a child plants it, they will absolutely eat it!"*

Sauerkraut and Apple Salad

Time to get that good flora activated in the old digestive tract. Probiotics are where it's at, according to most dietitians and health professionals, and this sauerkraut salad is a delicious dish to reboot with. Good quality kraut is a must, and we offer tips for making your own (*see page 237*). We have a great kraut source here in Baltimore, HEX Ferments, at the Belvedere Square Market. They ferment a number of high-quality products—kraut, kimchi, and kombucha, to name a few.

This is a refreshing salad that can be enjoyed for lunch, as a dinner appetizer, or as a side dish.

Serves 6 to 8

2   pounds sauerkraut
Generous pinch of salt
3   tablespoons apple cider vinegar
2   teaspoons local honey
¼   cup olive oil
3   tablespoons minced red onion
2   apples, peeled, cored, and diced
2   carrots, peeled and diced
Salt and freshly ground black pepper

Place the sauerkraut in a colander and rinse well with cold water. Ring out any excess water and place the kraut in a mixing bowl. Sprinkle a pinch of salt over the sauerkraut and toss. In a small bowl, whisk the cider vinegar, honey, and olive oil together.

Add the red onion, apples, and carrots to the bowl of sauerkraut. Pour the dressing over the kraut and toss well. Adjust seasoning with salt and pepper to taste. Chill the salad at least 1 hour before serving.

Watercress and Fresh Ricotta Salad with Apples, Walnuts, and Cider Vinaigrette

Growing up in Baltimore County, we would always play along the creeks and streams in the neighborhood and encounter this cool-looking leafy "stuff" growing along the stream beds. I soon learned from the grandmothers in the neighborhood that this "stuff" was a highly-prized ingredient for salads and soups. They would send us out to forage, and if we brought in a good supply, we'd get a dime or two. This refreshing salad is perfect for fall/winter dining with the warm flavors of honey, cider, and toasted walnuts.

But the star of the dish is the ricotta. Over on the Eastern Shore of Maryland, right outside of Cambridge, sits the little dairy farm of Nice Farms Creamery. The Miller family operates a truly sustainable, small-scale production operation, which is a boon to the local food economy and the environment. They gave me a winner recipe for fresh ricotta, which is a great product for novice cheese makers to try at home. It's not all that complicated, and you will feel the greatest sense of self-satisfaction, having made your very own cheese.

Serves 4

2   small tart apples, cored, peeled, and cut into slices
2   cups fresh ricotta (*recipe follows*)
1   teaspoon chopped fresh thyme
1   teaspoon chopped Italian parsley
1   clove garlic, minced
2   bunches watercress
2   tablespoons toasted walnuts
Freshly ground black pepper, to taste

Prepare the vinaigrette (*recipe follows*). Dip the apple slices into the vinaigrette and set aside. Place the ricotta into a bowl and add the thyme, parsley, and garlic. Mix well.

Divide the ricotta among 4 plates. Remove the bottom stems of the watercress and discard. Toss the remaining watercress with vinaigrette and arrange around the herbed ricotta. Arrange apple slices on the plates. Garnish with toasted walnuts and freshly ground black pepper.

HONEY–APPLE CIDER VINAIGRETTE

1   cup apple cider

3   tablespoons sherry wine vinegar

2   tablespoons local honey

1   teaspoon Dijon mustard

⅔   cup extra-virgin olive oil

Salt, to taste

Place the cider in a saucepan and bring to a boil. Reduce the cider until about 3 or 4 tablespoons remain. Set aside and cool before using.

In a mixing bowl, combine the reduced cider, vinegar, honey, and mustard and whisk together well. Add the olive oil gradually, whisking all the while to make an emulsified dressing. Salt to taste.

NICE FARMS CREAMERY HOMEMADE RICOTTA CHEESE

Makes about 4 cups

1   gallon Nice Farms Creamery creamline milk (*see note*)

2   teaspoons salt

¾   cup freshly squeezed lemon juice or vinegar, or combo of juice and vinegar

Pour milk into a non-reactive pot (glass, enamel, ceramic, or stainless—no aluminum!). Add the salt and stir until dissolved. Heat milk, stirring occasionally to prevent sticking, to 190°F. Reduce the heat to medium-low and add the lemon juice or vinegar. Turn off the heat.

Cover and allow to sit for 15 to 30 minutes. The greenish whey will separate from the curds. Strain through cheesecloth. The longer you allow the cheese to strain, the drier the cheese will be. Place into storage containers, cover, and refrigerate. Can be kept chilled for up to 3 to 5 days.

Note: "Creamline" designates milk that has not been homogenized. It has a higher fat content. For most people making this recipe at home, whole pasteurized milk will work beautifully. Do not use lowfat or nonfat milk to make the cheese.

Ultimate Chessie Chopped Salad with Herby Green Goddess Dressing

This salad is evil. Period. But oh, sweet mother of Goddess—so good! Chopped salads are all the rage right now but have been popular for generations. I think the appeal, besides the everything-but-the-kitchen-sink ingredient list, is that the chopped salad is a full meal but still essentially a salad. And how could a salad be bad? This is an indulgence, but one that will make for a memorable repast. As one could imagine, the room for variations on this are limitless. I invite you to allow your imagination to run wild.

Serves 4

Herby Green Goddess Dressing
   (*recipe follows*)
1   head romaine lettuce

2   cups arugula
1   bunch watercress
8   slices bacon or 4 thick-cut slices Taylor Pork Roll (*see note*)
Flour for dusting
4   slices scrapple (*see note*)
½   cup finely diced red onion
16 grape tomatoes
1   cup chilled Succotash (*page 147*), frozen succotash, or just corn kernels
1   cucumber, peeled and diced
1   small bunch radishes, sliced
1   apple or pear, cored and diced
1   cup shredded local sharp cheddar or crumbled local blue cheese
Corn bread croutons (*see note*)

Prepare the Herby Green Goddess Dressing.

Cut or tear the romaine lettuce into bite-sized pieces and place in a large salad bowl. Add the arugula and watercress and toss all the lettuces together. In a frying pan, fry the bacon or pork roll. When cooked, drain on paper towels, and then cut into small pieces. Lightly dust the scrapple with flour and fry until crispy. Drain on paper towels and then cut into bite-sized pieces. Set meats aside.

Dress the lettuces with just enough Herby Green Goddess Dressing to coat the leaves but not make them too soggy. Add the onion, tomatoes, succotash, cucumber, radishes, apple or pear, and ½ cup of the shredded cheese. Toss again to coat, adding a little more dressing if necessary. Add the meat pieces and toss again. Divide the salad onto chilled salad plates, sprinkle with the remaining cheese, and garnish with croutons. Serve immediately.

Notes on meats: Taylor Pork Roll is a traditional, Chesapeake/Mid-Atlantic staple, similar to ham but with a unique flavor profile. Any smoked ham would work well as a substitute. Scrapple is, well . . . scrapple. It contains various parts of the pig and is bound together with cornmeal and spices. I think of it as a Mid-Atlantic rillettes. It's a regional breakfast meat that has graced breakfast plates for generations and is best served nice and crispy.

Note on corn bread croutons: If you have any of the Chesapeake-Style Corn Bread (see page 204) on hand, it works well for croutons. It's best a little stale or dried out. Just cut it, or your favorite corn bread, into cubes, and allow them to air dry for an hour or so. Brush or toss the bread with a little melted butter or olive oil and toast in the oven until crispy. Of course, regular store-bought croutons will work, too.

HERBY GREEN GODDESS DRESSING

Yields about 1½ cups

1   cup flat-leaf parsley

1   cup tightly packed spinach leaves

3   tablespoons tarragon leaves

¼   cup minced chives

2   teaspoons minced garlic

3   tablespoons freshly squeezed lemon juice

2   tablespoons sherry wine vinegar

½   cup olive oil

½   cup sour cream

Salt and freshly ground black pepper, to taste

Place the parsley, spinach, tarragon, chives, garlic, lemon juice, and vinegar into a blender. Blend well and then slowly drizzle in the olive oil with the blender running. Pour into a bowl and beat in the sour cream to make a smooth mixture. Season with salt and pepper to taste.

8

VEGGIES GALORE

In this chapter we're putting the veggies first. Some recipes are entirely vegetarian or vegan friendly, and others are just loaded with vegetables and "accented" with seafood and poultry. There are various cooking techniques employed here—braising, sautéing, roasting, stir-frying, and some au naturel. Throughout the year the types of vegetables change seasonally, and consequently, so do our meals—which makes life exciting.

Fried Green Tomatoes and Hominy with Soft-Shell Crab

This is a dish composed of, basically, tomatoes and corn. The tomatoes are green and the corn is dried and transformed into hominy, but essentially it's a veg fest, accented with soft-shell crab. What a Chesapeake trio! I like to serve this with a zesty remoulade sauce for dipping—both the tomatoes and crabs.

Serves 6

Cheddar Hominy (*page 134*)

3 green tomatoes, cored and sliced ½-inch thick, soaked in milk

All-purpose flour seasoned with salt and freshly ground black pepper

3 tablespoons butter

3 tablespoons bacon fat or oil

Pinch of sugar

6 prime or jumbo soft-shell crabs, cleaned

All-purpose flour seasoned with salt, freshly ground black pepper, Old Bay seasoning, and cayenne, to taste

Vegetable oil or shortening for frying

Lemons, cut into wedges

Remoulade Sauce (*recipe follows*)

Prepare a batch of Cheddar Hominy.

To prepare the fried green tomatoes: Drain the tomatoes slightly and dust them with the seasoned flour. In a heavy skillet, heat the butter and bacon fat. Fry the tomatoes over a medium-high heat for 3 minutes on each side or until tender, sprinkling each side with a little sugar. Remove from the pan and drain on paper towels to absorb excess grease. Keep in a warm oven while frying the soft-shells.

To prepare the soft-shell crabs: Give the soft-shells a good dose of seasoned flour, and shake off excess. Melt the shortening or vegetable oil in a heavy skillet to a depth of about ¾ inch, then get it good and hot. Fry the crabs until golden brown, about 3 minutes on each side. Using tongs, place the crabs on paper towels to absorb excess oil.

To assemble, place a mound of hot hominy in the center of each plate. Cut the tomatoes in half and place them around the hominy. Cut the fried soft-shells in half and place 2 halves on each plate, resting on the hominy. Serve with lemon wedges and Remoulade Sauce on the side.

REMOULADE SAUCE

Yields 2½ cups

1   cup mayonnaise

6   tablespoons finely minced celery

2   tablespoons finely minced green onion

1   tablespoon chopped parsley

1   teaspoon minced garlic

2   tablespoons coarse-grain mustard

1   tablespoon chopped capers

2   tablespoons ketchup

1   tablespoon Worcestershire sauce

1   teaspoon paprika

½   teaspoon Tabasco sauce

½   teaspoon salt

Place all the ingredients in a bowl and whisk together well. Cover and chill for several hours before serving.

Potato Cakes with Catfish Creole

When I was doing my *Coastal Cooking* television series, this was one of my favorite recipes from the show. Catfish has some culinary detractors (you know—food snobs), but for my money, it is some of the best southern coastal cooking to be found. You are getting a bunch of terrific recipes here: bacon-enriched potato cakes, a spicy creole sauce, and a pan-fried catfish. They are perfect as a combo or on their own.

Serves 6

Potato Cakes (*recipe follows*)
Creole Sauce (*recipe follows*)
6   blue catfish fillets, 6 ounces each
    (*see page 108*)
Milk, as needed
1   cup flour
1   cup finely ground yellow or white cornmeal
1   tablespoon Old Bay seasoning or Cajun
    seasoning
½   teaspoon cayenne pepper
Salt and freshly ground black pepper
Vegetable oil, for frying
Flat-leaf parsley and lemon wedges, for garnish

Prepare the Potato Cakes and the Creole Sauce.

Soak catfish in a bowl with milk. In a second dish, mix the flour, cornmeal, Old Bay or Cajun seasonings, cayenne, salt, and pepper. Remove the fish from the milk, 1 fillet at a time, letting the excess milk drip back into the dish. Coat well with the flour-cornmeal mixture.

Pour oil into a frying pan to a depth of ½ inch and place over medium heat. When the oil is hot, add as many fillets as the pan will allow. Fry about 3 to 4 minutes on each side or until golden brown. Remove fish from the pan and drain well on paper towels.

On a warmed dinner plate, make a pool of hot Creole Sauce and top with 2 potato cakes. Place a catfish fillet on top of the cakes and top with a little more Creole Sauce. Repeat with each additional plate. Garnish with chopped flat-leaf parsley and lemon wedges. Greens are a perfect accompaniment, and don't forget to have freshly baked corn bread (*see page 204*) on hand.

POTATO CAKES

¼ pound sliced bacon

2 small yellow onions, diced

6 large potatoes, boiled, peeled, and cut into ½-inch pieces

Salt and freshly grated black pepper

Tabasco sauce, to taste

Cook the bacon in a large heavy skillet until fairly crisp. Remove from the pan and drain on paper towels. After bacon has cooled, coarsely chop and set aside.

Pour off all but 4 tablespoons of the bacon drippings and reserve the rest. Heat the skillet and add the onions. Cook over medium heat, stirring often, until the mixture begins to brown. Stir in the cooked potatoes and mix well. Continue to cook over medium heat, stirring often, for 5 minutes. Season with salt, pepper, and Tabasco.

Let cool to room temperature and then form into 12 cakes, about 2½- to 3-inch rounds. Set aside. When ready to serve, heat the remaining bacon fat in a cast-iron or heavy skillet. Brown the potato cakes on both sides, about 3 minutes per side. Drain on paper towels to remove excess grease. They are then ready to serve.

CREOLE SAUCE

Makes about 8 cups

5 tablespoons olive or vegetable oil

2 cups onions, finely diced

1½ cups celery, finely diced

1½ cups green onions, finely chopped

1½ cups green bell peppers, finely diced

2 tablespoons garlic, minced

¾ teaspoon cayenne pepper

1½ teaspoons salt

½ teaspoon freshly ground black pepper

½ teaspoon fennel seeds

1 teaspoon Tabasco sauce

1½ teaspoons dried basil

1½ teaspoons dried thyme

2 bay leaves

2 cups Fish Stock (*page 58*)

3 cups tomatoes, peeled and chopped, fresh or canned

2 tablespoons tomato paste

½ cup water

Heat the oil in a pot over medium heat and add the onions, cooking and stirring frequently for 8 to 10 minutes or until nicely browned. Add the celery, green onions, and bell peppers and cook for 5 minutes more. Add the garlic, cayenne, salt, pepper, fennel, Tabasco, basil, and thyme and cook for 3 minutes.

Add the bay leaves, fish stock, tomatoes, tomato paste, and water. Bring mixture almost to the boil, then reduce heat and let sauce slowly cook for 1 hour, stirring occasionally. The sauce should be prepared ahead and then reheated shortly before cooking the catfish.

"I Can't Believe It's Not Crab" Cakes

Alright, alright! I'm giving it all away here. Folks have been asking for this recipe for nearly twenty years and I keep saying, "the next cookbook, the next cookbook." Well, here you go. My sister, Kathleen Ashley, is the one who turned me onto this idea of a mock crab cake. She was overwhelmed by summer zucchini in the garden and started making mock crab cakes just to use up the supply. I'm sorry, Kath, but you know me—I can never leave well enough alone. Just have to jazz everything up, as I cannot help myself.

The recipe here can be made either vegetarian or vegan and is a crowd pleaser whether one is vegetarian or not. I like to serve it just like a crab cake, with coleslaw and French fries or roasted potatoes.

Serves 4

2   cups coarsely grated zucchini—salt lightly and let drain in a colander for 30 minutes
1   cup bread crumbs, plus additional for coating
2   eggs, or 1 tablespoon Ener G egg replacer mixed well with 4 tablespoons warm water (*see note*)
1   teaspoon Old Bay seasoning
1   teaspoon Dijon mustard
3   rounded tablespoons mayo or Vegenaise (or any eggless mayo)
¼   teaspoon Tabasco sauce
Juice of ½ lemon
¼   cup fresh parsley
Vegetable oil for frying
Three Mustard Sauce (*recipe follows*)

Place the drained zucchini in cheesecloth or a clean dish towel, and wring out any excess water. Place the zucchini and bread crumbs in a bowl. Toss together.

In another bowl, mix together the egg or egg replacer, Old Bay, mustard, mayo, Tabasco, lemon juice, and parsley. Beat well with a whisk. Combine the two mixtures and fold together well.

Form the mixture into cakes and dust in bread crumbs. Heat a frying pan with vegetable oil, about ¾-inch deep. Fry the cakes in the hot oil for 3 to 4 minutes or until well browned on both sides. Remove from pan and drain on paper towels to absorb any excess oil. Serve at once with Three Mustard Sauce, tartar sauce, or cocktail sauce.

Note: Ener G egg replacer is an egg substitute that can be found at many grocery and health food stores. It is made from potato starch, tapioca flour, and leavenings.

THREE MUSTARD SAUCE

Makes 1½ cups

1 cup mayonnaise

¼ cup Dijon mustard

¼ cup coarse-grain mustard

2 teaspoons dry mustard powder

1½ tablespoons Worcestershire sauce

¼ teaspoon cayenne pepper

¼ teaspoon freshly ground black pepper

1 teaspoon freshly squeezed lemon juice

¼ teaspoon Tabasco sauce

Place all the ingredients into a bowl and mix together well.

Roasted Eggplant Tenders

A recipe favorite of mine, developed by the brilliant chef Yotam Ottolenghi, is for eggplant croquettes. After making the recipe several times, I was inspired to transform the concept into another dimension. Children and adults alike go crazy for chicken tenders, with the adults slyly ordering extra tenders on the side, implying they are for the children. Well, we know what they're up to! This recipe, made from charred eggplant, is a great change of pace from the run-of-the-mill clucker tenders. The chevre gives the tenders a smooth texture, and the grated cheese packs a flavorful punch. In a nod to tradition, we've come up with a BBQ mayo for dipping the tenders.

Serves 6

Vegetable oil for coating pan

2 medium eggplants

2 potatoes, peeled, cooked, and mashed

2 eggs, beaten

1 clove garlic, minced

6 ounces sharp cheddar or Parmesan cheese

4 tablespoons goat chevre, softened

Salt and freshly ground black pepper

2 cups bread crumbs, divided

1 teaspoon chopped fresh thyme, or ½ teaspoon dried

1 teaspoon chopped fresh basil, or ½ teaspoon dried

Vegetable oil for frying

BBQ Mayonnaise (*recipe follows*)

Preheat oven to 425°F.

Lightly grease a baking pan with vegetable oil. Prick the skin of the eggplants in several places and place on the baking pan. Roast in the oven for about 40 to 45 minutes or until soft when pierced with a knife. Remove from oven and let sit until cool enough to handle. Cut the eggplants in half lengthwise and scoop out the flesh into a strainer. Let sit for 5 to 10 minutes to allow liquid to drain out. You should have about 2 cups of charred eggplant remaining.

Place the eggplant into a mixing bowl and add the potatoes, eggs, garlic, cheeses, and a little salt and pepper. Mix in about 1 cup of the bread crumbs a little at a time, until it is of a consistency that will hold its shape but is not dry. Form the mixture into "tenders," little patties about 3½ inches by 2 inches wide and ½- to ¾-inch thick.

Place the other cup of bread crumbs on a plate and add the chopped herbs. Lightly season the bread crumbs with salt and pepper and mix together. Place the tenders on the bread crumbs and coat well on both sides.

Heat a frying pan with vegetable oil about 1 inch deep. When the oil is quite hot, fry the tenders for about 2 minutes on each side or until nicely browned. Take care not to burn them. Remove from frying pan and drain on paper towels to absorb any excess grease. Serve at once with the BBQ Mayonnaise or dipping sauce of your choice on the side.

BBQ MAYONNAISE

1   egg yolk

1   whole egg

3   generous tablespoons of your favorite BBQ sauce

1   teaspoon freshly squeezed lemon juice

⅓   cup canola oil

⅓   cup olive oil

Salt, to taste

Place the egg yolk and whole egg in a blender or food processor. Add the BBQ sauce and lemon juice and blend until quite smooth and a bit frothy. With the blender or processor running, slowly drizzle in the oils until a nice emulsified mayonnaise is formed. Adjust the taste of the mayo with a touch of salt, if necessary.

Rebuilding Our Soils

It's just "dirt"—right?

No. It's *soil*, the essential sustenance of all life on planet Earth, and we'd best treasure it. Soil is made of weathered rocks (think minerals), organic matter, water, and air. But what transforms that mix into something truly magical is the hidden life that thrives down in the dark, in the rooting areas of the plants. There's a delicate give-and-take that goes on between the plants with green chlorophyll that grow above the ground in the sunlight and the microscopic bacteria and fungi below the ground in the dark. This is a complex ecology that can be damaged very easily. Soil compaction, poor drainage, agricultural runoff and low fertility, with the resultant misuse of chemical fertilizers, all wreak havoc on the health of our soil.

It's not difficult to see how intensive mono-cropping and heavy pesticide use can make a pretty big mess of things. In too many of our over-mechanized farms, the soil has been so utterly depleted that it merely serves as a dry, thirsty sponge, soaking up the massive chemical inputs necessary to get anything to grow there.

A better approach is known as the Integrated Farming System (IFS). In integrated systems, livestock and crops are carefully placed so that a healthy cycle is developed where the waste products of one component serve as a resource for the other. Manure is used to enhance crop production; crop residues and by-products feed the animals.

The soils around the Chesapeake have long been battered. Mono-cropping tobacco in the 1700s and 1800s took a massive toll. Since the 1960s, huge acreages of genetically modified corn have done great damage, and gigantic poultry operations polluting the ground and waterways with unhealthy amounts of nitrogen runoff surely have not helped. Good soil husbandry and an integrated approach can rebuild our precious soils. I've heard it said, and I know it's true: *"The soil is like a farmer's bank. You've got to keep making deposits into it all the time. If you withdraw from it until it's empty, you'll be out of business."*

Old-Timey Scalloped Tomatoes

I have been serving this wonderful Eastern Shore tomato recipe for what now seems like forever. *The Chesapeake Bay Fish & Fowl Cookbook,* a treasure of long-lost Chesapeake fare, inspired me to play around with this "scalloped" dish.

Serves 6

8   medium tomatoes, peeled, cored, and chopped
1   teaspoon salt
1   tablespoon brown sugar
Pinch of nutmeg
1   small onion, minced
4   tablespoons softened butter, divided
2   cups croutons

Preheat the oven to 400°F.

Place the tomatoes in a heavy-bottomed pot with a tight-fitting lid. Cover and cook the tomatoes for 15 minutes, stirring occasionally. Season the tomatoes with salt, brown sugar, nutmeg, onion, and 2 tablespoons butter.

Spray a casserole dish with pan spray and scatter 1 cup of the croutons evenly on the bottom of the casserole. Pour the tomatoes over the croutons, and then sprinkle the remaining croutons over the tomatoes. Dot the croutons with the remaining 2 tablespoons of butter.

Place in oven and bake for about 20 minutes or until nicely browned.

Roasted Brussels Sprouts

Who would think of Brussels sprouts going like peanuts? But just about everyone who snacks on these just-roasted, little cabbage-like vegetables goes crazy for them. There are a myriad of ways to gussy up Brussels sprouts, but here is a simple starter recipe that you can customize as you go along.

Serves 3 or 4

1   pound small Brussels sprouts, trimmed (if larger, cut in half)

3   tablespoons olive oil (try some virtually local olive oil from Dimitri Olive Oil)

Kosher salt and freshly ground black pepper

Preheat the oven to 400°F.

Toss the Brussels sprouts with the olive oil in a bowl and season with salt and pepper. Spread the Brussels sprouts out on a sheet pan and place in the oven, roasting for about 20 to 30 minutes. About every 5 minutes during the roasting, shake the pan to rotate the Brussels sprouts.

When the Brussels sprouts are nicely browned, remove them from the oven. They can be served hot, warm, or at room temperature.

Some variations:

Add 1 teaspoon Dijon mustard or 2 tablespoons balsamic vinegar to the olive oil mixture before coating the Brussels sprouts.

Charlottetown Farm Roasted Butternut Squash with Spicy Onions

Cheese maker Pam Miller has devised a tasty recipe to marry her signature goat cheese with winter squash. Feel free to substitute whatever type of nut you'd like; however, the hazelnuts (a.k.a. filberts) really are fantastic in this dish. Pam says that sometimes she leaves out the mint, but if you have fresh mint on hand it is a great addition.

Serves 4 to 6

1   cup toasted hazelnuts

2   large butternut squashes (about 4 pounds), seeded, peeled, and sliced ¼-inch thin

¼   cup plus 2 tablespoons olive oil

Salt and pepper

6   ounces Charlottetown Farm goat cheese crumbles (can use chevre, feta, or aged)

½   cup chopped fresh mint

2   tablespoons chopped fresh marjoram

Spicy Onions (*recipe follows*)

Preheat oven to 350°F. Toast the hazelnuts on a baking sheet, stirring occasionally, until golden brown, 6 to 8 minutes. Let cool and coarsely chop. Increase oven temperature to 400°F.

Toss the squash and ¼ cup oil in a medium bowl. Season with salt and pepper and divide between two rimmed baking sheets. Roast until tender, about 30 to 40 minutes.

Return the squash to the bowl, adding cheese, hazelnuts, mint, marjoram, and Spicy Onions. Toss to combine.

Transfer squash mixture to large serving platter and drizzle with remaining 2 tablespoons oil.

SPICY ONIONS

2   tablespoons olive oil

1   medium onion, sliced

1   teaspoon crushed red pepper flakes

¼   cup fresh lime juice

1   teaspoon finely grated lime zest

2   teaspoons honey

Heat oil in a large skillet over medium-high heat. Cook onion until lightly charred and softened. Add red pepper flakes and toss to combine. Remove pan from heat and mix in lime juice, zest, and honey. Let cool.

Spicy Onions can be made up to 3 days ahead. Cover and chill to keep them fresh.

Gertie's Sweet and Sour Cabbage

My grandmother Gertie was no slouch with cabbage dishes. She could make the cabbage *sing*. This recipe reflects Gertie's German parentage. The brown sugar gives the dish a caramelized nuance. When serving a beautiful pork roast, Gertie would often prepare this recipe with red cabbage. You may cook the cabbage to the desired doneness, but I suggest not overcooking.

Serves 4 to 6

1 medium cabbage, cored, and outer leaves removed

3 slices bacon

2 tablespoons butter

4 tablespoons brown sugar

3 tablespoons red wine vinegar or cider vinegar

2 tablespoons sweet pickle juice

Salt and freshly grated black pepper

Slice the cabbage into ¼-inch strips.

In a large pan, render the bacon until crisp. Remove the bacon and add the butter and brown sugar. Stir well until the butter is melted and the sugar is smooth.

Add the cabbage strips, tossing well to coat with the bacon-butter mixture, and sauté the cabbage for about 5 minutes. Add the vinegar and pickle juice. Mix well and continue to simmer on a low heat for about 5 to 8 minutes longer. Season with salt and pepper to taste.

If desired, chop the reserved bacon and sprinkle on top of the finished cabbage.

Vegetable Tofu-Young

I have been fascinated by Egg Foo Young from an early age. Not that we had many Chinese restaurants in the Baltimore neighborhood of my youth, but in Baltimore's tiny Chinatown, I would always order the Egg Foo Young because I loved the elevated serving platter, complete with dome. Presentation is everything! Truth be told, their Egg Foo Young was pretty greasy and not all that authentically Chinese. So, decades later I started playing around with the Foo Young concept, and I've come up with a vegan version that, if I do say so myself, is quite delightful.

Why, you may ask, is this dish in a Chesapeake cookbook? Obviously there are local veggies galore in this recipe, and we are fortunate to have two of the premier tofu producers in the United States located in our region: Twin Oaks Community Foods in Louisa, Virginia, and Fresh Tofu Inc. in the Susquehanna River watershed, in Allentown, Pennsylvania. Both businesses craft tofu products that rival those of Northern California, China, and Japan. No small feat.

I have arranged this recipe a little differently from most in this book due to the execution. In the majority of Chinese recipes, it's all about the *mise en place* (meaning "putting in place") before pulling all the ingredients together during the cooking process. These individual "omelets" need to be made one at a time—or in however many omelet-size pans you might have.

Serves 4

Tofu mixture for 4 servings:

2   packages (12 ounces each) firm tofu, well drained and mashed

¾   cup soy sauce

2   teaspoons miso, thinned in a little water

2   teaspoons minced ginger root

½   teaspoon turmeric

2   tablespoons Ener G egg replacer mixed with ¼ cup warm water (*see note*)

Mash and mix together all the ingredients in a bowl and set aside.

For each individual serving:

3   tablespoons chopped onion

Pinch of minced garlic

⅔   cup shredded cabbage

⅔   cup bean sprouts

¼   cup chopped mushrooms

2   teaspoons olive oil

2   teaspoons soy sauce

Canola or corn oil, for cooking

Drizzle of sesame oil

Ginger Citrus Gravy (*recipe follows*)

2   tablespoons chopped green onions

1   tablespoon or so chopped toasted peanuts

To assemble: Over medium-high heat, sauté the onion, garlic, cabbage, sprouts, and mushrooms in olive oil until they soften, about 3 minutes. Add the soy sauce and then put the cooked veggies into a mixing bowl. Add ¾ cup of the tofu mix to the bowl. Stir well.

Heat an omelet pan with about 2 teaspoons cooking oil until hot. Add one serving of the tofu-vegetable mixture and cook on medium heat until well browned but not burnt. Flip and cook until well browned on the other side. Slide onto a platter or serving plate. Drizzle with just a touch of sesame oil. Repeat the process for the other three servings.

Generously cover with Ginger Citrus "Gravy" and garnish with chopped green onions and chopped peanuts.

GINGER CITRUS GRAVY

2½ cups orange juice

2½ cups Vegetable Stock (*page 59*)

3   tablespoons soy sauce

2   tablespoons mirin rice wine

2   tablespoons sugar

2   tablespoons grated ginger

½   cup cornstarch, dissolved in a little water

In a saucepan, mix all ingredients together well and bring to a boil, whisking constantly. Cook for about 3 minutes and remove from heat until ready to use.

Note: Ener G egg replacer is an egg substitute that can be found at many grocery and health food stores. It is made from potato starch, tapioca flour, and leavenings.

Waverly Winter Market Cabbage and Tofu with Quinoa

Deborah Howard and I always kid around that she is my "separated-at-birth" sister. My former neighbor in Charles Village, she devised a tempting recipe just for this book. She challenged herself to find ingredients at the Waverly farmers' market to show that it is quite possible to feed oneself "locally," even during the winter months. Deb starts out by "roasting" or baking her tofu, which is an excellent technique to give the tofu a chewier, meatier texture. She also roasts winter beets to bring out the natural sugars. Savoy cabbage is her choice, but she adds that any cabbage of your liking will work well.

Serves 4

12-ounce package sprouted tofu (*see note*)
4 tablespoons grapeseed oil, divided
Salt, pepper, and Old Bay seasoning, to taste
2 large beets, peeled
1 cup quinoa
2 cups water
1 teaspoon salt
3 tablespoons olive oil
1 head Savoy cabbage, cored and cut into ribbons a bit wider than shoestring potatoes
1 teaspoon minced garlic
2–3 tablespoons soy sauce, or to taste
Freshly ground black pepper, to taste

Preheat the oven to 425°F.

Line two baking trays with parchment paper. Pat the tofu with paper towels to remove excess moisture. Cut into cubes. Toss the tofu with 2 tablespoons grapeseed oil and sprinkle with salt, pepper, and Old Bay seasoning. Place on one of the baking trays.

Cut the beets into small bite-size pieces. Toss with 2 tablespoons grapeseed oil and season with salt and freshly ground black pepper. Place on the other baking tray. Place both trays in the oven and bake for 20 minutes or until beets are tender.

Place the quinoa in a fine-mesh strainer and rinse well with cold water for about 2 to 3 minutes. Put the water and 1 teaspoon salt in a saucepan and bring to a boil. Stir in the quinoa, cover the saucepan, reduce the heat, and cook for 15 minutes. Remove from heat and let stand for 5 minutes. After 5 minutes, use the tines of a fork to fluff the quinoa. Cover and set aside.

In a large skillet, heat 3 tablespoons of olive oil. Add the cabbage and garlic and stir-fry for about 3 to 5 minutes, until a bit soft, but not mushy. Add the soy sauce and toss well. Add the cooked quinoa and cook for about 5 minutes with the cabbage. Add the roasted tofu and beets and toss all together. Adjust seasonings if necessary with soy sauce and pepper.

Note: Sprouted tofu is normally sold wherever regular tofu is sold. In this type of tofu, the soy beans are sprouted before the tofu is made. Sprouted tofu is touted as being more nutritious and easier to digest. If you cannot find sprouted tofu, I would suggest either firm or extra-firm organic tofu.

Rumbleway Farm Roasted Tomato Succotash with Chicken Confit on Johnnycakes

Here's another take on succotash from Robin Way of Rumbleway Farm. Robin says this recipe, especially the confit, is a huge hit. A few years ago, my restaurant, Gertrude's, was taking part in the governor of Maryland's Buy Local Cookout at the State House in Annapolis, Maryland. We were paired with Rumbleway, and this is the dish we featured at the event.

The confit can be made with chicken or duck, depending on what you like. And another tip— if you have a hankering for succotash with johnnycakes but have not the time to prepare a confit, try putting some pulled pork or shredded BBQ chicken thighs on top. Delish.

Serves 4

Johnnycakes (*page 205*)

1   cup young lima beans

Salt

1   cup fresh corn kernels (2 ears)

3   tablespoons butter

Juice of ½ lemon

Freshly ground black pepper, to taste

2   large Roasted Tomatoes (*recipe follows*), diced

3   tablespoons chopped fresh basil

Cecil County Chicken (or duck) Confit (*recipe follows*), heated

Prepare and bake the johnnycakes. Cut into rounds, squares, or triangles for serving.

Put the limas in a saucepan and add enough water to just cover the beans. Lightly salt the water. Bring to a boil, cover, and simmer until the beans are barely tender, about 15 to 20 minutes. Add the corn and simmer for 10 minutes more. Drain off the water and season with butter, lemon juice, salt, and pepper. After the succotash has cooled, mix in the Roasted Tomatoes and basil.

To assemble, place a spoonful of succotash on a warm or grilled johnnycake and top with a generous spoonful of warm shredded Cecil County Chicken Confit.

ROASTED TOMATOES

2 tablespoons olive oil

1 tablespoon sherry wine vinegar or balsamic vinegar

½ teaspoon minced garlic

2 large ripe tomatoes, cored

1 teaspoon brown sugar

½ teaspoon salt

Preheat oven to 450°F.

In a small bowl, mix together the olive oil, vinegar, and garlic. Cut the tomatoes in half and place cut-side up on a lightly oiled sheet pan. Drizzle the oil-vinegar mixture over the tomatoes. Sprinkle the tops of the tomatoes with the brown sugar and salt. Place in the oven and bake for about 20 minutes or until the tomatoes begin to brown and slightly caramelize. Let cool to room temperature.

CECIL COUNTY CHICKEN CONFIT

Yields about 2 cups

4 chicken leg portions with thighs attached, excess fat trimmed and reserved (about 2 pounds)

1 tablespoon plus ⅛ teaspoon kosher salt

½ teaspoon freshly ground black pepper

10 garlic cloves

4 bay leaves

4 sprigs fresh thyme

1½ teaspoons black peppercorns

½ teaspoon table salt

4 cups olive oil

Lay the chicken leg portions on a platter, skin side down. Sprinkle with 1 tablespoon of the kosher salt and ½ teaspoon black pepper. Place the garlic cloves, bay leaves, and sprigs of thyme on each of 2 leg portions. Lay the remaining 2 leg portions, flesh to flesh, on top. Put the reserved fat from the chicken in the bottom of a glass or plastic container. Place the sandwiched leg portions in the container as well. Sprinkle with the remaining ⅛ teaspoon kosher salt. Cover and refrigerate for 12 hours.

Preheat the oven to 200°F.

Remove the chicken from the refrigerator. Remove the garlic, bay leaves, thyme, and chicken fat and reserve. Rinse the chicken with cool water, rubbing off some of the salt and pepper. Pat dry with paper towels. Put the reserved garlic, bay leaves, thyme, and chicken fat in the bottom of an enameled cast-iron pot. Sprinkle evenly with the peppercorns and salt. Lay the chicken on top, skin-side down, and then add the olive oil. Cover and bake for 12 to 14 hours or until the meat pulls away from the bone.

Remove the chicken from the fat. Strain the fat and reserve. Pick the meat from the bones and place it in a stoneware container. Cover the meat with some of the strained fat, making a ¼-inch layer on top. The chicken confit can be stored in the refrigerator for up to 1 month.

Urban Gardening

Many inner-city residents around the country live in "food deserts"—neighborhoods that lack access to healthy and affordable food. Thankfully, urban gardens are popping up everywhere you look in the two major cities in our region. We have rooftop gardens, backyard gardens, barren and empty lots transformed into lush and bountiful gardens, and even larger community-run mini-farms. By transforming vacant land into growing spaces, urban agriculture can be a powerful tool to help combat a neighborhood's struggling economy as well, raising property values and providing affordable healthy food choices, while building a sense of pride, rootedness, and accomplishment that strengthens community spirit. It's a beautiful thing.

Baltimore's Power in Dirt, a citywide initiative, has made it easier for people to get permission to create gardens in empty city-owned lots since 2011. Since then, more than 1,100 lots have been adopted, totaling 49 acres of growing spaces. Many privately owned vacant lots are in need of improvements as well. Baltimore's Parks & People Foundation can explain the steps to obtaining legal access to a privately owned vacant lot. Working with the Community Law Center, they've broken down the policy to make it easy for you to understand. With the Parks & People Foundation's help, hundreds of community groups have navigated the process of getting their gardens started. Removing sometimes confusing barriers that can discourage prospective community groups helps empower low-income residents to actively revitalize their own communities.

Baltimore City's Farm Alliance is a network of thirteen farms located across the city. One of the most amazing projects in the Farm Alliance is Real Food Farm. Located in the city's Clifton Park, it's an 8-acre expanse of gardens, hoop houses, and a retention pond run by the nonprofit group Civic Works. Real Food Farm promotes urban agriculture as an economic engine in Baltimore by training and employing youth and adults in agricultural and horticultural jobs. Real Food offers an affordable CSA arrangement, partners with local restaurants, institutions, and retailers, and even takes the fresh produce out to inner-city neighborhoods in their Mobile Farmers Markets. They've created a replicable and sustainable model that shows the potential for urban agriculture to boost Baltimore's local economy.

In Washington, DC, the Department of Parks and Recreation is committed to promoting urban gardens. In 2014, the Urban Garden Division made increasing community gardens in the District of Columbia a top priority. In 2015, they launched a garden tool share program for DC gardeners to "check out" garden tools and larger equipment, such as rototillers, power tools, broad forks—even an apple press.

Bread for the City has DC's largest urban rooftop farm. This garden produces fresh, healthy food for use in their food pantries and cooking workshops. DC Greenworks, a nonprofit organization that promotes the environmental health of DC and the Chesapeake watershed, provided the technical support, transforming an existing 3,000-square-foot green roof into an intensive garden that has 30 raised beds, growing a variety of vegetables and herbs.

On three-quarters of an acre, the K Street Farm is home to 5,000 square feet of growing space, two honeybee hives, four egg-laying chickens, a variety of fruit trees, and many perennial herbs and flowers. The K Street Farm also serves as a training site for DC Greens's network of school garden coordinators from all eight wards of the city.

There are many more remarkable success stories from throughout the Chesapeake watershed I would love to share, but do a little detective work in your neighborhood and I'm sure you will find a number. Is there an eyesore lot in your neighborhood? Talk to your neighbors, and get things rolling. There's plenty of assistance available. You're only limited by the scope of your dreams. Look to the resources section in the back of the book for information about some civic organizations and municipal departments you can contact.

Lettuce Wraps Stuffed with Spring Veggies and Chicken

Here we have another recipe from the Rumbleway Farm Cooking School in Conowingo, Maryland. This is a plant-forward dish with big, cup-sized leaves of butter lettuce stuffed with a mélange of fresh veggies, seared marinated chicken, and a couple of Asian sauces. It's a party recipe for sure, with a buffet table full of ingredients and toppings for guests to assemble and build their own.

Serves 6 to 8

Asian Marinade (*recipe follows*)

3   pounds boneless chicken breasts or thighs

2   bunches scallions

3   regular-size carrots

1   cup finely chopped peanuts

4   tablespoons vegetable or grapeseed oil, divided

1   pound asparagus, bottom ends removed, cut into 1½-inch pieces

1   pound snow peas

2   heads Bibb or leafy lettuce

2   bunches cilantro, chopped

2   cups diced cucumber

Hoisin sauce (*see note*)

Sriracha sauce (*see note*)

Prepare the Asian Marinade. Cut the chicken into small bite-size strips and soak in marinade for at least 6 hours. If time is of the essence, poking the chicken with a fork can create a faster marination, but it disturbs the product a bit.

Chop the scallions, and julienne (matchstick cut) the carrots with a knife. Pulse the peanuts in a food processor until they are finely chopped. Place the scallions, carrots, and peanuts in their own individual serving dishes.

Remove the chicken from the marinade and pat dry with paper towels. Put 2 tablespoons vegetable or grapeseed oil in a skillet and heat until very hot. Cook chicken about 15 minutes, stirring occasionally until well seared and cooked through. Let rest, covered with aluminum foil.

Put 2 tablespoons vegetable or grapeseed oil in a skillet and heat until very hot. Put the asparagus in the skillet and toss, searing the whole outside evenly, for 3 minutes. Add snow peas, and stir for an additional 2 minutes.

Put the chicken and the asparagus–snow pea mixture in their own bowls for serving.

To serve: Set up a table with, left to right, plates, lettuce, cilantro, chicken, asparagus–snow peas, carrots, scallions, cucumber, hoisin, sriracha, and peanuts.

ASIAN MARINADE

1 cup soy sauce

½ cup rice wine vinegar

½ cup orange juice

2 tablespoons minced ginger

2 tablespoons minced garlic

2 tablespoons white miso

3 tablespoons sesame seeds

¼ cup cilantro

½ cup vegetable or grapeseed oil

½ teaspoon mayonnaise, if needed

¼ cup cornstarch

2 cups warm water

Put the soy sauce, rice wine vinegar, orange juice, ginger, garlic, miso, sesame seeds, and cilantro into a blender and blend on high until all ingredients are smoothly combined. With the blender running, slowly add vegetable oil to emulsify. (If the oil and vinegar do not blend together, add a half teaspoon of mayonnaise and it will do the trick.)

Create a loose slurry by stirring together the cornstarch and the warm water. Add the slurry to the marinade and place the mixture in a saucepan. Cook over medium heat, whisking frequently, until it begins to thicken slightly. Remove from heat and allow to cool.

Note: Hoisin sauce is a thick, fragrant Asian sauce that can be found at most grocery stores and international markets. Sriracha sauce, one of the most popular hot sauces on the market today, is made from chili paste and vinegar. It can be found at Asian markets, most grocery stores, and international markets.

9

BREAD BASKET

In the universe of bread are marvelous galaxies of grains, leavenings, and flavors baked together to nourish and delight our senses. Since before the written word, humans have been sustained by the simple, milled cereal grains particular to their regions. The Chesapeake is no exception, and has a long tradition of breads and muffins. These link to the various continents from which many of us came and to the traditions of the native people who made the Bay their home, long before the settlers arrived.

Here, I have collected a variety of recipes: from good sturdy wheat and rye breads, to yeasted breads enriched with butter and cheese; bread fashioned with milled corn in the Native American tradition; and quick-breads and muffins for our snacking pleasure.

Maple Whole Wheat Bread

There is nothing better, in my opinion, than a hearty loaf of bread. The smell of a fresh loaf baking in the oven is one of life's true joys. We have gotten away from the art of bread baking, much to the detriment of our households. There's something about baking fresh bread that is akin to gardening. It's rather miraculous seeing something come to life right before your eyes.

I've enjoyed this recipe for years, but some people shy away from denser, textured breads. However, this bread adapts well by using half white flour and half whole wheat. You will get a much lighter loaf, but still with all the wonderful maple flavor.

Yields 1 loaf

- 3 teaspoons active dry yeast
- ½ cup warm water (105–110°F)
- 4 tablespoons maple syrup, divided
- 1¾ cups water
- 4⅔ cups whole wheat flour, plus extra for kneading
- ½ cup wheat bran
- 2 teaspoons sea salt

Dissolve the yeast in the warm water and add 1 tablespoon maple syrup. Let sit until dissolved and foamy, about 10 minutes. Transfer to a large mixing bowl. Stir in the 1¾ cups water and the remaining 3 tablespoons maple syrup. In another bowl, mix together the flour, bran, and salt. Add the flour mixture to the wet ingredients, 1 cup at a time, stirring with a wooden spoon. When dough is too hard to stir with the spoon, use your hands. The dough should be moist but not sticky. Add a little more flour if necessary.

Knead the dough on a floured surface or breadboard for about 10 to 15 minutes, adding more flour as necessary. Place the dough in an oiled bowl, turning the dough to lightly coat all sides. Cover the bowl with a damp dish towel and set aside in a warm place to rise until double in bulk, about 1½ to 2 hours.

Oil a 9½ x 5½ inch loaf pan.

Punch the dough down with your fist and knead for 5 minutes longer on the floured surface. Form the dough into the shape of a loaf. Pinch the seam of the loaf together and place it, seam side down, in the pan. Cover with a damp towel and let stand in a warm spot until the dough has risen above the top of the loaf pan, about 30 to 45 minutes. Preheat the oven to 350°F.

Bake the loaf for 40 to 50 minutes, until done. To test, remove the loaf from the pan and tap the bottom of the loaf to see whether it sounds hollow. If it does, it's ready. Brush the top of the loaf with a little oil, and transfer to a wire rack to cool completely.

Johnny's Brown Bread

I've spent quite a bit of time visiting Ireland, and I fell in love with their brown bread on my first trip. This staple of the Irish kitchen is nothing like the sweet, raisin-filled, Irish-American version I grew up eating. I've experimented for years with variations of recipes, and this is the best one I've come up with. Because the bread flour sold in Ireland is much coarser than what is available here in the United States, the texture is never exactly like that of the breads in Ireland. But this recipe produces a loaf very similar to the ones I've enjoyed. Some people, like me, enjoy a little sweetness in the bread and a touch of butter to enrich the loaf. However, the authentic brown bread has no sweetener or butter.

Makes 1 loaf

3   cups stone-ground whole wheat flour
½   cup all-purpose flour
3   tablespoons oats
3   tablespoons bran
1   teaspoon baking soda
½   teaspoon salt
2   tablespoons brown sugar (optional)
2   tablespoons chilled butter, cut into pieces (optional)
1½ cups or so buttermilk

Preheat oven to 425°F.

Sift the flours, oats, bran, baking soda, salt, and sugar (if using) together into a mixing bowl. If using butter, rub the butter into the flour with the tips of your fingers or a pastry cutter. Make a well in the center of the flour and pour in the buttermilk all at once. Mix with a wooden spoon or by hand, just until all the liquid is incorporated.

Turn the dough onto a lightly floured board and shape into a loaf. Place in a lightly greased 8-inch loaf pan and make a deep "x" cut across the top of the dough with a sharp knife. Bake for about 40 minutes. Remove from pan. When the loaf is tapped on the bottom, it should sound hollow. Allow to cool on a baking rack before serving. This bread is great with butter and preserves.

Hutzler's Cheese Bread

Many of us have fond recollections of the big department stores of our youth. If you lived in the Baltimore, Maryland, area during the twentieth century, Hutzler's was the premier department store. The downtown flagship location was legendary for its local Chesapeake fare and its quite refined tea room. And for Hutzler's cheese bread the crowds went wild, waiting in line to secure a loaf or two to take home. When the local chain went dark, there was much wailing and gnashing of teeth over the loss of our treasured cheese bread.

Well, folks, the suffering is over. I found a reputed copy of the recipe and have adapted it for home use. A good, sharp local cheddar makes a world of difference, and my feelings wouldn't be hurt if you decided to add a couple extra ounces of cheddar.

Makes 2 loaves

1   package (¼ ounce) dry yeast
½   cup lukewarm water
4¾ cups all-purpose flour
1½ teaspoons salt
2   tablespoons sugar
1   cup milk
8   ounces sharp cheddar cheese, divided—4 ounces shredded, 4 ounces cut into small chunks
2   tablespoons butter, melted

Preheat the oven to 325°F.

Dissolve the yeast in lukewarm water and let it sit until dissolved and foamy, about 10 minutes. Transfer to a large mixing bowl. Add the rest of the ingredients and mix well. Knead the dough on a floured surface or breadboard for about 10 to 15 minutes, adding more flour as necessary.

Place the dough into an oiled bowl, turning the dough to lightly coat on all sides. Cover the bowl with a damp dish towel and set aside in a warm place to rise until double in bulk, about 2 hours.

Grease two 4 x 8 inch bread pans. Divide dough into two parts and tuck it into bread pans, seam side down. Cover with a towel and let rise again, for about 30 to 40 minutes.

Bake for 1 hour. Remove loaves from bread pans and place on a wire rack to cool completely.

Kitchen Garden Rye

It seems hard to find good rye bread these days. Not that long ago, neighborhood bakeries graced virtually every commercial block, and each had its own signature rye bread. There's nothing better than a nice, fresh crusty loaf of rye, for sandwiches, with smoked fish, or, most importantly, a bowl of soup or stew. In my hippie days, one of my go-to cookbooks was the *Moosewood Cookbook*—and sure enough, after thousands of studies on the effects of food on our health, it seems the hippies knew what they were talking about.

I must give a shout-out to my hero, John Robbins, author of *Diet for a New America*, a book that is loaded with information on our health and the direct role food plays in it. His follow-up companion cookbook, *May All Be Fed*, includes a variation on the Moosewood rye. This recipe was inspired by both. I highly recommend these books for your kitchen collection.

Yields two 1½-pound loaves

1   cup warm water (105–110°F)
1   package (¼ ounce) active dry yeast
1   tablespoon honey
1½   cups water
2   tablespoons molasses
3   tablespoons canola oil, plus extra for brushing loaves
4   cups unbleached white flour, plus extra for kneading
2   cups rye flour
1   medium carrot, grated
1   medium potato, peeled and grated
1   small parsnip, grated
1   small beet, peeled and grated
3   tablespoons chopped fresh dill
2   teaspoons salt
2   teaspoons caraway seeds

In a small bowl, combine the warm water, yeast, and honey. Let stand until the yeast has dissolved and is foamy, about 10 minutes. Transfer to a large bread bowl and stir in the 1½ cups of water, molasses, and oil. In another large bowl, mix the white and rye flours together. Using a wooden spoon, stir 4 cups of the flour mixture into the liquid, one cup at a time. Stir the mixture for about 3 minutes. Use a rubber spatula to scrape the dough from the sides of the bowl. Cover the bowl with a damp kitchen towel. Let stand in a warm place until the dough has doubled in size and resembles a sponge, with tiny holes appearing on the surface, about 1 to 2 hours.

Mix in the grated carrot, potato, parsnip, beet, dill, salt, and caraway.

To make the dough, use the wooden spoon (and your hands if necessary) and stir in the remaining 2 cups of flour mixture to make a soft, kneadable dough. Turn out onto a floured work surface or breadboard and form into a ball. Knead the dough, adding flour as necessary, for 12 to 15 minutes, or until the dough is smooth and elastic. The dough should be somewhat moist but not sticky.

Place the ball of dough in an oiled mixing bowl and turn it to lightly coat with oil. Cover the bowl with a moist towel, place it in a warm place, and let stand until the dough doubles in bulk, about 1 to 1½ hours.

Oil two 9½ x 5½ inch loaf pans.

Punch the dough down with your fist and knead for 5 minutes longer on the floured surface. Divide into two equal portions and form them into logs. Pinch the seams of the loaf together and place loaves, seam side down, in the pans. Cover with the damp towel and let stand in a warm spot until the dough has risen above the tops of the loaf pans, about 30 to 45 minutes.

Preheat the oven to 350°F.

Bake the loaves for 40 to 50 minutes. To test, remove a loaf from the pan and tap on the bottom of the loaf to see whether it sounds hollow. If it does, it's ready. Brush the tops of the loaves with a little oil and transfer to wire racks to cool completely.

Chesapeake-Style Corn Bread

Corn bread is the cornerstone of the Chesapeake bread basket. It has many shapes and
forms: quick-bread, muffins, johnnycakes,
hush puppies, and the like. In our region, the
corn bread is crafted with yellow cornmeal, as
opposed to the white cornmeal used by bakers
farther to the south. There are as many versions
of this bread as there are cooks, but this is the
recipe that I like best.

Serves 4 to 6

1	cup yellow cornmeal
1	cup white flour
3	tablespoons sugar
3	teaspoons baking powder
½	teaspoon salt
2	eggs, lightly beaten
1¼	cups milk
2	tablespoons butter, melted and cooled

Preheat the oven to 425°F. Grease and flour an 8-inch square pan.

Mix the cornmeal, flour, sugar, baking powder, and salt in a bowl. In another bowl, combine the eggs, milk, and butter. Add the wet ingredients to the dry ingredients and mix thoroughly without overbeating. Pour into the pan.

Bake for 30 minutes or until a toothpick inserted in the middle comes out clean. Let the corn bread rest for at least 15 minutes before cutting. (If you'd enjoy a sweet crust on your corn bread, take a piece of butter and rub it along the top of the corn bread when it first comes out of the oven. Sprinkle lightly with sugar.) Cut into 2-inch squares and serve.

Variations:

Add the juice of half an orange, along with the zest, to the batter.

Put 2 tablespoons of bacon fat into a cast-iron skillet and when very hot, add the batter and bake the corn bread right in the skillet.

Reduce sugar by 1 tablespoon, add ¼ cup grated onion and an extra ¼ cup of flour, and voilà—you have a hush puppy batter ready for deep-frying.

To "veganize" the recipe: use 1 tablespoon Ener G egg replacer mixed with 4 tablespoons warm water to replace the eggs, use plant milk instead of dairy milk, and use 2 tablespoons vegan butter or canola oil to replace the butter.

Johnnycakes

I found quite a number of recipes in old Chesapeake regional cookbooks when researching *The Chesapeake Bay Cookbook,* going on three decades ago. There is much disagreement about the origin of this dish, but it is found frequently in archives from the original thirteen colonies. The cakes are actually a cornmeal flatbread. Legend says they were actually called "journey cakes," which would make sense, as the original recipe had no leavening and only boiling water as the liquid. Nothing could go bad, and thus they were perfect for a long journey.

These johnnycakes have no baking powder but are lightened a bit with an egg and some white flour. They can be served as a breakfast item with butter and syrup or honey, but more often are served as the foundation of a plate with shredded meat or poultry resting on top. Check out the Roasted Tomato Succotash with Chicken Confit (*see pages 191–92*) for a perfect recipe using these cakes.

Serves 4 to 6

1   egg
1   tablespoon sugar
1½ cups milk or plant milk
½   teaspoon salt
¾   cups yellow cornmeal, stone-ground
¼   cup all-purpose flour
1   tablespoon butter, melted
3   tablespoons bacon drippings, melted (vegetable oil may be substituted for bacon drippings; for a very authentic taste, put 2 drops of Liquid Smoke into the batter if not using bacon fat)

Preheat the oven to 400°F.

Beat the egg and sugar together in a bowl. Stir in the milk and salt. Beat in the cornmeal and flour. Mix in the butter and 2 tablespoons of the bacon drippings.

Generously grease an 8-inch cast-iron skillet with the remaining tablespoon of bacon drippings. Put in the hot oven for about 5 minutes. Wearing oven mitts, remove from the oven and pour in the batter. (Alternatively, these can be made on a hot griddle as small individual cakes.)

Return to the oven and bake for 30 to 40 minutes or until well browned. Serve hot, cut into wedges.

The Interstate Highway System and the Demise of the Local Food Economy

"The best-laid plans of mice and men often go awry."
—Scottish poet Robert Burns

Or, in this case, we're talking about the best-laid *roads*. Before the explosion of the commercial trucking industry, most agricultural products were produced near where they were consumed. There was little long-distance transport of bulk agricultural products other than grains. What there was went relatively slowly, by water or by rail. Massively centralized processing, packaging, and marketing were almost unheard of.

Here in the Chesapeake region, hundreds of small, independent seafood packers and produce canners were thriving in our agricultural communities. In Baltimore, with good water transport and rail access, there were many medium-sized processing and canning industries. Still, most of the people who lived around here primarily ate what was grown, raised, or harvested nearby. Municipal and neighborhood markets offered truly fresh produce, meats, dairy products, and seafood. Food traveled from the neighboring counties into the city over a network of roads that wove directly from the farms and docks, through the small towns and into the city. The money folks spent on their food was threaded right back into the regional economy via the vendors' pockets.

The Dwight D. Eisenhower National System of Interstate and Defense Highways was authorized by the Federal Aid Highway Act of 1956. The bill was lobbied for heavily by a coalition of vehicle, oil, tire, cement, steel, and union interests, but in the process of laying 42,793 miles of limited-access pavement, the Interstate builders changed America in ways few could have imagined back then. In 1956, trucks moved just half a billion tons—now, an estimated 20 billion tons of goods each year are moved on the nation's highway system.

President Eisenhower's assistant secretary of agriculture, Earl Butz, had a vision of transforming American agriculture with a corporate farming model. He famously advised farmers across the country to "Get big or get out." The new interstate highway system, while providing much-needed access to connect all parts of the country, was also a perfect way to facilitate the distribution of massive amounts of agricultural products from large, centralized farms to destinations all over the country. Crop prices were manipulated, eventually driving many small farmers out of business. With the demise of the small farmer went the fortunes of rural towns and agricultural communities.

The monopolizing of processing, distribution, and marketing activities involved in transforming raw agricultural commodities into food products has resulted in the farmers' share of the money made selling foodstuffs shrinking significantly. The USDA computes that in 1956 more than 40 percent of consumer food expenditures went directly to farm producers. By 2012, that had dropped to a mere 17 percent, and I feel certain it's even lower today. We need to turn that around!

Nice Creamery Bran Muffins

With all the processed food we have at our disposal these days, most Americans get nowhere near enough fiber in their diets. And the consequences of a diet low in fiber can be seen in the plague of developed-world medical maladies. So here we have a delicious and healthy way to get an ample amount of fiber for the day. And thanks to the folks at Nice Creamery on the Eastern Shore, there's plenty of calcium and vitamin D to go around.

Makes 12 standard muffins
or 6 oversized muffins

2½ cups bran flakes
½   cup rolled oats
1   cup whole wheat flour
2   teaspoons baking soda
1   teaspoon baking powder
½   teaspoon salt
⅔   cup Nice Creamery creamline milk
     (whole milk works well)
⅔   cup vanilla yogurt
2   duck eggs or 3 chicken eggs, lightly beaten
⅓   cup butter, melted
⅓   cup sorghum molasses
⅓   cup raw honey

Preheat oven to 375°F.

Grease muffin tins.

In a mixing bowl, combine the bran flakes, oats, flour, baking soda, baking powder, and salt. Blend all dry ingredients together and set aside.

In another bowl, beat together milk, yogurt, and eggs. Add the melted butter, molasses, and honey. Whisk until well blended. Combine with the dry ingredients and spoon batter into muffin tins.

Bake standard muffins for 20 to 25 minutes and oversized muffins for 25 to 30 minutes or until a knife inserted into the center comes out clean.

Morning Glory Muffins

There's something to be said about starting out your morning with a nice hot cup of coffee and a freshly baked muffin. I'm obsessed with muffins and am always looking for a healthier, tastier morning morsel. I think these fit the bill beautifully. They are loaded with carrot, raisins, and apple, along with some pineapple and nuts to boot. If you are looking to reduce the fat, I suggest using ½ cup applesauce or mashed banana, mixed with only ¼ cup of the vegetable oil. The muffin may be just a tad heavier but still quite moist.

Makes 1 dozen muffins

2 cups whole wheat flour or 1 cup white and 1 cup whole wheat

1 cup brown sugar

1 teaspoon cinnamon

2¼ teaspoons baking soda

½ teaspoon salt

⅔ cup shredded coconut, unsweetened or sweetened

½ cup raisins

2 cups grated carrots

1 large tart apple, peeled, cored, and grated

⅔ cup walnuts, toasted and chopped

3 eggs

¾ cup vegetable oil

¾ cup drained, crushed pineapple

2 teaspoons vanilla extract

Zest and juice of 1 orange

Rolled oats, for top of muffins

Preheat oven to 375°F.

In a large mixing bowl, mix together the flour, sugar, cinnamon, baking soda, and salt. Stir in the coconut, raisins, carrots, apple, and walnuts.

In another bowl, beat the eggs and then add the oil, pineapple, vanilla, orange zest, and orange juice. Mix well.

Add the wet ingredients to the flour mixture and stir to mix together well. You want all the ingredients moistened, but do not overmix. Scoop muffin batter into lightly oiled muffin tins and top each muffin with a few oats for garnish. Bake for 20 minutes or until a toothpick inserted in the center comes out clean.

Rhubarb Muffins

Normally when we see a recipe for rhubarb, it is paired with strawberries. But actually, rhubarb stands quite well all on its own, as this recipe will attest. In the Chesapeake you will find rhubarb plentiful in the spring, and it can be cut up into pieces and frozen in ziplock freezer bags for use throughout the year.

Makes 12 muffins

2½ cups all-purpose flour
1   teaspoon baking soda
1   teaspoon baking powder
½   teaspoon salt
½   teaspoon ground cinnamon
1½ cups brown sugar
⅓   cup vegetable oil
1   egg, beaten
1   teaspoon vanilla extract
1   cup buttermilk or 1 cup soy milk mixed with 1 teaspoon apple cider vinegar
2   cups diced rhubarb
½   cup chopped walnuts
3   tablespoons sugar
½   teaspoon ground cinnamon

Preheat oven to 400°F.

In a mixing bowl, sift together the flour, baking soda, baking powder, salt, and cinnamon. In another bowl, mix the brown sugar and oil together. Add the beaten egg and vanilla. Mix very well until smooth and creamy. Whisk in the buttermilk (or soy milk) and mix well.

Add the wet ingredients to the dry and mix well, without overbeating. Fold in the rhubarb and walnuts. Ladle the batter into a lightly oiled muffin tin.

In a small bowl, mix together the sugar and cinnamon and sprinkle the mixture over each muffin. Place muffin tin into the oven and bake for 22 to 25 minutes. A toothpick inserted into the center of a muffin should come out clean.

Remove muffins from oven and let stand for 5 minutes before removing muffins from the tin. Serve warm or at room temperature.

Zucchini Bread for Miss Molly

If you do any home gardening, you are well aware of the zucchini invasion that comes at the end of summer. It's everywhere, and it just won't stop growing. Zucchini bread is one of the solutions to an overabundance of this vegetable. It's a quick-bread that does not involve yeast, but rather is leavened with baking soda and a touch of baking powder.

The traditional recipe is loaded with sugar and oil. I sent one to my cousin-in-law in Ireland, Annie Gilligan Browne, who wanted to make a loaf for her daughter, Molly. She was startled by the amount of sugar, and it made me take another look at the recipe. So we played around with it and came up with a healthier, and I think tastier, version of the classic loaf. Give it a try.

Makes 2 loaves

3   eggs
¾   cup granulated sugar
½   cup vegetable oil
2   cups firmly packed grated zucchini
     (do not peel)
1   tablespoon vanilla extract
1½   cups all-purpose flour
1½   cups whole wheat flour
1   teaspoon salt
1   teaspoon baking soda
½   teaspoon double-acting baking powder
1   tablespoon ground cinnamon
1   cup coarsely chopped walnuts or pecans
¼   cup raisins

Preheat oven to 350°F.

In a bowl, beat the eggs until light and foamy. Add the sugar, oil, zucchini, and vanilla and mix lightly but well. In another bowl, combine the flours, salt, soda, baking powder, and cinnamon and add to the egg-zucchini mixture. Stir until well blended, but do not overmix. Fold in the nuts and raisins, and pour the batter into two 8 x 4 x 2½ inch greased loaf pans.

Bake in a preheated oven for 1 hour. Cool on a rack.

Chocolate Chunk Ginger Scones

A well-made scone is a sight to behold and a delightful accompaniment to a strong cup of tea. It's what afternoons are made for. These scones are crafted in the classic manner, with sweet butter rubbed into the flour, and raised primarily by the baking soda's reaction to the buttermilk. The addition of chocolate chunks and bits of candied ginger will make this recipe a staple of your scone-making repertoire.

Makes 12 large or 18 small scones

2	cups whole wheat flour
2	cups unbleached white flour
1	teaspoon baking soda
½	teaspoon baking powder
1½	tablespoons ground ginger
½	teaspoon cinnamon
¼	teaspoon ground allspice
⅓	cup sugar, plus extra for sprinkling
½	teaspoon salt
¼	cup cold butter
1¼	cup lowfat buttermilk
1	egg, beaten
1	teaspoon pure vanilla extract
5	ounces dark chocolate (a chocolate bar or bag of chocolate chips)
⅓	cup candied ginger, cut into tiny pieces

Preheat the oven to 400°F.

Line two baking sheets with parchment paper or lightly grease them.

In a large bowl, whisk together the flours, baking soda, baking powder, ground ginger, cinnamon, allspice, sugar, and salt. Cut the butter into small bits and add to the flour mixture. Work the butter into the flour with the tips of your fingers or with a pastry cutter until it resembles a coarse meal.

In a small bowl, mix together the buttermilk, egg, and vanilla. Add wet ingredients to dry ingredients and mix until just combined. If using a chocolate bar, chop the chocolate into chunks. Add chocolate and ginger to the bowl of dough and mix until evenly distributed.

Turn the dough out onto a floured surface or a breadboard, and roll out to about ½-inch thick. Cut out 12 large or 18 small scones with a fluted cutter. Arrange the scones on the baking sheets, spaced well apart. Bake for 15 to 20 minutes or until the scones are golden brown. Cool on wire racks.

10

DESERTS AND SWEET TREATS

For those of you who may never have written a cookbook, I'd like to tell you that the dessert chapter is always the most difficult. Wherever you go to talk with folks about regional food and look for recipes, seven out of ten recipes you get will be for dessert. I guess it's just human nature that we are fond of sweet things, and often they are part of traditional celebrations, making them much beloved.

As this is *The New Chesapeake Kitchen*, I tried to go for a more fruit-centered approach with the desserts. We have a goodly sampling of pies, cobblers, and cakes that are embedded with fruit. For a number of the recipes, I've given ideas on how you might "veganize" the desserts as well, should you be so inclined. Many of the recipes are adaptable to other fruit during the various seasons. So as always, I encourage experimentation with your recipes by trying different renditions throughout the year.

Apple and Mango Chutney Cobbler

Fruit crisps rule. Our local orchards are the source for beautiful apples, pears, peaches, apricots, and anything crisp-able. Mangoes in the Chesapeake? Well, maybe not, but this is one of my all-time favorite apple crisp recipes. Just about any type of chutney will work to scent and lightly sweeten the apples, but a good mango chutney from an Asian or Indian market does the job quite well.

Serves 6

6–8 tart apples, peeled, cored, and sliced
1   cup coarsely puréed mango chutney
1   cup flour
¾   cup brown sugar
½   cup sugar
¼   teaspoon salt
2   teaspoons cinnamon
½   teaspoon ground coriander
½   pound butter, cut into pieces
Vanilla ice cream or lightly sweetened whipped
     cream (optional)

Preheat the oven to 350°F.

In a bowl, mix the apples with mango chutney and set aside.

Mix the flour, brown sugar, sugar, salt, cinnamon, and coriander in a bowl. Incorporate the butter pieces with fingertips to make a coarse meal.

Butter an 8-inch Pyrex glass pan and spread out the chutney-coated apples in it. Top evenly with the sugar-flour mixture. Bake for about 45 to 50 minutes or until well browned.

Serve the crisp at room temperature or slightly warmed, with whipped cream or a scoop of vanilla ice cream.

Note: For a plant-based presto-change-o, replace the butter with a vegan "butter" and serve with a nut-based ice cream. Or if gluten free is needed, substitute 1 cup ground almond meal for the flour.

Apple Rhubarb Pandowdy

Here's a tasty, old-fashioned pandowdy that is gluten free and vegan optional. What distinguishes a "pandowdy" is the step after the initial baking, where you press down on the crust to allow the juices to seep through and then bake a little longer, allowing the juices to caramelize. It gives the dish a distinctive topping that is quite unique. The pandowdy can be served with lightly sweetened whipped cream or vanilla ice cream—regular or plant based.

Makes 8 servings

2 tablespoons butter or vegan butter, divided

5 cups (4–5) Gala or other cooking apples, peeled, quartered, cored, and sliced thin

1 pound rhubarb, cleaned and cut into ½-inch pieces (about 3 cups)

1 tablespoon lemon juice

¾ cup brown sugar or ½ cup maple syrup

Almond Flour Pastry Crust (*recipe follows*)

1 tablespoon granulated sugar

½ teaspoon cinnamon

Preheat the oven to 375°F. Use 1 tablespoon of the butter to grease an 8 x 8 x 2 inch glass baking dish.

In a mixing bowl, toss the fruit first with the lemon juice, then with the sugar or maple syrup. Pour the fruit into the prepared pan. Roll out the pastry to a diameter of about 9 to 10 inches and place the pastry over the fruit, tucking the edges down around the filling. Cut the remaining tablespoon of butter in small pieces and dot them around the top of the pastry. Mix the sugar and cinnamon together in a small bowl and sprinkle over the pastry.

Bake for about 30 minutes or until crust is golden. Remove from oven and, using a sharp knife, score the crust diagonally into diamond shapes about 2 inches wide. Use a spatula to press the crust down gently into the fruit. Return to oven and bake until the crust is browned, about 15 minutes more. Remove from oven and serve warm.

ALMOND FLOUR PASTRY CRUST

2   cups almond flour

½   teaspoon salt

2   tablespoons canola oil

1   egg or 1 tablespoon Ener G egg replacer whisked with 3 tablespoons warm water

2   tablespoons cold water

Mix together the almond flour and salt in a mixing bowl. Use your fingers or a fork to work the canola oil into the flour mixture until it is the consistency of coarse meal. In a small bowl, beat the egg (or the mixed Ener G egg replacer) and add to the pastry, mixing with a fork. Add the cold water to the pastry 1 tablespoon at a time, mixing with a fork after each addition. Add only enough water to make the dough stick together. When you can form it into a ball, dust a pastry board with almond (or rice) flour and roll out dough to fit the top of the baking dish.

PASTRY DOUGH FOR A DOUBLE PIE CRUST

Makes pastry for 1 double-crust 9-inch pie

2½ cups all-purpose flour

1   teaspoon salt

1   cup vegetable shortening or ½ cup shortening and ½ cup butter, cut into small pieces

6–8 tablespoons very cold water

Sift together the flour and salt into a mixing bowl. Work the shortening (and butter if using) into the flour with your fingertips or a pastry blender, until the mixture is the consistency of a coarse meal. Add the water 1 tablespoon at a time, mixing with a fork after each addition.

Dough should not be wet but just moist enough to hold together. Form the dough into a ball. Wrap and refrigerate for at least 15 to 30 minutes before rolling. Divide dough into two pieces, one slightly larger than the other. Roll out the larger piece on a lightly floured board to ⅛-inch thickness and line the bottom of the pie pan. Roll the second piece to the same thickness and use to top the pie.

Black Rock Orchard Slab Pie

Emily Zaas knows her apples and is a master of pies. This is a very cool technique, and I was much impressed when she first served it to me and even more so when I tasted it. The slab pie is definitely a change of pace from the classic apple pie, and I find it so much fun to prepare. If memory serves me well, there was ice cream involved with the warm pie.

Serves 8

Pastry Dough for a Double Pie Crust (*recipe opposite*)

12–18 tart pie apples (Ida Red, Red Winesap, or Stayman Winesap preferred), peeled and cored

1 generous teaspoon ground cinnamon

1 cup sugar

¼ cup (½ stick) butter, cut into small pieces

1½ cups crushed cereal flakes (wheat flakes, corn flakes, etc.)

¼ cup milk

Prepare pie dough and refrigerate for at least 30 minutes.

Preheat the oven to 400°F.

Set aside a 15½-inch jelly roll pan or a 13 x 9 inch cake pan. A larger pan and a flatter pie are good. Slice the apples into a mixing bowl. Add the cinnamon and sugar and mix well. Add the butter pieces to the apple mixture and stir together well.

Roll out half of the pie dough to fit the bottom of your pan. Sprinkle the cereal flakes over the dough to within a half-inch of the edge. Spoon the apple mixture over the cereal flakes. Roll out the remaining dough and fit over the apples. Seal the edges by pinching the dough together. Brush the dough with a little milk.

Bake for 20 minutes, and then lower the temperature to 350°F and bake for 50 minutes longer, until top crust is nicely browned.

Serve warm or cold.

Schnitz Pie

There is a thriving Amish community in the Chesapeake region, and their cooking traditions have greatly influenced the cuisine. During the fall apple harvest, Amish women gather to make large batches of cider, apple sauce, and "dry" apples, which are known as "schnitz," from the Old German "to cut."

Not wasting anything and always wanting to preserve and "put up" their fruits and vegetables, schnitz was a pretty nifty innovation, extending the life of apples. The dry apples need to be reconstituted by soaking and cooking in water. Schnitz makes an exceptional apple pie, with the soaked fruit creating a very creamy filling. There are numerous Amish markets and specialty stores around the Bay that sell schnitz.

Serves 8

1 pound of schnitz (dried apples)

Zest of 1 orange, chopped finely

Juice of 1 orange

Pastry Dough for a Double Pie Crust (*page 216*) or prepared pie crust

2 cups sugar

2 tablespoons cinnamon

2 tablespoons softened butter

Place the apples in a saucepan with just enough water to cover them, and allow to soak overnight. The next day, add the orange zest, orange juice and, if necessary, a little more water to barely cover the apples. Cook over medium heat until the apples are soft, about 15 to 20 minutes. Push the softened apple mixture through a colander into a mixing bowl. Drain excess liquid from apple mixture. Add the sugar and cinnamon and mix well.

Preheat oven to 425°F.

Pour apple mixture into pastry shell and dot with pieces of the softened butter. Cover with the top crust or make lattice strips if you like. Bake in hot oven for 10 minutes. Reduce the heat to 350°F and continue baking for 30 minutes. Allow the pie to sit for at least 1 hour before serving. Serve as you would normally serve an apple pie, with either lightly sweetened whipped cream or vanilla ice cream.

Thomas Jefferson

Thomas Jefferson once wrote, "I have lived temperately, eating little animal food, and that, not as an aliment so much as a condiment for the vegetables, which constitute my principal diet." He was not only our third president but also a very serious gentleman farmer. He is respected as one of America's early agronomists, for he understood and insisted upon the importance of many good land practices that were being disregarded in his day. He cultivated 170 varieties of fruits and 330 different kinds of vegetables, including 40 types of beans, 2 dozen kinds of English peas, and 17 types of lettuce. Integrated farming systems, with good animal husbandry included, were imperative to Jefferson. He kept detailed farm journals on his Virginia estate, Monticello, where he held fast to a seven-year plan for rotating his crops:

1. Wheat, followed the same year by turnips, to be fed to the sheep.

2. Corn and potatoes mixed, and in autumn the vetch to be used as fodder in the spring if wanted, or to be turned in as a dressing.

3. Peas or potatoes, or both according to the quality of the fields.

4. Rye and clover sown on it in the spring. Wheat may be substituted here for rye.

5. Clover.

6. Clover, and in autumn turn it in and sow the vetch.

7. Turn in the vetch in the spring, then sow buckwheat and turn that in, having hurled off the poorest spots for cowpenning (so these spots could be improved by the manure).

While he was serving as secretary of state in 1793, Jefferson received a letter from his daughter Martha, complaining about the insect damage to the gardens in Monticello that year. He responded: "We will try this winter to cover our garden with a heavy coating of manure. When earth is rich it bids defiance to droughts, yields in abundance, and is of the best quality. I suspect that the insects which have harassed you have been encouraged by the feebleness of your plants; and that has been produced by the lean state of the soil."

I've been inspired by the wisdom of Jefferson's relationship with nature, the health of the soil, the importance of responsible growing, and his thoughts on diet. He felt that animal protein should be used as a condiment to vegetables. That food philosophy has been instrumental in the development of my thoughts on Bay- and body-friendly food and the vision for a twenty-first century Chesapeake kitchen. As the Desert Fathers and Mothers (early ascetics and hermits living in Egypt) have reminded us, to see our way to the future we must keep one foot rooted in the past.

Today the Thomas Jefferson Foundation engages a national and global audience in a dialogue with Jefferson's ideas. At www.monticelloshop.org you can even purchase seed packs of heirloom plants still cultivated there. Many are unusual and hard to find, like Purple Calabash Tomato seeds and Hyacinth Bean seeds.

Baltimore Peach Cake

This peach cake is the thing that memories are made from. Every Baltimore neighborhood bakery had its signature peach cake recipe, and customers were fiercely loyal to their favorites. My grandmom made a fine peach cake, but I could not find her recipe after she passed. After searching for many years, I came up with a version I think Grandma Gertie would be pleased with.

I futzed with an old recipe from the *Baltimore Sun* and here is the resulting butter-enriched dough that holds and envelops the ripe summer peaches. This recipe calls for an optional addition of food coloring to the glaze. This is a nod to the bakeries of yesteryear that added a bright red sheen to their peach cakes. For a natural non-chemical red color, add a pinch of beet root powder to the glaze.

Serves 8 to 10

3½ cups flour
½ cup sugar
1 teaspoon salt
2 packages dried yeast
6 tablespoons softened butter
1 cup warm water (120–130°F)
2 eggs

For the topping:
4–6 cups fresh, peeled, sliced peaches
½ cup sugar
1 teaspoon cinnamon
1 cup apricot jam
2 drops red food coloring (optional)

In a large mixing bowl, thoroughly mix 1 cup flour, sugar, salt, and the undissolved yeast. Beat in the butter and slowly add the very warm water. You can mix this dough in a mixer using a dough hook, but I prefer to mix the dough in a bowl with a sturdy wooden spoon for about 5 minutes. Add the eggs and 1 cup flour, just enough to make a thick, but not stiff, batter. Vigorously stir the dough batter for another 5 minutes while gradually adding the remaining flour.

Spread the batter into a greased 13 x 9 x 2 inch baking pan. Arrange the peaches evenly on top of the batter. Sprinkle with the combined cinnamon and sugar. Cover the pan with a tea towel and let rise for about 1 hour or until doubled in bulk.

Preheat oven to 375°F.

After the dough has completed its rise, bake for about 25 to 35 minutes or until done.

Remove the pan from the oven and let sit for about 15 minutes. Warm the apricot jam over low heat and add the food coloring (if using). Gently brush the glaze on the warm peaches.

Cornmeal Peach Shortcake with Fluffy Cornmeal Pecan Topping

Just imagine—slices of ripe peaches, lightly sweetened and tucked into a dish by a mound of shortcake batter. The peaches release their juices upon baking and seep into the shortcake crust. Sounds heavenly. The slight grittiness of the cornmeal gives great texture to the cakes, especially as it is dotted with small pieces of candied pecans. A dollop of sweetened whipped cream is all that's needed as an accompaniment.

Serves 8 to 10

6 cups peaches, pitted and sliced

¼ cup sugar

¼ cup packed light brown sugar

½ teaspoon cinnamon

Pinch of salt

2 tablespoons butter, cut in small pieces

Fluffy Cornmeal Pecan Biscuit Dough
(*recipe follows*)

Preheat the oven to 450°F.

Toss the peaches in a large bowl with the sugar, brown sugar, cinnamon, and salt. Pour peach mixture into a 9-inch deep-dish pie pan or a square baking dish. Dot the top with the butter. Spread the biscuit dough rounds over the top—the covering doesn't have to be neat, and all the fruit doesn't have to be covered.

Bake until the pastry is nicely browned and the fruit filling is bubbling, 20 to 25 minutes. Remove from the oven to cool on a rack.

FLUFFY CORNMEAL PECAN BISCUIT DOUGH

2   cups all-purpose flour, or more as needed

1   cup fine-ground white or yellow cornmeal

4   teaspoons baking powder

1   teaspoon salt

1   teaspoon sugar

¼   teaspoon cream of tartar

¼   cup vegetable shortening

4   tablespoons (½ stick) butter, cut into small pieces

½   cup milk

1   cup candied pecan pieces (see note)

Into a mixing bowl, sift together the flour, cornmeal, baking powder, salt, sugar, and cream of tartar. Cut in the shortening and butter with a fork, pastry blender, or your fingers until the mixture resembles coarse meal. Add the milk, stirring until a stiff batter forms. Fold in the candied pecan pieces. If the batter is too sticky, add a little more flour.

Form the dough into a ball, wrap in plastic, and chill the dough for at least 30 minutes. When ready to use, unwrap and roll out on a lightly floured surface to about ½-inch thick. Cut into rounds.

Note: To candy the pecans, melt 1 cup of sugar in a heavy-bottomed saucepan over high heat, stirring with a wooden spoon. When the sugar starts to darken, lower the heat and cook, stirring, until the sugar becomes a light caramel color. Add 1 cup of pecan pieces and stir to coat thoroughly, cooking for another 30 seconds. Spread the mixture onto an oiled baking sheet and set aside to cool and harden. When the mixture is cool, break it into small bits. You can use a food processor to do this, but don't over-process; you want small chunks, not crumbs or dust.

Peach Upside-Down Cake

Where do chefs get their ideas? Some come from cooking schools or grandmothers, or from reading magazines or cookbooks, or from watching cooking shows on TV. This cake is inspired by a recipe in *Cook's Illustrated* for a pineapple upside-down cake. Our chef at Gertrude's, Doug Wetzel, adapted it for peaches, with great results. Make sure the peaches are small—if they are not, use only two.

Serves 8 to 10

4 tablespoons unsalted butter, plus extra for greasing pan

¾ cup packed brown sugar

3 small-to-medium ripe peaches, pitted and sliced

1½ cups all-purpose flour

1½ teaspoons baking powder

4 tablespoons cornmeal

⅓ teaspoon salt

1 stick unsalted butter, softened

1 cup sugar

4 large eggs, separated

2 teaspoons vanilla extract

⅔ cup milk

Preheat the oven to 350°F.

Butter a 9-inch round cake pan.

In a medium saucepan, melt the 4 tablespoons of butter over medium heat. Add the brown sugar and cook until mixture is foamy and pale, about 3 minutes, stirring occasionally. Pour into the prepared cake pan and make sure to coat bottom of pan completely with the mixture. Arrange the sliced peaches over the topping and set aside.

In a mixing bowl, combine the flour, baking powder, cornmeal, and salt. Mix well. In the bowl of an electric mixer, cream the butter with the paddle attachment. Then slowly add the sugar, a little at a time, and beat for about 3 minutes or until the mixture is light and fluffy. Beat in the yolks and vanilla. Add the dry mixture and milk alternately in batches, beginning and ending with the dry ingredients, until the batter is smooth.

In a separate bowl, beat the egg whites until stiff peaks are formed. Fold half of the egg whites into the batter until well combined. Fold the remaining egg whites into the batter just until no white streaks remain. Pour the batter evenly into the cake pan. Bake for about 55 to 60 minutes or until the top is golden brown and a toothpick inserted in the center comes out clean.

Remove cake from oven and let set for 15 minutes. Run a knife around the edge of the cake to loosen it from the pan. Place a serving platter face down on top of cake pan and, while holding tightly, flip/invert the cake onto the plate.

Strawberry Rhubarb Shortcake

Just like there's bread and butter, around these parts, we have strawberries and rhubarb. A good pie is nice, but I really like this shortcake rendition, which is not only delicious but makes a beautiful presentation. Check out the shortcake, as it is a little different from the classic. As you may notice, it has no butter. The creamy richness of the shortcake comes from the coconut milk. I read about this technique in my new favorite cookbook, *Thug Kitchen,* and was a little dubious, but it really works. I've adapted it for use here.

Serves 8

1	pound rhubarb, lightly peeled and cut into 1-inch pieces
½	cup sugar
¼	cup water
2	quarts strawberries, hulled and sliced
2	tablespoons sugar
2	cups heavy whipping cream, very cold
1	teaspoon vanilla extract
3	tablespoons powdered sugar

Shortcake Biscuits (*recipe follows*)

Combine the rhubarb with the sugar and ¼ cup water in a medium-size pot. Bring to a simmer over medium heat and continue to cook, stirring, until the rhubarb cooks down into a thick purée, about 18 to 20 minutes. Cool completely, and then fold in half of the strawberries. Stir the 2 tablespoons of sugar into the remaining berries and chill slightly.

In a chilled mixing bowl, combine the whipping cream, vanilla, and powdered sugar. Whisk vigorously until soft peaks are formed. An electric mixer can be used for whipping the cream.

Cut the shortcake biscuits in half and place a large dollop of the strawberry-rhubarb mixture on the bottom half of the biscuit. Top generously with whipped cream and sliced strawberries.

Replace the top of the biscuit and garnish with more whipped cream and strawberries. Repeat for each serving. Or if it's a casual party, you can put the strawberry-rhubarb mixture, sliced strawberries, and whipped cream in separate bowls and let the guests make their own.

SHORTCAKE BISCUITS

1¼ cups whole wheat pastry flour

1 cup white flour

1 tablespoon baking powder

2 tablespoons sugar

½ teaspoon salt

1 cup canned coconut milk

½ teaspoon vanilla extract

Preheat oven to 425°F.

Sift together the flours, baking powder, sugar, and salt into a mixing bowl. Make a well in the middle and stir in the coconut milk and vanilla extract. Stir together until everything is combined into a shaggy-looking dough. If you need more liquid, add a tablespoon or two more of coconut milk.

Turn the dough out onto a floured board and pat it into a rectangle about 1½ inches thick. Using a biscuit cutter, cut out all the biscuits possible, with 8 being the desired number. Place the biscuits on a baking sheet and bake for about 12 to 15 minutes or until nicely browned. Place on a wire rack and allow to cool before using.

Gateaux Mont Saint Michel—Julia Child's Apple Crepe Cake

Who doesn't love Julia Child? I learned many of my cooking skills and techniques from her as a young chef, carefully studying her well-researched cookbooks and eagerly awaiting each new episode of her cooking shows. I am an apple pie fan—like big time—and here is the ultimate apple pie.

I know, it says "gateaux," but you try this recipe and tell me it isn't the best apple pie you've ever had! The name comes from an island off the coast of Normandy in France, Mont St. Michel. The centerpiece of the tiny island is an abbey and monastery that sit atop the "mound" of the island. This gateaux, when baked in a bowl-shaped vessel and inverted after baking, is said to resemble the island.

You may, if you like, haul out your favorite Julia cookbook and make your own crepes, but actually there are many fine prepared crepes available in the frozen food section of most grocery stores. So whatever you decide is good with me, but do try this dish.

Serves 8 to 10

12 tart apples, peeled, cored, and sliced

Juice of 1 lemon

½ cup sugar

½ cup melted butter

1⅓ cups blanched almonds, toasted until medium-brown (not burnt)

⅔ cup sugar

2 eggs, beaten

½ teaspoon vanilla extract

1 teaspoon almond extract

8 tablespoons (1 stick) butter, at room temperature

1 tablespoon dark rum

Pinch of salt

Prepared crepes

Preheat the oven to 425°F.

Toss the apples, lemon juice, sugar, and melted butter together in a bowl. Place into a buttered baking dish and bake for about 30 minutes or until the apples have softened somewhat. Remove from oven and set aside.

Place the almonds into the bowl of a food processor and pulse to chop fairly fine. Add the sugar, eggs, extracts, butter, rum, and a pinch of salt. Process to a smooth paste consistency. Scrape the almond mixture out of the processor with a rubber spatula and transfer to a bowl.

To assemble the gateaux, butter a glass pie plate or a wide, ovenproof glass bowl. Place a crepe on the bottom, and spread a layer of the almond cream on the crepe. Top with a layer of apples. Repeat the layering until all the crepes, apples, and almond cream are used and you have a crepe on top. Refrigerate for about 20 minutes before baking.

Preheat the oven to 375°F.

Bake for 30 minutes or until nicely browned and bubbling. Let sit for at least 20 minutes before serving. Cut into wedges and serve warm or cold, with plenty of lightly sweetened whipped cream. For a more impressive serving, the gateaux may be inverted onto a platter or large cake plate and presented at the table, where it may be cut into servings.

Firefly Farms Goat Cheese Cheesecake

This cheesecake was developed by cheese maker–chef Pablo Solanet of FireFly Farms. When we first served this dessert at our restaurant, people were taken aback that we would put goat cheese in a cheesecake. One bite, and they were sold. The goat cheese imparts the slightest tang to the cheesecake and provides a smooth, silky texture. The idea of adding walnuts to the graham crackers for the crust was brilliant. I've substituted black walnuts from time to time in the crust with great success.

Makes 12 to 16 servings

2¼ cups graham cracker crumbs

½ cup finely chopped English walnuts

½ cup melted butter

3 (8-ounce) packages cream cheese, at room temperature

8 ounces chevre goat cheese, at room temperature

1½ cups sugar

1 cup sour cream

3 eggs

1 tablespoon cornstarch

¼ cup heavy cream

1 teaspoon vanilla

Topping (*recipe follows*)

Preheat the oven to 350°F.

In a mixing bowl, combine 2 cups of the graham cracker crumbs, walnuts, and butter. Press the mixture into the bottom and slightly up the sides of a 10-inch springform pan. Refrigerate.

In a food processor or mixer, combine the cream cheese, goat cheese, sugar, and sour cream and mix until smooth. Add the eggs, one at a time, until incorporated.

Dissolve the cornstarch in the cream and add to the cream cheese mixture. Fold in the vanilla. Pour the filling into the springform pan and bake for 1 hour or until the cake has set. Remove the pan from the oven and spread the topping evenly over the top. Return cake to the oven and continue baking for 15 minutes.

Remove from the oven and run a knife around the edge of the pan to prevent the cake from cracking. Place on a wire rack to cool. After the cake has cooled a bit, sprinkle the remaining ¼ cup of graham cracker crumbs on top. Allow to cool completely before serving.

TOPPING

¼ cup sour cream

¼ cup softened goat cheese

3 tablespoons honey

½ cup jarred caramel sauce

½ cup coarsely chopped English walnuts

Combine all ingredients and mix until smooth.

Peach and Cherry Enchiladas

Wow, what summertime fun we have going on here. Peaches and cherries are generally both in good supply at the summer farmers' markets, and they pair up beautifully in this Hispanic-themed, crepe-like dessert.

Serves 3 to 6

4 tablespoons white sugar

1 teaspoon cinnamon

3 cups sliced or diced peaches

2 cups pitted cherries, quartered

6 (8-inch) flour tortillas

½ cup softened butter

½ cup honey

½ cup brown sugar

¼ cup dark rum

¼ cup heavy cream

Whipped cream or ice cream for topping

Preheat the oven to 350°F.

Mix together the white sugar and cinnamon. Place the peaches and cherries in a bowl and toss with the sugar-cinnamon mixture.

Place a tortilla on a plate and spoon one-sixth of the fruit along the middle. Roll up the tortilla and place, seam side down, in a lightly buttered baking dish. Repeat for the other five tortillas.

In a small pot, combine the softened butter, honey, brown sugar, rum, and heavy cream and bring to a boil, whisking constantly. Reduce heat and, stirring frequently, continue cooking for 3 minutes.

Pour sauce evenly over the tortillas. Cover the baking dish with aluminum foil and bake for 15 minutes. Remove foil from baking dish and bake another 5 minutes.

Serve enchiladas warm, topped with ice cream or lightly whipped cream.

Old Bay Peanut Brittle

I love my Old Bay seasoning. Of course, I was (along with everyone else in the Chesapeake Bay region) raised on it. I also enjoy putting together sweet and slightly hot, spicy tastes. And that combination makes a truly enjoyable savory brittle.

This is the master recipe, but feel free to play around a little. For instance, you could turn it into a pecan or hazelnut brittle or alter the amount of "heat" by adjusting the cayenne and Old Bay. Take care when stirring, pouring, and stretching the brittle. We are talking about a hot molten liquid. I don't normally make a lot of candy, but it really feels satisfying when you've made a batch of this brittle and are able to hand out small tins of it as gifts.

Makes about 3 pounds

Vegetable oil, for greasing cookie sheets
1   tablespoon Old Bay seasoning
½   teaspoon cayenne pepper
1   teaspoon baking soda
1   teaspoon vanilla
3   cups sugar
1¼ cups white corn syrup
1   cup water
2   tablespoons butter
4   cups shelled and peeled roasted peanuts

Generously oil three cookie sheets. Mix the Old Bay, cayenne, baking soda, and vanilla together in a small container. Set aside.

Place the sugar, corn syrup, water, and butter into a heavy-bottomed saucepan and bring to a boil. Continue cooking over high heat, brushing down any crystals that may form on the side of the pan with a pastry brush moistened with water, until the syrup reaches hard crack stage (300–310°F) on a candy thermometer.

Remove from heat and add the peanuts. Return the saucepan to the heat and bring back to a full boil. Remove from heat again and carefully (it may foam up a little) stir in the Old Bay mixture.

Working quickly, pour a third of the peanut mixture onto each of the well-oiled cookie sheets. Spread it out with a greased spatula, making sure the peanuts are distributed evenly.

When the brittle is beginning to cool and congeal but is still very hot, put on a pair of clean garden gloves. Lightly grease the fingers and palms of the gloves, grasp the brittle, and turn it over. Allow to cool slightly, and then grasp the sides of the brittle and gently stretch it until it is very thin between the nuts. When the brittle is completely cool, break it into pieces.

I store my brittle in small tins lined with wax paper and covered with a tight-fitting lid. It may also be stored in plastic bags, but make sure you store it in a dry place.

11

PUTTIN' IT UP

As we envision our new Chesapeake kitchen, we once again look to the past to see our way to the future. This is especially true when looking at the age-old traditions of preserving food. Growing seasons are what they are. Humans learned quickly that there would be periods of scarcity and that preserving, or "putting up," was the solution. Even though we live in a world of international food sourcing, with products coming to us from around the globe, we are also realizing the finite extent of this industrialized food system. Bottom line—it just ain't sustainable. It's not good for the land, for the quality of the water and air, and most importantly, for the health of our bodies.

We're talking about rebuilding our local food economy here in the Chesapeake, rebuilding it so that it can sustain and feed all the residents around the Bay. It's a big challenge, but as you may have gathered from some of the writings in this book, it's happening. And so if we're growing it, we need to preserve it as well. Okay, it's time to haul out our pressure cookers and canners and get started.

I watched my grandmother Gertie put up her vegetables when I was young, but I still have much to learn and am experimenting as I go. It's fun and exciting. But I thought it best to bring in an expert for us to learn about the many preservation techniques for our local foods. So I'd like to introduce you to my very good friend and colleague, Bonnie North. She has been involved in the local Chesapeake food movement since the early days and was the leader of the Slow Food Baltimore organization, as well as the editor and publisher of *Baltimore Eats* magazine. She has conducted numerous sold-out classes on canning and preserving. Let's sit back here and take a listen as Bonnie walks us through the ins and outs of preserving food.

PUTTIN' IT UP, BY BONNIE NORTH

What does that mean? It means using a method for preserving a seasonal overabundance of food-stuffs so they can be stored for eating during leaner times. Humans, all over the world, have been puttin' it up since long before recorded history. Archaeological evidence shows that in the Middle East, people used the hot sun to dry foods as early as 12,000 BC. Later cultures on every continent left more evidence; their methods for preserving food reflect their climates and the types of food supplies they stored.

Today we don't tend to think much about long-term storage of food, what with our refrigerators in the kitchen and nearby grocery stores restocked daily. But it must be said that there's something tremendously satisfying about doing your own food preserving, from simply making up your very own jams to give as special, and especially thoughtful, gifts to hauling out the pressure canner and doing up quarts of fresh tomatoes to be savored come winter. Convenient or not, there's nothing you'll find in the grocery store that will compare with summer's home-preserved tomatoes for making your winter soups and sauces!

There are many ways to preserve a summer's bounty, and we'll explore several of them here. They really aren't difficult, either. Since we're talking about the *process*, we'll be focused on that, and as far as actual recipes go—well, take some inspiration from the recipes here, then use what you have on hand, coupled with your own good taste and imagination!

DRYING/DEHYDRATION

Drying, or dehydration, is one of the oldest and probably very simplest ways to preserve foods. It's the method used to make meat jerkies, fruit leathers, dried vegetables, teas, and culinary herbs. Microorganisms require moisture to grow, so removing the water from food is a very effective method of preservation.

The key to dehydration is to complete the process faster than the food can spoil. To do that, you want to promote evaporation by providing some heat (but not enough to cook the food) and air circulation. Starting out by attempting your own beef jerky might not be advisable, but you can certainly try your hand at drying some herbs or fruits. Dried fruits have a sweetness and a chewiness that are hard to beat, and harvesting the last of a little herb patch out back, before frost hits it, will give you some super-tasting (and cost-free) herbs for your winter's kitchen.

You can invest in an electric food dehydrator, like the Excalibur, which comes with a timer and nine trays for really loading it up. But sun drying requires very little in the way of equipment—just a table or shelves that can be set up outside in a sunny spot, some cookie sheets, aluminum foil, or butcher paper on which to dry the edibles, and a protective netting (cheesecloth, for instance) to keep insects off the food.

Your food should be *clean* and *ripe*. Juicy fruits, such as tomatoes or peaches, should be cut up before they're dehydrated. The chunks of food must be arranged so that air can circulate freely among them. If you crowd the pieces together, mold can quickly ruin the entire batch.

Drying herbs is easy. All you do is cut near the base of the stem, tie the plants upside down in bundles, and hang them in a warm and dry place (such as the attic) for a week or so. When the leaves are "crackling dry," crumble with your hands, put into freezer bags or jars, and store in a dark place. You can infuse them in hot water for teas or crumble them real fine and use for cooking.

FERMENTING

Fermenting is simply a form of *controlled* food spoilage. Certain microorganisms involved in the process produce desirable effects while inhibiting the growth of other, harmful organisms. The science of fermentation is known as zymology. The bacteria or yeast active in the fermentation process produce an acid environment where potentially harmful bacteria can't thrive. As a bonus, many fermented foods, such as kimchi and sauerkraut, can provide healthy additions to the natural flora of the human gastrointestinal tract. And as for beer and wine—well, as A. E. Housman famously said: "Malt does more than Milton can to justify God's ways to man." If you want to learn more about fermentation, I highly recommend *The Art of Fermentation* by Sandor Katz.

Cabbage is easily fermented, and here are a couple of my all-time favorite fermented cabbage dishes. In the first stage, the vegetable is soaked in a salty brine that kills off harmful bacteria. In the second stage, the remaining *Lactobacillus* bacteria (the good guys!) convert the plant's sugars into lactic acid, which preserves the vegetables and gives them that wonderful, tangy flavor.

Kimchi

Napa cabbage kimchi is a traditional Korean dish that opens the doors to your creativity. You don't need stoneware crocks or special jars to make it—just good cabbage, some fresh vegetables and spices, and your personally preferred taste profile. Though there are countless varieties of kimchi, the most common is made with fermented napa cabbage flavored with chilies, scallions, and plenty of garlic.

You can make vegan kimchi or you can add fish or shrimp. You can make it fiery, with lots of red pepper powder, or not; you can make it crunchy, with slivered carrots perhaps, or not; you can make it sweet, pungent, or garlicky. Rely on your own sense of smell and taste and you'll end up with a fine batch. Just bear in mind that too much garlic can make the kimchi bitter, and too much ginger can make it sticky.

Here's a simple vegan kimchi that I enjoy.

Makes about 1½ quarts

1 large head napa cabbage, cored and separated into individual leaves, about 1 pound total
1 small daikon radish (about 4 ounces)
8 scallions, greens roughly chopped, whites reserved separately
Kosher salt
8 cloves garlic
2-inch knob ginger root, peeled and chopped
⅓–½ cup Korean chili powder (kochukaru), depending on heat desired (*see note*)
2 tablespoons white or red miso paste
1 tablespoon sugar
1 cup water, or as needed

Place cabbage leaves, daikon, and scallion greens in a large bowl and sprinkle with 2 tablespoons kosher salt. Toss to combine, cover, and let sit at room temperature until cabbage is wilted, at least 1 hour and up to 12 hours. It should release about ¼ to ½ cup of liquid.

Meanwhile, combine scallion whites, garlic, ginger, chili powder, miso paste, and sugar in the bowl of a food processor or blender. Process until rough paste is formed—about 30 seconds—scraping down sides as necessary.

Once the cabbage is wilted, add the chili mixture and turn to coat evenly. Add water to the mixture. Taste liquid and add more salt as necessary (it should have the saltiness of seawater). Using a slotted utensil, pack kimchi into Mason jars, pressing down firmly to pack tightly and using a knife or chopstick to release any air bubbles trapped in the bottom or on the sides of the jar. Cover the kimchi with its liquid.

Seal the jars tightly and allow them to sit at cool room temperature for 24 hours, then transfer to the refrigerator. Some folks like their kimchi "new," but it will gather more tang if you let it sit for several days. When it tastes good to you—it's done. It will keep in the fridge for 3 to 4 weeks, getting more pungent as time goes by.

Note: Kochukaru is available in Asian grocery stores; a mixture of red pepper flakes and smoked paprika can be used in a pinch, but the flavor won't be as authentic.

Sauerkraut

Makes about 2 gallons

15 pounds fresh cabbage
9 tablespoons Kosher salt

Slice cabbage thin (about ¹⁄₁₆-inch to ⅛-inch thick—using a mandoline works best) and place in a large bowl. Sprinkle the salt over the sliced cabbage and toss well.

Take one-third of the salted cabbage and place it in a sturdy crock. Smash the cabbage with your fist or a wooden mallet until it becomes very juicy. Continue to add cabbage a third at a time, smashing well after each addition. You want to create an anaerobic environment, so the cabbage must ultimately be completely submerged underneath the brine of its juices for the lactic acid bacteria to proliferate.

Place a clean towel right on top of the cabbage, set a platter on top of that, and press it down with weights or something good and heavy—I've used a glass gallon jug filled with water as an effective weight.

Store at a cool room temperature and give it time—at least 2 weeks. Check every third day and skim off any foam that may have gathered on the top of your kraut. Wring out the towel, letting the liquid go back into the crock, and replace the towel with a clean one. Once the sauerkraut has developed the taste and crunch that you like, it's done. Store your kraut in the fridge.

Pickles are the hottest in healthy living now. They are being credited with everything from a top-notch intestinal tract full of good gut flora to improved mental health. Lactic acid fermentation is the technical process, but around these parts we just call it "pickling," be it cucumbers, beets, or other local veggies. One might figure that it would be an extremely complicated process to get all those health benefits, but not so much. Now, get your pickle juices flowing and here's the basic approach.

- When you pickle something, you are simply preserving it in vinegar. Always store pickled food in glass containers; vinegar will corrode metal.
- Prepare the jars: Wash wide-mouth pint jars, lids, and rings in warm soapy water and rinse well. Set aside to dry, or dry completely by hand.
- Prepare the vegetables: Wash and dry the vegetables. Peel carrots, trim the end of beans, etc. Cut vegetables into desired shapes and sizes.
- Add the flavorings: Divide the herbs, spices, or garlic you are using among the jars.
- Add the vegetables: Pack the vegetables into the jars, making sure there is a half-inch of space between the rim of the jar and the tops of the vegetables. Pack them in as tightly as you can without smashing.
- Make the pickling liquid: Combine the vinegar, water, salt, and sugar (if using) in a small saucepan over high heat. Bring to a boil, stirring to dissolve the salt and sugar. Pour the brine over the vegetables, filling each jar to within half an inch of the top. You might not use all the brine.
- Remove air bubbles: Run a knife around the inside wall of the jar a few times to remove all the air bubbles. Top off with more pickling brine if necessary.
- Seal the jars: Place the lids over the jars and screw on the rings until tight.
- Cool and refrigerate: Let the jars cool to room temperature. Store the pickles in the refrigerator. The pickles will improve with flavor as they age—try to wait at least 48 hours before cracking them open.
- Pickled food can be stored in the refrigerator for up to 2 months. If you process for 10 minutes by the hot water bath method (*see page 250*), they can be stored unopened at room temperature for a year or more.

All About Vinegar

Vinegar is a totally natural food that literally makes itself when any substance capable of fermentation encounters any aerobic bacteria while it is exposed to oxygen. Acetic acid will be formed, and that is the acid that we find in all vinegars.

The benefits of and uses for vinegar are pretty astounding, and it's been produced and used by various groups of people for over five thousand years! Residues of vinegar are found in some Egyptian urns that have been dated to 3000 BC. Written mention of vinegar as a preservative occurs in Chinese texts dated to 1200 BC, and Cleopatra is reported to have used apple cider vinegar to keep her complexion fine.

Vinegar inhibits the formation of bacteria, so it has long been used as a wound-cleansing and general sanitizing agent. Its acidity can dissolve mineral deposits from glass and demineralize your steam iron and coffee maker. The same properties make it great for preserving food such as pickles. It aids digestion, lowers blood sugar, lowers cholesterol, repairs the pH levels of the skin, and does nice things to your hair. A great way to keep drains clear and sweet smelling: pour a little baking soda in your sink drain, follow with a splash of white vinegar, and watch what happens!

Flavored and specialty vinegars do wondrous things in the culinary world as well. Here are some of my favorite culinary vinegars:

Apple cider vinegar—made from fermenting apples (the "must"). Amber-colored, with a very slight sweetness, apple cider vinegar is often used in salad dressings, where a little honey accompanies it.

Balsamic vinegar—a mellow, aromatic aged vinegar produced in the Modena and Reggio Emilia areas of Italy. Traditional balsamic vinegar is made from the must of white Trebbiano grapes. Aged for 12 to 25 years, it will be marked "tradizionale" or "DOC" to denote its "Protected Designation of Origin" status and is pretty expensive. A more everyday version, commercially called "aceto balsamico di Modena" (balsamic vinegar of Modena), is typically made with concentrated grape juice mixed with a strong vinegar, then colored and slightly sweetened with caramel and sugar.

Malt vinegar—also known as alegar, is made from malt ale that is allowed to turn to vinegar, and then aged. Light brown in color, malt vinegar is a favorite sprinkled over hot, fresh French fries.

Rice vinegar—popular in the cuisines of East and Southeast Asia, rice vinegar comes in "white" (actually light yellow), red, and black varieties. The mild white rice variety is the one most commonly used, and it is often sold sweetened or flavored with Asian spices.

Sherry vinegar—made from sherry, the best comes from the Jerez region of Spain. It's dark mahogany in color, is quite concentrated, has generous aromas, and is ideal for vinaigrettes and marinated foods.

Wine vinegar—both red and white wine vinegars have a slightly lower acidity than cider vinegars. Just as with wine itself, the quality varies considerably. Better-quality wine vinegars are usually aged in wooden casks for up to 2 years, imparting them with complex and mellow flavors.

Garlic Dill "New" Pickles

The "new" part of these pickles simply means that they are not fully cured, or "full dills." I really enjoy these "half sours," because they retain their beautiful green color and stay quite crispy and refreshing. As they are so quick and easy to prepare, you could always make a half batch of these at a time if you are not planning on using them quickly. You can just keep them in a large glass bowl in the fridge until they've all been devoured!

Makes about 4 quarts

2   cups white wine vinegar
6   cups water
⅓   cup pickling or kosher salt
10 cloves garlic
5   pounds pickling cucumbers, washed well
8   sprigs dill

Bring the vinegar, water, salt, and garlic to a boil. Place the cucumbers in a container and cover with the brine. Add the dill.

Cover with a towel and refrigerate. It will take several days to reach a crisp, "new" pickle stage.

Quick Pickled Radishes

Makes 2 cups

2   cups sliced radishes
1   small onion, cut into thin wedges and separated
½   cup seasoned rice vinegar
½   cup sugar
1½   teaspoons salt

Slice radishes by hand or use the slicing blade of a food processor. Place radish slices and onions in a large bowl or crock. In another bowl, stir together vinegar, sugar, and salt until sugar is dissolved. Pour over radish mixture.

Cover and refrigerate at least 8 hours or overnight before serving. Radish mixture will have a very pungent aroma.

Dilly Beans

Makes 7 pints

4   pounds fresh green beans, washed, with ends trimmed

For each pint jar:

1 or 2 sprigs of fresh dill

1   clove of garlic, or to taste

Pinch hot pepper

5   cups water

5 c ups vinegar

½   cup pickling salt

Place dill, garlic, and hot pepper in each pint jar, then pack jar with green beans (wide-mouth jars work best). Bring water, vinegar, and pickling salt to a boil and pour it over beans, filling to half an inch from top of jar.

Process for 15 minutes using the hot water bath canning method (*see page 250*).

Pear and Cucumber Pickles

Makes 1 quart

1   cup sugar

1   cup salt

1   cup white wine vinegar

1   cup apple cider vinegar

1   teaspoon crushed red chili pepper

2   tablespoons mustard seed

1   tablespoon peppercorns

1   tablespoon minced garlic

3   Asian pears, cored and cut into 1⅛-inch wedges

3   cucumbers, cut into ½-inch rounds

In a bowl, whisk together the sugar, salt, vinegars, chili pepper, mustard seeds, peppercorns, and garlic. Place the sliced pears and cucumbers in clean glass jars or a glass bowl, and pour the brining liquid on top. Cover and refrigerate. The taste comes together in about 3 to 6 hours. These will keep in the fridge for 2 to 3 weeks.

JELLIES, JAMS, PRESERVES, MARMALADES, AND CHUTNEYS

Preservation with the use of honey or sugar was well known to the earliest cultures. In ancient Greece, for instance, we know that the season's quince harvest was mixed with honey and packed tightly into jars for later consumption.

Jellies are made from just the juice of a fruit, with pectin, a kind of fiber naturally found in the cell walls and rinds of certain fruits, added. Pectin is commercially available in both powdered and liquid form. When heated with sugar in water, it gels, giving jelly its thickness. In marmalades, the rind of the fruit provides the pectin, so none needs to be added.

Jams and preserves get their thick structure from the actual flesh of the fruit. Jams use mashed-up fruit, while preserves use whole or large pieces of fruit. In a chutney, vinegar and sugar are often used together, so chutneys are not necessarily sweet. Chutney recipes often combine fruits, vegetables, and spices for a complex, nuanced flavor.

Always wash and remove the stems or cores, if any, of your fruit. Peel if necessary. For cherries and berries, of course, you don't need to peel, but skinned fruits, such as pears, apples, and peaches, will need peeling. Scorching is more likely to happen to jams and preserves, so to avoid that problem, take care and stir your mixture often.

Blackberry Jalapeño Jelly

Makes about four 1-cup jars

1.75-ounce package powdered pectin

½   cup white sugar

4   cups blackberry juice

1   green jalapeño pepper, minced

1   red jalapeño pepper, minced

3½ cups white sugar

Mix the pectin crystals with ½ cup sugar in a bowl. Stir the blackberry juice, pectin mixture, green jalapeño, and red jalapeño together in a saucepan; bring the mixture to a boil for 1 full minute.

Add the 3½ cups sugar and return to a rolling boil until the sugar has fully dissolved, about 1 minute. Remove from heat; stir while off the heat for about 5 minutes to remove bubbles and foam.

Ladle into jars, leaving ¼ inch of headspace. Process jars in a hot water bath for 10 minutes (*see page 250*).

Plum Preserves

Makes about 5 pints

5   cups plums, pitted and diced

4   cups sugar

1   cup water

Combine all ingredients in a large saucepot. Bring to a boil, stirring until sugar dissolves. Bring to a low boil and cook rapidly until the mixture thickens—about 20 to 30 minutes. Stir frequently toward the end of the cooking time so that the preserves do not stick to the bottom of your saucepot.

Ladle into jars, leaving ¼ inch of headspace. Process jars in a hot water bath for 15 minutes (*see page 250*).

Tangerine Vanilla Bean Marmalade

A creative addition to the ranks of citrus marmalades, this makes an especially charming gift if you spruce up the jar with a bow or a cloth cap.

Makes four 1-cup jars

2 pounds tangerines, peeled, each cut into 4 wedges
1 lemon, cut into 4 wedges
5 cups water
2 vanilla beans, split lengthwise and crosswise
3½ cups sugar

Cut tangerine and lemon wedges crosswise into ¼-inch-thick slices. Remove all seeds from the fruit. Slice tangerine rind into thin strips and set aside. Transfer fruit to a large bowl. Add 5 cups of water, covering fruit. Cover bowl with plastic wrap; let stand at room temperature for 1 day.

Transfer fruit mixture to large, heavy pot. Scrape seeds from vanilla beans, cut vanilla pods into 1-inch lengths, and add seeds and pods to fruit mixture. Add the strips of tangerine rind. Bring mixture to a low boil. Reduce heat and simmer until rind is very tender, stirring occasionally—about 1 hour 15 minutes.

Remove from heat. Add sugar; stir until sugar dissolves. Boil gently, stirring often, until mixture is 210°F, about 1 hour 20 minutes—your marmalade should be "gloppy" and cling to a spoon.

Scoop hot marmalade into four warmed 1-cup jars, being sure to get a roughly equal number of vanilla pods into each jar. Cover tightly. It will keep in the refrigerator up to 1 month.

Apple Fig Chutney

Makes about 1 pint

2 cups coarsely chopped Gala apples, peeled and cored
¼ cup dried figs, chopped
1 cup sugar
½ cup apple cider vinegar
¼ cup finely chopped slivered almonds
¼ cup raisins
1 teaspoon ground cinnamon
1 teaspoon ground fennel seed
½ teaspoon ground allspice
Zest of 1 orange
Juice of 1 orange

Add all the ingredients to a pan and bring to a boil. Reduce heat, and simmer on low for 35 minutes. Pack into jars and process according to hot water bath method for 20 minutes (*see page 250*).

Tomato and Fruit Chutney

Makes five 1-cup jars

4–5 plum tomatoes, peeled, cored, and diced
6 apricots, pitted and diced
½ cup dried peaches, diced
½ cup dried dates, chopped
1 cup apple cider vinegar
1 cup light brown sugar
1 teaspoon brown mustard seeds
½ teaspoon garam masala
½ teaspoon kosher salt
1 medium yellow onion, diced
1 small serrano chili, seeded and diced
2 cloves garlic, peeled and sliced

Combine all ingredients in a large bowl and toss to combine. Refrigerate overnight.

Pour mixture into a large saucepan; bring to a low boil, stirring constantly, then reduce the heat to medium-low. Cook until thickened, stirring occasionally, for about 45 minutes.

Fill jars, leaving about ½ inch of headspace, and process for 20 minutes according to hot water bath method (*see page 250*).

EZ Chunky Applesauce

Well . . . no, this isn't a jelly, a jam, a preserve, a marmalade, or even a chutney—but it's a great, super-easy, and delicious way to make use of all those apples!

Yields 6 cups

10–12 medium-sized tart apples, peeled, cored, and cut into pieces
1 cup apple cider
1 teaspoon ground cinnamon
¼ teaspoon freshly grated nutmeg
Juice of ½ lemon
Maple syrup, to taste

Place the apples in a heavy-bottomed pot. Add the cider, cinnamon, nutmeg, and lemon juice. Cover the pot and cook over medium heat until the apples are soft, about 20 to 25 minutes.

Remove lid, and season with maple syrup. Let simmer, uncovered, for about 10 minutes longer, stirring often so applesauce does not scorch. Remove applesauce from heat. Use within 1 week or process using the hot water bath method for 20 minutes (*see page 250*).

Ok—here's where we get serious about this! You may remember your mother's or grandmother's stories about "puttin' up" tomatoes or green beans every summer. Especially in rural communities, this was a yearly ritual, and women often gathered together to spend afternoons around a picnic table snapping the ends off green beans for hours, drinking sweet iced tea and enjoying the camaraderie. And come those dark chilly days, there was nothing to compare with the flavor of home-preserved foods, bringing the scents and tastes of summertime to the winter's table.

Now, home canning can be some work—but it's also fun and satisfying. Once you've canned your own summer tomatoes, you'll never again be quite satisfied using store-bought for your sauces and soups. Doing it properly and safely is important, though. A steam-pressure canner creates a lot of raw force and needs to be handled properly. Thankfully, modern steam-pressure canners are much safer and easier to use than the older versions our parents and grandparents managed with—I won't even mention stories I've heard about a dozen quarts of hot beans flying all over the kitchen!

THE BASICS

Understanding how to prevent food spoilage is the key to canning safety. Molds, yeasts, and bacteria are the major causes of food spoilage, and the most important factor in controlling these "spoilers" is controlling the environment that encourages their growth. The "processing" in canning destroys potentially harmful microorganisms and drives air from the jar. As the jars cool, a vacuum is formed and the lid seals tightly to the jar, preventing other microorganisms from entering and contaminating the food. That's how canning interrupts the natural decaying process—by heating the food to a specific temperature and holding it there for a specific period of time. The word "specific" is important here! Refer to reliable recipes or other good sources for instructions. The *Ball Complete Book of Home Preserving*, edited by Judi Kingry and Lauren Devine, is an *excellent* source and well worth the investment.

THE TWO METHODS

There are two methods of home canning: the hot water bath method and the steam-pressure canner method. The pH, or the natural acidity, of the food you are preserving determines which method must be used. The processing methods are not interchangeable. Foods naturally high in acid, such as tomatoes, sauerkraut, or pickles, are safe to process by the hot water bath method since the acidity of the food prevents the growth of hard-to-kill bacteria such as *Staphylococcus* or *Clostridium botulinum*.

However, *Staphylococcus* and *botulinum* can be dangerous in a low-acid environment. These bacteria cannot be destroyed by the hot water bath method, since temperatures above the boiling point of water must be reached and maintained. The steam-pressure canner is designed to seal so tightly that the water cannot all turn to steam and escape, and thus pressure builds and a higher temperature can be reached. A steam-pressure canner *must* be used to preserve low-acid foods safely.

Select the method of canning based on the acid level of the food being canned (*see the acidity chart*). The processing methods are NOT interchangeable. Also, the "headspace," the room left for the contents to expand inside the jar during heating, will vary, since some foods swell more than others and require additional headspace. Generally, leave 1 inch of headspace for low-acid foods, like meats or vegetables; ½ inch for acidic foods such as fruits and tomatoes; and ¼ inch for juices, jams, jellies, pickles, and relishes. Processing times also vary greatly depending upon the type of food being canned, the jar size you are using, and, in steam-pressure canning, even the altitude where you are working! Refer to each recipe for correct processing information regarding length of processing, pressure required, etc.

If all the steps to canning are followed properly, your food will be safely preserved and can be stored at room temperature almost indefinitely. Once you have cracked the seal and opened the jar, your food must be stored in the refrigerator.

Foods on the pH (Acidity–Alkalinity) Scale

Strong Acid

Lemons
Pickles
Apricots
Plums
Apples
Blueberries
Sour Cherries
Peaches
Sauerkraut
Sweet Cherries
Pears
Tomatoes

Process at 212°F
with Hot Water Bath Method

Okra
Carrots
Beets
Turnips
Green Beans
Spinach
Asparagus
Lima Beans
Peas
Corn

Process at 240°F
in a Steam-Pressure Canner

Strong Alkali

BASIC CANNING EQUIPMENT

Glass canning jars

Packing funnel

Clean sponge for cleaning jar rims

Jar lids—can only be used once

Magnetic lid lifter

Spatula or butter knife for removing
air bubbles from packed jars

Metal jar rings—will be removed after
processing and can be reused over and over

Steam-pressure canner for pressure canning, or
large canning pot with cover for hot water bath

Rack for elevating jars within the canner

Timer

Tongs for removing hot jars

Pot holders and towels

Jar opener

THE STEPS

- When you are ready to can, carefully remove any small diseased areas or bruised spots on your food. Discard moldy, insect-damaged, and over-ripe foods. Prepare food for loading into jars.

- Place lids in a pan of warm water and heat gently to soften the rubberized rim. Do not allow the water to boil, which could crack the rubber.

- Load jars using the funnel, leaving proper headspace for contents to expand during processing.

- Run a spatula or butter knife down the sides of each jar to tease out any air bubbles that may be inside.

- Wipe the rim of each jar carefully so there will be a clean and uninterrupted seal between the glass rim of the jar and the rubberized circle inside the lid.

- Lift each lid from the warm water without touching it by using the magnetized lid lifter and gently drop onto the rim of each jar without touching the rubberized circle inside the lid. If you touch the rubber rim of the lid, it may not properly seal while processing. Position lids well centered on the jars.

- Screw jar rings onto the jars. The ring should be fully screwed on but not overly tight. It's the rubberized lid that makes the seal as the jars cool and the product contracts. You may even hear a bunch of snapping sounds while they cool—that's the seal being made. You'll remove the ring to check the seal when the jars have fully cooled. Rings can be reused. Lids cannot; they won't seal a second time.

HOT WATER BATH METHOD

- Fill canning pot half full of warm water.

- Load jars into rack and lower rack into the water.

- Add additional hot water until the water level is at least 2 inches above jar tops.

- Cover canner.

- Bring to a hard rolling boil and adjust down to a soft rolling boil.

- Set timer for the number of minutes for processing.

- When timer sounds, turn off heat and allow to cool down for about 15 minutes before opening canner. Be certain to lift the canner lid toward you so that the steam moves away from your face. There will be steam coming out!

- Using tongs, remove the jars and set on a towel to finish cooling. Remove rings and check seals only when the jars are fully cooled. Do not replace the rings. If the rings are stored on the sealed jars, they can corrode and become difficult to remove. Rings can be kept for reuse, but the lids cannot.

STEAM-PRESSURE CANNER METHOD

These are the important parts of a steam-pressure canner:

Bottom base

Rack

Locking lid with rubber gasket

Pressure vent pipe

Pressure gauge

Pressure regulator cap

Safety valve, in case of over-heating or over-pressurizing

THE STEPS

- Check canner equipment, making certain all vents are cleared, rubber sealing gasket is secure, etc.

- Put rack in bottom of canner.

- Load filled jars onto rack and add water to reach a height of 3 inches around the sides of the jars.

- Lock canner lid firmly into place.

- Heat until steam begins to flow from the steam vent pipe.

- Allow steam to escape for a full 10 minutes.

- Place pressure regulator cap on steam vent.

- Allow pressure to build until the desired pressure is reached, and adjust heat to maintain pressure at that level.

- Set timer.

- When processing is complete, turn off the heat and allow canner to cool naturally. Do not remove the pressure regulator or open the canner until the canner has depressurized and returned to zero pressure.

- Remove pressure regulator and wait at least 2 minutes more before opening canner. Be certain to lift the canner lid toward you so that the steam moves away from your face.

- Allow jars to sit for 5 to 10 minutes in the canner to adjust to the lowering of temperature.

- Using the tongs, lift jars from canner and set on a towel to continue cooling. Remove rings and check seals when jars are completely cooled. Do not replace the rings. If the rings are stored on the sealed jars, they can corrode and become difficult to remove. Rings can be kept for reuse, but the lids cannot.

STORAGE

Before placing the cooled jars in your pantry, wipe off the lids and jars to clean off any food residue that may have escaped during the canning process. Label each jar with the date it was canned and the type of food preserved. Food that has been properly canned can last almost indefinitely, but chemical changes will occur over time. This can affect the color, flavor, texture, and nutritional value of the canned food, so labeling, dating, and using old stock first are important.

When opening the jars, check to be certain that the lids are still tightly sealed. You'll need the handy jar opener to crack the seal and open the jars. If the lid is easily removed, do not use the product.

Check for any disagreeable odors, mold, sliminess, gassiness, or fermentation. If a jar has become contaminated, discard the jar, lid, contents, and any cloths or sponges that may have come into contact with them immediately.

Canned foods are best stored at temperatures between 50°F and 70°F. Freezing can cause the contents to expand and break the glass.

Now, have fun!

CHEERS!

Cocktails made from locally crafted distilled spirits are what it's all about these days. They are actually not a new phenomenon here in the Chesapeake region. For over two hundred years (not counting Prohibition) there were hundreds of distilleries around the Bay. Maryland and Virginia's whiskeys were legendary and much sought after. As a result of Prohibition and then later through the purchase of smaller brands by large national brands, many distilleries and breweries were put out of business. But just as the tide has turned for local agriculture, so it has for the craft breweries, local wineries, and now regional distilleries.

Just a few of the names: Ironclad Distillery in Newport News, Virginia; Chesapeake Bay Distillery in Virginia Beach, Virginia; The Baltimore Whiskey Company; Lyon Distillery in Easton, Maryland; Sagamore Distillery in Baltimore, Maryland; and Catoctin Creek Distillery in Purcellville, Virginia, near Catoctin Mountain. And new operations are opening all the time.

We are fortunate to have so many award-winning, locally crafted beers and wines throughout the Chesapeake watershed. It seems only fair that the distilleries are now coming back into their own, so we locals may be able to enjoy our cocktails made from locally crafted hooch. Get out your cocktail shakers, and let's get the party started!

Jon Carroll is a man for all seasons. He is a master gardener, master chef of exquisite ramen pop-ups around Baltimore, and a whiz mixologist. For years he worked as bar manager at our restaurant, Gertrude's. He was our "mad scientist" of cocktail crafts. He had brews, potions, nectars, bitters, and infusions all percolating simultaneously throughout the restaurant. He is quite the genius crafter and lover of all things locally grown. Here's a small collection of some of his favorites and those of Gertrude's.

Saint Sangria

2 ounces Old Westminster carbonic-style Cabernet Franc red wine, or a pinot noir

1 ounce elderflower liqueur

Juice chips (*see note*)

Chilled sparkling wine (cava or similar)

Add red wine and liqueur to a cocktail shaker and stir. Pour into a chilled glass and add juice chips. Top with the sparkling wine.

Note: To make juice chips, take a little apple, orange, or cranberry juice and pour into an ice-cube tray about ¼- to ½-inch deep. Freeze.

Baltimore Shot Tower Gin Cucumber Cooler

6 mint leaves

¼ of a lime, sliced

2 teaspoons sugar, more or less to taste (optional)

1½ ounces Baltimore Shot Tower gin

5 thin cucumber slices

4 ounces tonic water

Sprig of mint for garnish

In a cocktail shaker, place the mint leaves, lime, and sugar and muddle together. Add the gin and cucumber slices. Put the top on the cocktail shaker and shake vigorously.

Pour into a glass filled with ice, and top with tonic water. Garnish with a sprig of mint.

Blackberry Patch

2 ounces blackberry-infused Lyon white rum (*see note*)

5 mint leaves

1 ounce lime juice

Ginger beer

Put 2 ounces of blackberry rum, mint leaves, and lime juice into a cocktail shaker. Put the top on the shaker, and shake well. Strain into a glass with ice. Top with ginger beer.

Note: To make your blackberry-infused rum, fill a 1-quart canning jar with fresh blackberries and add rum to cover. Allow to steep for 1 week, shaking the jar every day. After a week, strain through a coffee filter into a container and refrigerate until ready to use.

Bloody Maryland

Mix makes 6 tall cocktails

Mix together well:

36 ounces tomato juice

⅓ cup lemon juice

2 tablespoons pickle juice

2 tablespoons Worcestershire sauce

1 tablespoon celery salt

3 tablespoons grated horseradish

1 tablespoon black pepper

12 dashes Tabasco sauce

1 tablespoon Old Bay seasoning

For garnish:

Old Bay seasoning for rimming glasses

Celery sticks with leaves

Jumbo lump crab

Rim each tall glass with Old Bay seasoning and fill with ice. Pour in 2 ounces (about ¼ cup) vodka and fill with Bloody Maryland mixture. Stir well. Garnish each with a spear of fresh celery and a lump piece of crab.

Jon's Gin 'n Juice

1½ ounces Baltimore Shot Tower gin

2   ounces Concord grape syrup (*see note*)

Club soda

Lemon peel for garnish

Mix the gin and grape syrup in a cocktail shaker. Put the top on the shaker and shake well. Pour into a 10-ounce highball glass with ice and top with club soda. Garnish with a lemon peel.

Note: To make simple syrup, mix equal parts white sugar and water in a saucepan. Bring to a boil, stir, and simmer for 2 minutes. Allow to cool before using. To make grape syrup, mix 2 cups Concord grapes with 1 quart simple syrup in a saucepan. Stir and simmer for 10 minutes. Allow to cool and strain through a fine-mesh strainer.

Mimosa Flight

Flights are very popular now. They are small tastes of beer, whiskey, rum, or, as we have here, mimosas. Make at least three seasonal juices for a flight. Or, if you are crazy for one of them, fly solo!

1   part seasonal juice (*see note*)

3   parts dry Champagne or sparkling wine (cava)

Pour seasonal juice into champagne flute and add sparkling wine.

Note: A few examples of seasonal juices:

Persimmon—1 part persimmon purée and 1 part orange juice

Pawpaw—1 part pawpaw custard (flesh of the pawpaw fruit) and 1 part mango nectar

Mulled cider—2 ounces apple cider with 1 tablespoon mulling spice; simmer and strain

Rosemary Lemon Soda

Steep fresh rosemary leaves in simple syrup (*see note*) for several days, then strain. Then mix 3 parts rosemary syrup to 1 part lemon juice.

To serve: Mix 2 ounces prepared syrup to 8 ounces soda water over ice. Garnish with a sprig of rosemary.

Note: To make simple syrup, mix equal parts white sugar and water in a saucepan. Bring to a boil, stir, and simmer for 2 minutes. Allow to cool before using.

Southern Belle

1½ ounces Bourbon
¼ of a fresh peach
¾ ounce lemon juice
4 ounces sweet iced tea

In a cocktail shaker, muddle together the Bourbon and fresh peach. Add the lemon juice and tea, put the top on the shaker, and shake well. Strain into a rock glass filled with ice.

HEX FERMENTS COCKTAIL IDEAS

Here are some fabulous cocktail ideas from Baltimore's own HEX Ferments. What better than getting a dose of healing probiotics in your cocktail glass? Sounds like a win-win to me. The folks at HEX suggest it's best to use local distilleries such as Lyon Distilling, Blackwater Distilling, Baltimore Whiskey Company, or Sagamore Spirit, whenever possible.

Easy Breezey

4 parts HEX Butterfly Lime kombucha

1 part clear white spirits, such as vodka, gin, or white rum

3 thin, round slices of fresh lime

Lay 3 lime slices in bottom of tumbler-sized glass, and add crushed ice to fill. Pour spirits over ice. Add HEX Butterfly Lime kombucha to the top and stir. *Toast to our microbiomes!*

Pom-Ade (courtesy of Rocket to Venus restaurant)

1 part River Rose gin

1 part lemonade

½ part Cartron pomegranate liqueur

3 parts HEX ginger kombucha

Lemon (or lime) wedge as garnish

Add ice to fill glass. Layer in gin, lemonade, pomegranate, then HEX kombucha. Present in layers with citrus as garnish, but stir before consuming. *Toast to our healthy drinking!*

Cocobucha

1   part white rum

1   part coconut water

4   parts HEX Turmeric Tonic kombucha

Lime wedge as garnish

Pour all ingredients over ice and stir. Add lime garnish. Drink—yum. *Toast to feeling good about enriching our inner ecosystems!*

HEX Rum Manhattan

2   parts aged rum (or whiskey)

1   part sweet vermouth

½   part maple syrup

2   parts HEX ginger kombucha

Cherry as garnish

Stir rum/whiskey, vermouth, and maple syrup together to blend. Shake over ice, strain into glass, and top with HEX ginger kombucha and a cherry. *You make a toast!*

KEY LOCAL RESOURCES

Maryland's Best

Here you'll find just about everything you need to get on board with eating local and supporting our local food economy. The searchable website includes links to each of Maryland's farmers' markets and pick-your-own farms as well as recipes, nutrition information, and "Maryland's Best" seafood. http://marylandsbest.net

Maryland Department of Agriculture

http://mda.maryland.gov

Virginia Is for Lovers

This state slogan webpage includes a complete list of Virginia's farmers' markets. www.virginia.org/farmersmarkets/

Virginia Department of Agriculture and Consumer Services

www.vdacs.virginia.gov

Chesapeake Bay Program

The Chesapeake Bay Program is renowned as a regional, national, and international leader in ecosystem science, modeling, and restoration partnerships. You could spend all day exploring their gorgeous website, especially the Discover the Chesapeake section that has everything from a comprehensive field guide to the thousands of species of plants and animals that call the Chesapeake region home to a fascinating History of the Bay, beginning thirty-five million years ago in the Eocene. www.chesapeakebay.net

Bay Journal

The Bay Journal is published by Bay Journal Media, a 501(c)(3) nonprofit, to inform the public about issues and events that affect the Chesapeake Bay. www.bayjournal.org

Chesapeake Bay Foundation

The Chesapeake Bay Foundation has offices, restoration facilities, and education centers throughout Maryland, Pennsylvania, Virginia, and Washington, DC. Current work is focused on ensuring that these key watershed states meet their 2025 Bay cleanup goals under the Chesapeake Clean Water Blueprint. www.cbf.org

Chesapeake Bay Trust

The mission of the Chesapeake Bay Trust is to promote public awareness and participation in the restoration and protection of the water quality and aquatic and land resources of the Chesapeake Bay region and other aquatic and land resources of the state. www.cbtrust.org

Citizens for a Better Eastern Shore

Dedicated to promoting balanced growth, enhancing the quality of life of all our citizens, and preserving our cultural and natural resources, while promoting open government and citizen engagement. www.cbes.org

Future Harvest

Future Harvest CASA's (Chesapeake Alliance for Sustainable Agriculture) mission is to provide education, networking, and advocacy to help build a sustainable Chesapeake foodshed. www.futureharvestcasa.org

Parks and People Foundation

Dedicated to developing and reviving green spaces throughout the city. Working with the Community Law Center, Parks and People has increased access to abandoned lots within the city. parksandpeople.org

Civic Works Real Food Farm

An innovative urban agricultural enterprise engaged in growing fresh produce on 8 acres in and around Clifton Park in northeast Baltimore. realfoodfarm.civicworks.com

Power in Dirt

A Baltimore City initiative, this organization assists people in adopting and revitalizing vacant lots. powerindirt.com

Farm Alliance of Baltimore

A network of producers working to increase the viability of urban farming and improve access to urban-grown foods. farmalliancebaltimore.org

DC Department of Parks and Recreation Urban Garden Division

Works with communities across the District of Columbia to establish outdoor gardens. dpr.dc.gov/page/urban-garden-education-program

The K Street Farm

This ¾-acre demonstration farm in downtown Washington, DC, is used to educate community members about food access issues in their city. The farm is home to 5,000 square feet of growing space, honeybee hives, egg-laying chickens, a variety of fruit trees, and many perennial herbs and flowers. dcgreens.org/k-st-farm

City Blossoms

Dedicated to fostering healthy communities by developing creative, kid-driven green spaces in Washington, DC. cityblossoms.org

SUGGESTED READING

Wendell Berry, *Bringing It to the Table: On Farming and Food.* Counterpoint, 2009.

Terence J. Centner, *Empty Pastures: Confined Animals and the Transformation of the Rural Landscape.* University of Illinois Press, 2004.

Janet Chadwick, *The Beginner's Guide to Preserving Food at Home.* Storey Publishing, 2009.

Wenonah Hauter, *Foodopoly: The Battle Over the Future of Food and Farming in America.* New Press, 2014.

Michael Pollan, *Food Rules: An Eater's Manual.* Penguin, 2011.

Michael Pollan, *In Defense of Food: An Eater's Manifesto.* Penguin, 2008.

Michael Pollan, "Naturally." *New York Times Magazine,* May 13, 2001.

Michael Pollan, *The Omnivore's Dilemma: A Natural History of Four Meals.* Penguin, 2007.

John Robbins, *The Food Revolution: How Your Diet Can Help Save Your Life and Our World,* with foreword by Dean Ornish. Conari, 2010.

Gene Stone, *Forks Over Knives: The Plant-Based Way to Health,* with foreword by T. Colin Campbell and Caldwell B. Esselstyn. Experiment, 2011.

Stone Barns Center for Food and Agriculture, Martha Hodgkins, editor, *Letters to a Young Farmer: On Food, Farming, and Our Future.* Princeton Architectural, 2017.

Eunice Wong with Kip Andersen and Keegan Kuhn, *What the Health.* Xlibris, 2017.

INDEX

Agriculture, US Department of, 28
Allen, Standish K., 48
almond milk
    in Apple and Raisin Cornmeal
        Mush, 21
    in "Buttermilk" Buckwheat
        Pancakes with Mixed Berry
        Compote, 25–26
    in Health-Defining Green
        Smoothies, 32–33
    in Rhubarb Muffins, 209
almonds
    in Gateaux Mont Saint Michel—
        Julia Child's Apple Crepe Cake,
        227–28
    in Schillinger Farm Watermelon
        Gazpacho, 85
animal husbandry, 106
Annville Mill, 144
apple cider vinegar, 239
apples, 248
    Apple and Mango Chutney
        Cobbler, 214
    Apple and Raisin Cornmeal Mush,
        21
    Apple Fig Chutney, 52, 244
    Apple Rhubarb Pandowdy, 215–16
    Black Rock Orchard Slab Pie,
        216–17
    Champagne Cabbage and Apples,
        113
    Gateaux Mont Saint Michel—Julia
        Child's Apple Crepe Cake,
        227–28
    Herring, Apple, and Red Onion
        Salad, 158
    Sauerkraut and Apple Salad, 165
    Schnitz Pie, 218
    Watercress and Fresh Ricotta Salad

with Apples, Walnuts, and Cider
        Vinaigrette, 166–68
applesauce
    EZ Chunky Applesauce, 245
apricots, 248
    Tomato and Fruit Chutney, 245
aquaculture, 3, 8, 48–49, 64
Arcadia Center for Sustainable Food
    and Agriculture, 108
Art of Fermentation, The (Katz), 235
arugula
    Arugula, Tomato, and Tabbouleh
        Salad, 160
    in Asparagus, Fennel, and Roasted
        Beet Salad with Walnuts and
        FireFly Farms MountainTop Blue
        Vinaigrette, 162
    Fig, Arugula, and Goat Cheese
        Flatbread, 118–19
    in Health-Defining Green
        Smoothies, 32–33
    Ultimate Chessie Chopped Salad
        with Herby Green Goddess
        Dressing, 170
    in Warm Lentil Salad with
        Medallions of Liberty Farm
        Tenderloin and Cherry Balsamic
        Reduction, 148–49
Ashley, Kathleen, 179
asparagus, 248
    Asparagus and Broom's Bloom
        Cheddar Frittata, 14
    Asparagus and Crab Tart, 98–99
    Asparagus, Fennel, and Roasted
        Beet Salad with Walnuts and
        FireFly Farms MountainTop Blue
        Vinaigrette, 162
    Farfalle with Pea Tendril and Mint
        Pesto and Roasted Asparagus,

120–21
    in Lettuce Wraps Stuffed with
        Spring Veggies and Chicken,
        194–95
    in Moroccan Chickpea Vegetable
        Tagine, 80–81
Atwater, Ned, 144
Atwater's Bakery, 144
Avocado Cream, 39–41

bacon
    Beans and Bacon with Grilled
        Goat, 150–51
    in Champagne Cabbage and
        Apples, 113
    in Colonial Mushroom Tart, 110
    in Gertie's Sweet and Sour
        Cabbage, 186–87
    in Hot Butter Beans Come to
        Supper, 143
    in Potato Cakes with Catfish
        Creole, 176–77
    in Prize-Winning Spinach-Wrapped
        Oysters Casino, 37–38
    in Ultimate Chessie Chopped
        Salad, 170
Ball Complete Book of Home Pre-
    serving (Kingry and Devine), 247
balsamic vinegar, 239
    Cherry Balsamic Reduction,
        148–49
    in Curry Ketchup, 47
Baltimore, 108, 159, 164, 193
Baltimore Farmers' Market, 6
Baltimore Urban Gardening with
    Students, 164
barley, 144
    Mr. Al's Old-Timey Chessie
        Porridge, 23

beans, green, 248
    Dilly Beans, 241
beans (legumes)
    Beans and Bacon with Grilled
        Goat, 150–51
    Big Pot o' Beans and Greens with
        Ham Hocks, 151
    Fishing Creek Seafood Chili, 61–62
    Hot Butter Beans Come to Supper,
        143
    in Huevos and No-Huevos
        Rancheros, 15–17
    Rumbleway Farm Roasted Tomato
        Succotash with Chicken Confit
        on Johnnycakes, 191–92
    in Springfield Farm Brunswick
        Stew, 91
    Succotash, 147
    See also chickpeas; lentils; tofu
beef
    Bavarian Hunter's Stew, 89
    Beef Brisket with Tangy Peaches,
        104
    Beef Stock, 60
    Bison Ragu with Pappardelle, 128
    Bison Sliders with Talbot Reserve
        Cheese and Curry Ketchup, 47
    Emily's Hungarian Brisket, 100
    and plant-based diet, 127
    Warm Lentil Salad with Medallions
        of Liberty Farm Tenderloin
        and Cherry Balsamic Reduction,
        148–49
beer
    South Mountain Creamery
        Cheddar Cheese and Blackwing
        Lager Soup, 79
beets, 248
    Asparagus, Fennel, and Roasted
        Beet Salad with Walnuts and
        FireFly Farms MountainTop Blue
        Vinaigrette, 162
    Roasted Carrot and Beet Soup, 84
beverages. *See* cocktails; smoothies;
    soda
biscuits
    Cornmeal Peach Shortcake with

    Fluffy Cornmeal Pecan Topping,
        221–23
    Strawberry Rhubarb Shortcake,
        225–26
bison
    Bison Ragu with Pappardelle, 128
    Bison Sliders with Talbot Reserve
        Cheese and Curry Ketchup, 47
blackberries
    Blackberry Patch, 255
    Mixed Berry Compote, 26
Black Rock Orchard, 100
blueberries, 248
    Mixed Berry Compote, 26
bluefish
    Bluefish with Tomatoes and
        Capers, 95
bread
    Chesapeake-Style Corn Bread,
        204
    Chocolate Chunk Ginger Scones,
        211
    Hutzler's Cheese Bread, 200–201
    Johnnycakes, 191, 205
    Johnny's Brown Bread, 199
    Kitchen Garden Rye, 89, 202–3
    Maple Whole Wheat Bread, 198
    Zucchini Bread for Miss Molly,
        210
    See also biscuits; flatbread; muffins
Bread for the City, 108, 193
Broom's Bloom Dairy, 14, 54, 134
Browne, Annie Gilligan, 210
bruschetta
    Lump Crab and Roasted Corn
        Bruschetta, 42
    Sweet Pea and Mint Bruschetta
        with Chesapeake Chevre, 53
Brussels sprouts
    Roasted Brussels Sprouts, 184
    Shaved Brussels Sprout Salad
        with Spring Onions, Orange, and
        Toasted Black Walnuts, 161
butter
    Casino Butter, 37, 38

cabbage

    in Caribbean Vegetable Stew, 77
    Champagne Cabbage and Apples,
        113
    Gertie's Sweet and Sour Cabbage,
        186–87
    Lime-Jicama Slaw, 39
    Waverly Winter Market Cabbage
        and Tofu with Quinoa, 190–91
    See also kimchi; sauerkraut
cakes
    Baltimore Peach Cake, 220
    Firefly Farms Goat Cheese
        Cheesecake, 229–30
    Peach Upside-Down Cake, 224
Calvert, Rita, 47, 150
candy
    Old Bay Peanut Brittle, 231
canning, 247–51
    equipment for, 249
    hot water bath method, 247–48,
        250
    steam-pressure canner method,
        247, 248, 250–51
    steps in, 249–51
    and storage, 251
cantaloupe
    Spaghetti with Cantaloupe, 125
Carpenter, Meaghan and Shane, 141
Carroll, Jon, 254
carrots, 248
    in Morning Glory Muffins, 208
    Roasted Carrot and Beet Soup, 84
    in Winter Root Vegetable Stew, 88
catfish, blue, 78, 108
    Blue Cat Seafood Hash, 18
    Potato Cakes with Catfish Creole,
        176–78
    in Shrimp, Maryland Crab, and
        Rockfish Seafood Stew, 67–68
    Wide Net Blue Catfish Catties, 36
    Wide Net Blue Catfish in Banana
        Leaves, 94
cauliflower
    Roasted Cauliflower Linguine, 124
celery
    in Potato Cakes with Catfish
        Creole, 176–78

in Sydney's Mid-Atlantic Etouffee,
72–76
Chapel's Country Creamery, 54
Charlottetown Farm, 54, 105
cheese
artisanal, 54, 106
Asparagus and Broom's Bloom
Cheddar Frittata, 14
Bison Sliders with Talbot Reserve
Cheese and Curry Ketchup, 47
Broom's Bloom Cheddar and
Sausage Potato Puffs, 50–51
Broom's Bloom Cheddar Hominy,
134
Charlottetown Farm Swiss Chard
and Goat Cheese Gratin, 105
Fig, Arugula, and Goat Cheese
Flatbread, 118–19
Firefly Farms Goat Cheese
Cheesecake, 229–30
Firefly Farms Mountaintop Blue
Vinaigrette, 162–63
Hutzler's Cheese Bread, 200–201
Nice Farms Creamery Homemade
Ricotta Cheese, 168
Shady Goat Farm Stuffed
Portabella Mushrooms, 51
South Mountain Creamery
Cheddar Cheese and Blackwing
Lager Soup, 79
Sweet Pea and Mint Bruschetta
with Chesapeake Chevre, 53
Watercress and Fresh Ricotta Salad
with Apples, Walnuts, and Cider
Vinaigrette, 166–68
Chefs Collaborative, 83
cherries, 248
Peach and Cherry Enchiladas,
230
Warm Lentil Salad with Medallions
of Liberty Farm Tenderloin
and Cherry Balsamic Reduction,
148–49
Cherry Glen, 54
Chickahominys, 24
chicken, 10
Cecil County Chicken Confit,

191–92
Chicken Pot Pie with Sweet Potato
Crust, 101–2
Chicken Stock, 59
and Concentrated Animal Farming
Operations vs. integrated
farming, 103
factory-farmed vs. local
free-range, 8, 10
Lettuce Wraps Stuffed with Spring
Veggies and Chicken, 194–95
and organic standards, 28
Rumbleway Farm Roasted Tomato
Succotash with Chicken Confit
on Johnnycakes, 191–92
in Springfield Farm Brunswick
Stew, 91
See also poultry
chickpeas
Moroccan Chickpea Vegetable
Tagine, 80–81
Child, Julia, 227
children, education of, 3, 164
Chittister, Joan, 143
chocolate, 54
Chocolate Chunk Ginger Scones,
211
in Spelt Waffles with Crystallized
Ginger and Chocolate Chips,
27
chowder. See under soups
chutney, 242
Apple Fig Chutney, 244
Apple Fig Chutney "Creme
Fraiche," 52
Tomato and Fruit Chutney, 245
City Blossoms, 164
Civic Works, 193
clams
in Shrimp, Maryland Crab, and
Rockfish Seafood Stew, 67–68
Cleary, Gertie, 10, 19, 143, 159, 186,
220, 233
cocktails, 253–59
Baltimore Shot Tower Gin
Cucumber Cooler, 254
Blackberry Patch, 255

Bloody Maryland, 255
Cocobucha, 259
Easy Breezey, 258
HEX Rum Manhattan, 259
Jon's Gin 'n Juice, 256
Mimosa Flight, 256
Pom-Ade, 258
Saint Sangria, 254
Southern Belle, 257
coconut milk
in Health-Defining Green
Smoothies, 32–33
in Roasted Carrot and Beet Soup,
84
in Strawberry Rhubarb Shortcake,
225–26
collard greens
Big Pot o' Beans and Greens with
Ham Hocks, 151
Health-Defining Green Smoothies,
32–33
Community Law Center, 193
community-supported agriculture
(CSA), 8, 9, 193
compote
Mixed Berry Compote, 26
Peach Compote, 25
Concentrated Animal Farming
Operations (CAFOs), 3, 103
corn, 248
Cybee's Radish and Sweet Corn
Salad, 163
in Frogmore Stew, 62–63
Lump Crab and Roasted Corn
Bruschetta, 42
Succotash, 147
Sweet Corn, Red Bell Pepper, and
Lump Crab Salad, 154
Wild Shrimp and Sweet Corn
Chowder, 69–70
cornmeal
Chesapeake-Style Corn Bread,
204
Cornmeal Peach Shortcake with
Fluffy Cornmeal Pecan Topping,
221–22
Johnnycakes, 205

cornmeal (*cont.*)
  See also grits; hominy; masa harina;
    polenta
crab, 8, 71, 78, 83
  Asparagus and Crab Tart, 98–99
  Aunt Bessie's Crab Pudding, 97
  Doug's Crab Dip Flatbread, 116–17
  in Fishing Creek Seafood Chili,
    61–62
  Lump Crab and Roasted Corn
    Bruschetta, 42
  Mama Maria's Seafood Tamales,
    132–33
  Minted Crab and Shrimp Salad, 155
  Mrs. Kitching's EZ Crab Soup, 65
  Mrs. O'Linder's Crabby (or Not)
    Deviled Eggs, 44
  in Old Line Creole Oyster Stew, 66
  Shrimp, Maryland Crab, and
    Rockfish Seafood Stew, 67–68
  Svelte Crab and Veggie Salad,
    156–57
  Sweet Corn, Red Bell Pepper, and
    Lump Crab Salad, 154
crab, soft-shell
  Fried Green Tomatoes and Hominy
    with Soft-Shell Crab, 174
crab cakes, mock
  "I Can't Believe It's Not Crab"
    Cakes, 179–80
crepes
  Gateaux Mont Saint Michel—Julia
    Child's Apple Crepe Cake,
    227–28
  Sweet Potato Crepes, 45, 46
Cruz, Maria, 132
cucumber
  Baltimore Shot Tower Gin
    Cucumber Cooler, 254
  in Minted Crab and Shrimp Salad,
    155
  in Svelte Crab and Veggie Salad,
    156–57
  See also pickles

Daisy Flour, 144
dashi, 142

DC Greens, 193
DC Greenworks, 193
diet. *See* food
Diet for a New America (Robbins), 202
disease and diet, 127
Dodd, Marilyn and Lew, 106
Dowell, Susan Stiles, 65
drum fish (redfish)
  in Sydney's Mid-Atlantic Etouffee,
    72–76
duck
  Rumbleway Farm Molasses-
    Scented Duck Breast with Sweet
    Potato Crepes, 45–46
  Rumbleway Farm Roasted
    Tomato Succotash with Confit
    on Johnnycakes, 191–92
Dumbwaiter Bistro, 72
Dupont Circle farmers' market, 6,
  144

ecology, 3–4, 5, 48, 71, 78, 182
economy, 4, 11
  and community-supported
    agriculture, 8
  and farmers' markets, 5–6
  and gardening, 10
  and interstate highway system,
    206
  and oyster farming, 48, 49
  and preserving food, 233
  and regional markets, 7–8
  and small-scale animal husbandry,
    106
  and urban gardening, 193
  and Wide Net Project, 108
education, 3, 164
eggplant
  Ratatouille with Spelt Penne, 123
  Roasted Eggplant Tenders, 180–81
eggs
  Asparagus and Broom's Bloom
    Cheddar Frittata, 14
  Asparagus and Crab Tart, 98–99
  Aunt Bessie's Crab Pudding, 97
  Blue Cat Seafood Hash, 18
  Huevos and No-Huevos

Rancheros, 15–17
  Mrs. O'Linder's Crabby (or Not)
    Deviled Eggs, 44
  Svelte Crab and Veggie Salad,
    156–57
enchiladas
  Peach and Cherry Enchiladas, 230
etouffee
  Sydney's Mid-Atlantic Etouffee,
    72–76
Evergrain Bread Company, 144
Everona Dairy, 54

Farm Alliance, 193
farmers' markets, 5–7, 8, 29, 80, 89,
  159, 206
farming/agriculture, 3–4, 5–7, 8
  community-supported, 8, 9, 193
  corporate model of, 206
  education about, 164, 193
  and grains, 144
  and interstate highway system,
    206
  and Jefferson, 219
  and mono-cropping, 3, 144, 182
  organic, 28–29
  and pesticides and herbicides, 29,
    144, 182
  and plant-based diet, 127
  and pollution, 103
  and poultry, 103
  small-scale animal husbandry, 106
  and soils, 3, 4, 9, 144, 182, 219
  urban, 193
Feniger, Susan, 155
fennel
  Asparagus, Fennel, and Roasted
    Beet Salad with Walnuts and
    FireFly Farms MountainTop Blue
    Vinaigrette, 162
fermented foods, 235
  See also kimchi; kombucha;
    sauerkraut
figs
  Apple Fig Chutney, 52, 244
  Fig, Arugula, and Goat Cheese
    Flatbread, 118–19

Fig Spread, 119
FireFly Farms, 54, 162, 229
fish
    underutilized, 83
    See also aquaculture; bluefish;
        catfish, blue; drum fish; herring;
        rockfish; smoked fish; *under*
        stocks
fisheries
    community-supported, 64
    diminishing, 71
    and invasive species, 78
    and oyster farming, 3, 48
    trash fish in, 83
    and Wide Net Project, 108
    See also aquaculture
Fishing Creek, 61
flatbread, 115
    dough for, 117
    Doug's Crab Dip Flatbread, 116–17
    Fig, Arugula, and Goat Cheese
        Flatbread, 118–19
food
    Bay- and body-friendly, 8, 10, 127,
        219
    locally grown, 5–7, 29
    organic, 28–29
    for plant-centered diet, 8, 10, 127,
        219
    seasonal, 4–5
    See also farmers' markets
food preservation, 233–35, 239, 242
    canning, 247–51
    drying/dehydration, 234–35
    fermenting, 235
    jellies, jams, preserves,
        marmalades, and chutneys,
        242–45
    pickling, 238
FreshFarm Markets, 6
Fresh Tofu Inc., 188
frittata
    Asparagus and Broom's Bloom
        Cheddar Frittata, 14

gardening, 10–11, 164, 193
genetically modified (GM) food, 3,

103, 182
Gertrude's, 85, 118, 126, 191, 224, 252
gluten intolerance, 144
goat meat
    Beans and Bacon with Grilled
        Goat, 150–51
grains, 4, 8, 106, 115, 127, 131, 144, 197
    See also bread; *specific grains*
granola
    YVOK (Your Very Own Kitchen)
        Granola, 22
gratin
    Charlottetown Farm Swiss Chard
        and Goat Cheese Gratin, 105
gravy
    Ginger Citrus Gravy, 189
    Hominy and Gravy with Turkey
        Sausage Patties, 19–20
Great Kids Farm, 164
greens. *See* arugula; collard greens;
    kale; mustard greens; spinach;
    Swiss chard
grits
    Apple and Raisin Cornmeal Mush,
        21
    Grit Cakes with a Peachy
        Compote, 24–25
Gruber, Sharon Feuer, 108
Gunpowder Bison & Trading
    Company, 128

ham
    Big Pot o' Beans and Greens with
        Ham Hocks, 151
    in Mrs. Kitching's EZ Crab Soup, 65
    in New Earth Farm's Savory Oats
        "Risoatto," 138–39
    in Sydney's Mid-Atlantic Etouffee,
        72–76
    in Ultimate Chessie Chopped
        Salad with Herby Green
        Goddess Dressing, 170
hash
    Blue Cat Seafood Hash, 18
Hedgeapple Farm, 106
herring
    Herring, Apple, and Red Onion

Salad, 158
HEX Ferments, 141, 165, 258
Hochheimer, David, 5
hominy, 24
    Broom's Bloom Cheddar Hominy,
        104, 134
    Cheddar Hominy, 174
    Fried Green Tomatoes and Hominy
        with Soft-Shell Crab, 174
    Hominy and Gravy with Turkey
        Sausage Patties, 19–20
Howard, Deborah, 190

Institute of Wine and Food, 164
Integrated Farming Systems (IFSs),
    103, 106, 144, 182, 219

Jaffres, Loic, 37
Jamison, Kevin, 138
jams, 242
Jefferson, Martha, 219
Jefferson, Thomas, 219
jellies, 242
    Blackberry Jalapeño Jelly, 243
Johnson, Robert "RJ," 66
Johnson, Winnie Lee, 71
Johnson, Yolanda, 85
Jorgensen Family Foundation, 106

kale
    Big Pot o' Beans and Greens with
        Ham Hocks, 151
    Farmer Joan's Pasta and Greens,
        122
    in Health-Defining Green
        Smoothies, 32–33
Katz, Sandor, 235
Katzen, Mollie, 202
Keswick Creamery, 54
ketchup
    Curry Ketchup, 47
Khan, Riva, 164
kimchi, 235
    HEX Miso Kimchi Bowl with Crispy
        Green Onions, 141–42
    HEX Miso Kimchi Nut Butter
        Sauce, 141–42

kimchi (*cont.*)
    Kimchi, 236–37
Kingry, Judi, and Lauren Devine, 247
Kitching, Frances, 65, 96
kombucha, 141
    in cocktails, 258–59
    in Health-Defining Green
        Smoothies, 32–33
K Street Farm, 193

Lan, Mama, 126
Lands End Farm, 144
Lawrence, Vint, 144
leeks
    in Shrimp, Maryland Crab, and
        Rockfish Seafood Stew, 67–68
    in Winter Root Vegetable Stew, 88
lemons, 248
    Pom-Ade, 258
    Rosemary Lemon Soda, 257
lentils
    Lentil Shepherd's Pie with Potato-
        Parsnip Topping, 109
    Warm Lentil Salad with Medallions
        of Liberty Farm Tenderloin
        and Cherry Balsamic Reduction,
        148–49
lettuce
    Asparagus, Fennel, and Roasted
        Beet Salad with Walnuts and
        FireFly Farms MountainTop Blue
        Vinaigrette, 162–63
    Herring, Apple, and Red Onion
        Salad, 158
    Lettuce Wraps Stuffed with Spring
        Veggies and Chicken, 194–95
    Svelte Crab and Veggie Salad,
        156–57
    Ultimate Chessie Chopped Salad
        with Herby Green Goddess
        Dressing, 170–71
Lewis, Tre, 128
lobster
    in Shrimp, Maryland Crab, and
        Rockfish Seafood Stew, 67–68
    as trash fish, 83

malt vinegar, 239
mangoes
    Apple and Mango Chutney
        Cobbler, 214
markets, regional, 7–8, 206
marmalade, 242
    Tangerine Vanilla Bean Marmalade,
        244
masa harina
    Fishing Creek Seafood Chili, 61–62
    Mama Maria's Seafood Tamales,
        132–33
May All Be Fed (Robbins), 202
McGeary Organics, 144
McGuire, Tim, 144
Meers, Sydney, 71–72
Miller, Pam, 105
Miller family, 166
Milliken, Mary Sue, 155
Miriam's Kitchen, 108
Mobile Farmers Markets, 193
Moosewood Cookbook (Katzen), 202
Mrs. Kitching's Smith Island Cookbook
    (Dowell), 65
muffins
    Morning Glory Muffins, 208
    Nice Creamery Bran Muffins, 207
    Rhubarb Muffins, 209
mushrooms
    in Bavarian Hunter's Stew, 89
    Colonial Mushroom Tart, 110, 112
    in Kevin's Hearty Crock Pot
        Venison and Chevre Stew, 90
    Robin's Mushroom Risotto with
        Turkey Schnitzel and Shredded
        Confit, 146–47
    Shady Goat Farm Stuffed
        Portabella Mushrooms, 51
mussels, 78
    in Shrimp, Maryland Crab, and
        Rockfish Seafood Stew, 67–68
mustard greens
    in Health-Defining Green
        Smoothies, 32–33

National Aquarium, Baltimore, 108
National Days of Taste, 164

Neibuhr, Kevin, 90
New Earth Farm, 138
Next Step Produce, 144
Nice Farms Creamery, 166
Nick's Organic Farm, 106
Norfolk School Garden Collective,
    164
Norman, Joan and Drew, 106, 122
North, Bonnie, 233
nuts
    in Charlottetown Farm Roasted
        Butternut Squash with Spicy
        Onions, 185
    See also almonds; peanuts; pecans;
        walnuts

oats, 144
    Mr. Al's Old-Timey Chessie
        Porridge, 23
    New Earth Farm's Savory Oats
        "Risoatto," 138–39
    YVOK (Your Very Own Kitchen)
        Granola, 22
Oil, Tarragon Truffle, 87
okra, 248
    in Caribbean Vegetable Stew,
        77
    Polenta with Stewed Tomatoes
        and Okra, 135–37
    Stewed Tomatoes and Okra, 136
Old Beach Farmers Market, 51
Old Line Fish Company CSF, 64
O'Linder, Joanne, 44
One Straw Farm, 29, 106, 122
onions
    Charlottetown Farm Roasted
        Butternut Squash with Spicy
        Onions, 185
    Herring, Apple, and Red Onion
        Salad, 158
    Shaved Brussels Sprout Salad
        with Spring Onions, Orange,
        and Toasted Black Walnuts,
        161
    Spicy Onions, 185
    in Sydney's Mid-Atlantic Etouffee,
        72–76

oranges
    Shaved Brussels Sprout Salad
        with Spring Onions, Orange,
        and Toasted Black Walnuts, 161
Ottolenghi, Yotam, 180
oyster farming, 3, 48–49, 71
Oyster Recovery Partnership, 64
oysters
    Old Line Creole Oyster Stew, 66
    Prize-Winning Spinach-Wrapped
        Oysters Casino, 37–38

pancakes
    "Buttermilk" Buckwheat Pancakes
        with Mixed Berry Compote,
        25–26
    Pumpkin Pancakes with Candied
        Pumpkin Seeds, 30–31
Parks & People Foundation, 193
parsnips
    Lentil Shepherd's Pie with Potato-
        Parsnip Topping, 109
pasta
    Bison Ragu with Pappardelle, 128
    Farfalle with Pea Tendril and Mint
        Pesto and Roasted Asparagus,
        120–21
    Farmer Joan's Pasta and Greens,
        122
    HEX Miso Kimchi Bowl with Crispy
        Green Onions, 141–42
    Mama Lan's Tangy Noodles, 126
    Ratatouille with Spelt Penne, 123
    Roasted Cauliflower Linguine, 124
    Spaghetti with Cantaloupe, 125
    Ziti with Sauerkraut and Kielbasa,
        129
peaches, 248
    Baltimore Peach Cake, 220
    Beef Brisket with Tangy Peaches,
        104
    Cornmeal Peach Shortcake with
        Fluffy Cornmeal Pecan Topping,
        221–23
    Grit Cakes with a Peachy
        Compote, 24–25
    Peach and Cherry Enchiladas, 230

Peach Upside-Down Cake, 224
peanuts
    African-Inspired Sweet Potato and
        Peanut Soup, 82
    in Lettuce Wraps Stuffed with
        Spring Veggies and Chicken,
        194–95
    Old Bay Peanut Brittle, 231
pears, 248
    Pear and Cucumber Pickles, 241
peas, 248
    Farfalle with Pea Tendril and Mint
        Pesto and Roasted Asparagus,
        120–21
    in New Earth Farm's Savory Oats
        "Risoatto," 138–39
    Spring Pea Soup with Tarragon
        Truffle Oil, 86–87
    Sweet Pea and Mint Bruschetta
        with Chesapeake Chevre, 53
    Sweet Pea Stock, 87
pecans
    Cornmeal Peach Shortcake with
        Fluffy Cornmeal Pecan Topping,
        221–23
    Zucchini Bread for Miss Molly, 210
pectin, 242
peppers, bell
    in Moroccan Chickpea Vegetable
        Tagine, 80–81
    in Ratatouille with Spelt Penne, 123
    in Sydney's Mid-Atlantic Etouffee,
        72–76
pesto
    Pea Tendril and Mint Pesto, 120–21
pickles
    Dilly Beans, 241
    Garlic Dill "New" Pickles, 240
    Pear and Cucumber Pickles, 241
    Quick Pickled Radishes, 240
pie crusts
    Almond Flour Pastry Crust, 216
    for a double-crust pie, 216
    Flaky Pastry Crust, 112
    for a single-crust pie, 98
    Sweet Potato Crust, 101–2
pies, dessert

Apple and Mango Chutney
    Cobbler, 214
Apple Rhubarb Pandowdy, 215–16
Black Rock Orchard Slab Pie,
    216–17
Gateaux Mont Saint Michel—Julia
    Child's Apple Crepe Cake,
    227–28
Schnitz Pie, 218
pies, savory
    Asparagus and Crab Tart, 98–99
    Chicken Pot Pie with Sweet Potato
        Crust, 101–2
    Colonial Mushroom Tart, 110, 112
    Lentil Shepherd's Pie with Potato-
        Parsnip Topping, 109
pilaf
    Patsy's Veggie Rice Pilaf, 140
plant-based diet, 127
plums, 248
    Plum Preserves, 243
polenta
    Polenta with Stewed Tomatoes and
        Okra, 135–37
Pollan, Michael, 28, 127
pollution, 3, 8, 10, 29, 103, 127, 182
porridge
    Mr. Al's Old-Timey Chessie
        Porridge, 23
potatoes
    in Blue Cat Seafood Hash, 18
    Broom's Bloom Cheddar and
        Sausage Potato Puffs, 50–51
    Lentil Shepherd's Pie with Potato-
        Parsnip Topping, 109
    Potato Cakes with Catfish Creole,
        176–78
    Smith Island Rockfish with
        Potatoes, 96
poultry, 8, 10, 28, 103, 106, 173, 182
    See also chicken; turkey
Power in Dirt, 193
preserves, 242
    Plum Preserves, 243
preserving food. See food
    preservation
Preston, Cybil, 163

pudding, savory
    Aunt Bessie's Crab Pudding, 97
Pumpkin Pancakes with Candied
    Pumpkin Seeds, 30–31

quinoa
    and HEX Miso Kimchi Bowl with
        Crispy Green Onions, 141–42
    and Moroccan Chickpea Vegetable
        Tagine, 80–81
    Waverly Winter Market Cabbage
        and Tofu with Quinoa, 190–91

radishes
    Cybee's Radish and Sweet Corn
        Salad, 163
    Quick Pickled Radishes, 240
Rae, Doug, 144
Ratatouille with Spelt Penne,
    123
Ratcliffe Foundation, 64
ray, red, 71
Real Food Farm, 193
rhubarb
    Apple Rhubarb Pandowdy, 215–16
    Rhubarb Muffins, 209
    Strawberry Rhubarb Shortcake,
        225–26
rice
    HEX Miso Kimchi Bowl with Crispy
        Green Onions, 141–42
    in Mr. Al's Old-Timey Chessie
        Porridge, 23
    Patsy's Veggie Rice Pilaf, 140
    Robin's Mushroom Risotto with
        Turkey Schnitzel and Shredded
        Confit, 146–47
    Sydney's Mid-Atlantic Etouffee,
        72–76
Rice, Shannon, 106
rice vinegar, 239
risotto
    Robin's Mushroom Risotto with
        Turkey Schnitzel and Shredded
        Confit, 146–47
Robbins, John, 11, 202
Rocket to Venus restaurant, 258

rockfish, 71
    Crispy Rockfish Tacos with Lime-
        Jicama Slaw and Avocado
        Cream, 39–41
    in Fishing Creek Seafood Chili,
        61–62
    Shrimp, Maryland Crab, and
        Rockfish Seafood Stew, 67–68
    Smith Island Rockfish with
        Potatoes, 96
Rodale Institute, 144
Rohr, Richard, 3
Rowan, John, 83
Rumbleway Farm, 45, 103, 106, 146,
    191, 194

salad dressings
    Firefly Farms Mountaintop Blue
        Vinaigrette, 162–63
    Herby Green Goddess Dressing,
        170–71
    Honey-Apple Cider Vinaigrette,
        166–68
    Skinny Balsamic Dressing, 156
salads
    Arugula, Tomato, and Tabbouleh
        Salad, 160
    Asparagus, Fennel, and Roasted
        Beet Salad with Walnuts and
        FireFly Farms MountainTop Blue
        Vinaigrette, 162–63
    Cybee's Radish and Sweet Corn
        Salad, 163
    Herring, Apple, and Red Onion
        Salad, 158
    Lime-Jicama Slaw, 39, 41
    Minted Crab and Shrimp Salad,
        155
    Sauerkraut and Apple Salad, 165
    Shaved Brussels Sprout Salad
        with Spring Onions, Orange, and
        Toasted Black Walnuts, 161
    Svelte Crab and Veggie Salad,
        156–57
    Sweet Corn, Red Bell Pepper, and
        Lump Crab Salad, 154
    Ultimate Chessie Chopped Salad

with Herby Green Goddess
        Dressing, 170–71
    Watercress and Fresh Ricotta Salad
        with Apples, Walnuts, and Cider
        Vinaigrette, 166–68
Salsa Fresca, 15–17
sauces
    Asian Marinade, 195
    Avocado Cream, 39, 41
    BBQ Mayonnaise, 180–81
    Creole Sauce, 176–77
    HEX Miso Kimchi Nut Butter
        Sauce, 142
    Remoulade Sauce, 174–75
    Rouille, 67–68
    Three Mustard Sauce, 180
    See also gravy
sauerkraut, 235, 237, 248
    Champagne Cabbage and Apples,
        113
    Sauerkraut and Apple Salad, 165
    Ziti with Sauerkraut and Kielbasa,
        129
Saunders, Al, 23
sausage
    Broom's Bloom Cheddar and
        Sausage Potato Puffs, 50–51
    Homemade Turkey Breakfast
        Sausage Patties, 19–20
    in Sydney's Mid-Atlantic Etouffee,
        72–76
    Ziti with Sauerkraut and Kielbasa,
        129
schnitzel
    Robin's Mushroom Risotto with
        Turkey Schnitzel and Shredded
        Confit, 146–47
seafood. See clams; crab; crab, soft-
    shell; lobster; mussels; oysters;
    shrimp
Seafood Smart, 108
Seaver, Barton, 108
seaweed, 142
Shady Goat Farm, 54, 106
sherry vinegar, 239
Shields-Davis, Patricia, 140
shrimp

in Farmer Joan's Pasta and Greens, 122

in Fishing Creek Seafood Chili, 61–62

in Mama Maria's Seafood Tamales, 132–33

Minted Crab and Shrimp Salad, 155

Shrimp, Maryland Crab, and Rockfish Seafood Stew, 67–68

in Sydney's Mid-Atlantic Etouffee, 72–76

Wild Shrimp and Sweet Corn Chowder, 69–70

Smith, John, 4

smoked fish
in Blue Cat Seafood Hash, 18

smoothies
Health-Defining Green Smoothies, 32–33

soda
Rosemary Lemon Soda, 257

soils, 3, 4, 9, 144, 182, 219

Solanet, Pablo, 162, 229

soups, 57
African-Inspired Sweet Potato and Peanut Soup, 82

Maryland crab soup, 8

Mrs. Kitching's EZ Crab Soup, 65

Roasted Carrot and Beet Soup, 84

Schillinger Farm Watermelon Gazpacho, 85

South Mountain Creamery Cheddar Cheese and Blackwing Lager Soup, 79

Spring Pea Soup with Tarragon Truffle Oil, 86–87

Wild Shrimp and Sweet Corn Chowder, 69–70

See also stews

soy beans, 3, 103, 191
See also tofu

soy milk
in Apple and Raisin Cornmeal Mush, 21

in "Buttermilk" Buckwheat Pancakes with Mixed Berry

Compote, 25–26

in Health-Defining Green Smoothies, 32–33

in Rhubarb Muffins, 209

species, invasive, 3, 78

spelt
Doug's Crab Dip Flatbread, 116–17

Ratatouille with Spelt Penne, 123

Spelt Waffles with Crystallized Ginger and Chocolate Chips, 27

spinach
in Charlottetown Farm Swiss Chard and Goat Cheese Gratin, 105

in Farmer Joan's Pasta and Greens, 122

in Health-Defining Green Smoothies, 32–33

Prize-Winning Spinach-Wrapped Oysters Casino, 37–38

squash, summer
in Moroccan Chickpea Vegetable Tagine, 80–81

Ratatouille with Spelt Penne, 123
See also zucchini

squash, winter
Charlottetown Farm Roasted Butternut Squash with Spicy Onions, 185

Stang, Michael, 125

stews
Bavarian Hunter's Stew, 89

Caribbean Vegetable Stew, 77

Frogmore Stew, 62–63

Kevin's Hearty Crock Pot Venison and Chevre Stew, 90

Moroccan Chickpea Vegetable Tagine, 80–81

Old Line Creole Oyster Stew, 66

Shrimp, Maryland Crab, and Rockfish Seafood Stew, 67–68

Springfield Farm Brunswick Stew, 91

Sydney's Mid-Atlantic Etouffee, 72–76

Winter Root Vegetable Stew, 88

stocks, 58
Beef Stock, 60

Chicken Stock, 59

Fish Stock, 58

Sweet Pea Stock, 86–87

in Sydney's Mid-Atlantic Etouffee, 72–76

Vegetable Stock, 59

Strawberry Rhubarb Shortcake, 225–26

Stuart, Wendy, 94, 108

succotash, 147
Rumbleway Farm Roasted Tomato Succotash with Chicken Confit on Johnnycakes, 191–92

in Ultimate Chessie Chopped Salad with Herby Green Goddess Dressing, 170

sweet potatoes
African-Inspired Sweet Potato and Peanut Soup, 82

in Caribbean Vegetable Stew, 77

Chicken Pot Pie with Sweet Potato Crust, 101–2

Rumbleway Farm Molasses-Scented Duck Breast with Sweet Potato Crepes, 45–46

Spicy Sweet Potato Cakes with Apple Fig Chutney "Creme Fraiche," 52

Swiss chard
Charlottetown Farm Swiss Chard and Goat Cheese Gratin, 105

in Health-Defining Green Smoothies, 32–33

tabbouleh
Arugula, Tomato, and Tabbouleh Salad, 160

tacos
Crispy Rockfish Tacos with Lime-Jicama Slaw and Avocado Cream, 39–41

tamales
Mama Maria's Seafood Tamales, 132–33

tangerines
    Tangerine Vanilla Bean Marmalade,
      244
tarts. *See* pies, savory
32nd Street Farmers' Market,
    Baltimore, 6, 90, 190
Thomas Jefferson Foundation, 219
tofu, 127
    Fu-Scramble, 15–17
    and HEX Miso Kimchi Bowl with
      Crispy Green Onions, 141–42
    in Huevos and No-Huevos
      Rancheros, 15–17
    Vegetable Tofu-Young, 188–89
    Waverly Winter Market Cabbage
      and Tofu with Quinoa, 190–91
tomatoes, 248
    Arugula, Tomato, and Tabbouleh
      Salad, 160
    Fried Green Tomatoes and Hominy
      with Soft-Shell Crab, 174
    in Huevos and No-Huevos
      Rancheros, 15–17
    Lump Crab and Roasted Corn
      Bruschetta, 42
    Old-Timey Scalloped Tomatoes,
      183
    Polenta with Stewed Tomatoes and
      Okra, 135–37
    Rumbleway Farm Roasted Tomato
      Succotash with Chicken Confit
      on Johnnycakes, 191–92
    Salsa Fresca, 15–17
    Smoked Tomatoes, in etouffee,
      73
    Stewed Tomatoes and Okra,
      136
    Tomato and Fruit Chutney, 245
tortillas
    Huevos and No-Huevos
      Rancheros, 15–16
trucking industry, 206
turkey
    Homemade Turkey Breakfast
      Sausage Patties, 19–20
    Robin's Mushroom Risotto with
      Turkey Schnitzel and Shredded

Confit, 146–47
Twin Oaks Community Foods, 188

venison
    Kevin's Hearty Crock Pot Venison
      and Chevre Stew, 90
vinegars, 239
    See also balsamic vinegar
Virginia Beach Farmers Market, 6

waffles
    Spelt Waffles with Crystallized
      Ginger and Chocolate Chips, 27
walnuts
    Asparagus, Fennel, and Roasted
      Beet Salad with Walnuts and
      FireFly Farms MountainTop Blue
      Vinaigrette, 162
    Shaved Brussels Sprout Salad
      with Spring Onions, Orange, and
      Toasted Black Walnuts, 161
    Watercress and Fresh Ricotta Salad
      with Apples, Walnuts, and Cider
      Vinaigrette, 166–68
Washington, DC, 6, 108, 164, 193
Washington Youth Garden, 164
watercress
    in Ultimate Chessie Chopped
      Salad with Herby Green
      Goddess Dressing, 170
    Watercress and Fresh Ricotta Salad
      with Apples, Walnuts, and Cider
      Vinaigrette, 166–68
watermelon
    Schillinger Farm Watermelon
      Gazpacho, 85
Waters, Alice, 164
Waverly farmers' market, 6, 90, 190
Way, Mark, 45
Way, Robin, 45, 106, 146, 191
Wetzel, Doug, 116, 224
wheat, 144
Wide Net Project (WNP), 78, 94, 108
wine vinegar, 239

Zaas, Emily, 100, 217
zucchini

in "I Can't Believe It's Not Crab"
    Cakes, 179–80
in Moroccan Chickpea Vegetable
    Tagine, 80-81
Zucchini Bread for Miss Molly, 210